Financial Update
2019/20

Pearson

At Pearson, we have a simple mission: to help people make more of their lives through learning.

We combine innovative learning technology with trusted content and educational expertise to provide engaging and effective learning experience that serve people wherever and whenever they are learning.

We enable our customers to access a wide and expanding range of market-leading content from world-renowned authors and develop their own tailor-made book. From classroom to boardroom, our curriculum materials, digital learning tools and testing programmes help to educate millions of people worldwide — more than any other private enterprise.

Every day our work helps learning flourish, and wherever learning flourishes, so do people.

To learn more, please visit us at: www.pearson.com/uk

Financial Update
2019/20

 Pearson

Harlow, England • London • New York • Boston • San Francisco • Toronto • Sydney • Dubai • Singapore • Hong Kong
Tokyo • Seoul • Taipei • New Dehli • Cape Town • São Paulo • Mexico City • Madrid • Amsterdam • Munich • Paris • Milan

Pearson
KAO Two
KAO Park
Harlow
Essex CM17 9NA

And associated companies throughout the world

Visit us on the World Wide Web at:
www.pearson.com/uk

ISBN 978-1-787-64525-7

Printed and bound in Great Britain by Ashford Colour Press, Gosport,
Hampshire.

CONTENTS

The University of Lincoln does not necessarily agree with views expressed in this *Update*.

HOW TO USE THIS UPDATE

Financial Update 19/20 **covers a period from mid June 2018 to mid June 2019**, and is compiled to provide case studies and information on topical issues in the financial environment for Business, Finance and Economics students.

There are many welfare diagrams for level one and two students, plus discussions of macro and micro policy and a long introduction related to simple supply and demand analysis. Housing features strongly. Moreover, there are several topics concerning the use of numbers for levels one, two or three. Increasingly, the emphasis is not to provide information, but assist in the utilisation of information.

Read the Financial Times/ Use FT.com

THE SUPPLY AND DEMAND TEST

Supply and Demand analysis is one of those elements an undergraduate Business Studies student MUST grasp. Price and quantity decisions are featured in strategic management, marketing, management, accounting and finance. The bluff of putting an × in the middle of some text and hoping that that will do merits nothing. By considering how you apply theory to a case study, your tutor discriminates between those who understand a topic and those that do not. Knowing that something occurs directly after something else should be distinguished from knowing WHY that something occurs directly after something else. The 'no idea student' will bluff; the 'descriptive student' will identify a process without demonstrating a solid grasp of the underlying causes; but the 'analytical student' will MAKE it CLEAR that they have an understanding of a process that guides the relationship between these phenomena.

Let us begin with a basic issue and see how we can apply theory to a case. One example is the nature of property markets, which is featured later in this text. We will assume the forces of supply and demand determine both rents and house prices. Moreover, in this discussion we can talk about elasticity.

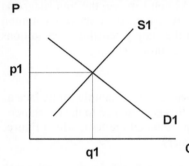

Here, we have the standard product of our analysis, the equilibrium or market-clearing price. At this price, the number of units fabricated by the collection of small producers is equal to the number of units that consumers as a whole wish to acquire. Sadly for the non-engaged student, this is as far as it goes.

How can an increase in price come about? From the figure left there are three possibilities: the demand schedule shifts right; the supply schedule shifts left; or price rises for non-market reasons. Why might the demand shift right? Here, we consider those factors that affect the consumer group, such as their preferences, their number, their wealth, etc.. Why might the supply curve shift left? Here, we consider those factors that affect the producer group, such as their costs, profit preferences, etc.. Why might price rise otherwise? Here, we consider non-market factors, such as government regulation on a price minimum, say price of cigarettes.

When is it that there is a move along a schedule, and when is there a shift? A change in the price level will lead to a move *along* a demand or supply schedule. Otherwise, with a change in conditions there is a shift. When answering a question on prices, demand and supply mechanics should be illustrated and this key issue ought to be addressed.

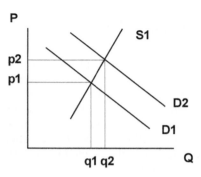

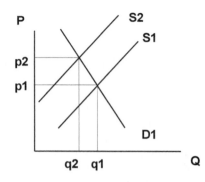

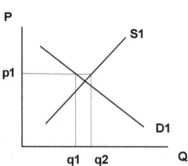

It gets more complicated when one turns to elasticity. We will discuss arc elasticity where the change in quantity demanded or supplied is reflected in the slope or gradient. As a guide, the shallower the schedule, the greater the adjustment in quantity (sensitivity) to a given change in price. As you can see, the four diagrams below are arranged to show a common shift in the supply schedule – conditions change for producers.

For a shift to the left, supply conditions have hardened. Say for example, firms face a higher employment tax. One could consider whether this is passed on to the consumer. Let us assume that the tax shifts the supply curve upwards. Of the four, which figure reflects the tax being absorbed entirely by the consumer?

Fig1

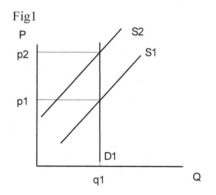

Fig2

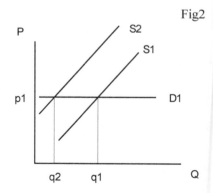

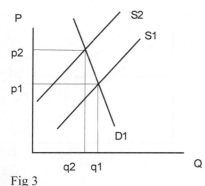

Fig 3

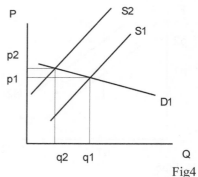

Fig4

With Fig1 there is no change in quantity at all and in Fig2, there is no change in price. These are logical extremes. The vertical demand curve reflects a good where its demand is not sensitive to a price change. Fig3 shows that it takes a large change in price to alter consumers' demand. Fig4 entails a small change in price provoking a large change in quantity demanded. Fig2 is an extension of that line. An infinitely small change in price leads to large change in quantity demanded.

Commonly, you are expected to relate these to a formula. Here, price elasticity of demand entails the % change in the quantity demanded divided by % change in price. The negative sign reflects the downward sloping demand curve.

$$P\varepsilon_D = (-)\frac{\%\Delta Q_D}{\%\Delta P}$$

❑ With Fig1, the change in quantity is zero. As a result the % change in Qd is zero. Thus, the good has zero price elasticity of demand or is perfectly inelastic.

❑ With Fig2, the change in price is zero. As a result, the % change in P is zero. Thus, the good has infinite price elasticity of demand, or is perfectly elastic.

❑ Figs 3 and 4 are in between. Fig 3, the steep schedule, is described as relatively inelastic and the formula generates a value between 0 and −1. Whereas Fig 4, the shallow schedule, is described as relatively elastic and the formula generates a value between −1 and −∞.

Try calculating: Original quantity $q_1 = 40$, $q_2 = 20$; original price $p_1 = 4$, $p_2 = 5$

%Δq = 100×(20–40)÷40 = –50%   %Δp = 100×(5–4)÷4 = +25%;

–50% ÷ +25% = –2.   Which figure would this reflect? –2 is in the range –1 to –∞, suggesting the demand curve is shallow and is described as relatively price elastic.

To answer the earlier question, all the tax is paid by the consumer when the demand curve is vertical (zero - perfectly inelastic).

Focusing on the slope of the supply curve, there is a corresponding set of figures.

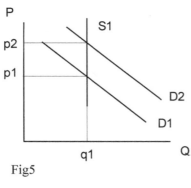

Fig5

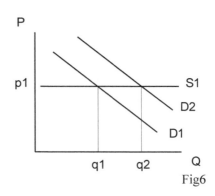

Fig6

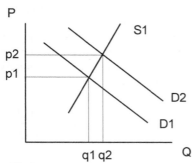

Fig7

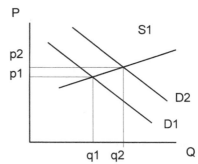

Fig8

Again, you can relate these to a formula. Here, the % change in the quantity supplied is divided by % change in price. The positive sign reflects the upward sloping supply curve.

$$P\varepsilon_S = (+)\frac{\%\Delta Q_S}{\%\Delta P}$$

Range of elasticity	0	<	+1	<	+∞
Figure	5	7		8	6

Uses of the concept of elasticity of demand

Price sensitivity is a very important measure in Economics. As the exchange rate changes relative prices, the goods must be price sensitive to make a devaluation of the currency worthwhile. It can be successful if the price elasticities of the imported and exported goods sum to over one. This is bound up with the next point; elasticity and revenue are related. Depending on whether the demand curve is elastic or inelastic, a given price change results in different revenue changes. If the good's demand curve is steep, a raised price increases revenue.

In Marketing, a focus is market segmentation. In Economics, this is known as price discrimination. Here, the market is segmented into distinct groups, each with different price sensitivities. The groups that are relatively price insensitive are charged a higher price for, essentially, the same product as the others. Using data mining techniques,

Accenture has been able to identify which spare car parts in a manufacturer's range customers are less price elastic to. Using this, at least seven car and truck makers charge an extra $415m/yr. As this is monopoly rent, this broke European competition rules. Although trivial, appearance matters. It advised Mitsubishi to raise the price of a 'silvery model badge' from €14.42 to €87.49. The point is that margins on cars can be 10% but spare parts could be nine times that. However, price hikes are avoided where insurers pay attention. Securite Reparation Automobile (SRA) measures car parts inflation and publishes this in the hope it will exert downward pressure on parts inflation.

The caché associated premium brand is, in part, based on the quality, price and the exclusivity. How it is sold and who sells it matters. Although it seems wasteful but Burberry burns bags, clothes and perfume. In 2017, unsold merchandise worth £28.6m contributing greatly to the total of over £90m over five years. Richemont (Cartier and Montblanc) spent €480m on watch buy-backs recently over two years. This avoids the grey market and the discounters that might devalue the brand – keeping the brand from becoming cheapened.

So, having suggested that the slopes of the demand and supply schedules are important considerations when answering a question, what influences these slopes?

Factors affecting price elasticity of demand
- ❑ If there are close substitutes, in the event of a price change, it is easier for consumers to switch from one product to another … so the slope will be shallower with more/closer substitutes.
- ❑ The consumer's income relative to their necessary expenditure is important. If there is little discretionary expenditure, consumers will tend to be more penny-wise…. this implies that the demand curve will be shallower.
- ❑ If the good is an essential, the demand curve will be steeper.
- ❑ Luxury goods are ones that are nurtured over years. A luxury product's image is handled carefully and reinforced through heavy advertising. The advertising should reduce the influence of substitutes, so one would expect that the demand curve is steeper.
- ❑ Information is key; consumers make choices on the basis of relative prices. Where price changes are easily noted and where consumers are more sophisticated about prices and alternatives, the demand curve will be shallower.
- ❑ Time is a factor. In the very short run, consumers have little time to respond to a change in price. It takes time to find, and become comfortable with alternatives.

Factors influencing elasticity of supply
- ❑ The element of time is perhaps even more important in supply. In the very short run, there is no scope to respond to a change in demand. Some perishable products must be sold that day so will have elasticity of supply of (close to) zero e.g. perishable fish on Friday. In the short run, some factors are fixed whilst the variable costs of labour and raw materials can be altered. As the period of analysis

is extended, there is greater scope to adjust these fixed factors. A farmer cannot increase the crop easily during the year, but can plant more in the next season. As all factors of production are variable, elasticity of supply tends to be greater in the long run. Thus, with an extension of the time frame, the supply curve is shallower.

❑ Cost of attracting factors of production into the firm/industry influences price sensitivity. It depends on the price sensitivity of the factors of production and how easy it is to substitute one factor for another. The easier it is to draw in labour from other industries without wages rising, and the more readily the producer can replace capital with labour, the shallower supply curve for the product is.

❑ A further factor is elasticity of demand for substitutes in production. The demand for it may vary as a result of a change in the demand for any one of its alternative uses. Steel may be used for making motor vehicles, fridges, ships, etc.. As demand increases for cars so the amount of steel made available to the motor vehicle industry will increase, increasing the price elasticity of supply of steel for ships.

Cross elasticity of supply

Cross elasticity of supply measures responsiveness of quantity supplied of one good to a change in price of another. **Substitutes in production** are goods for which producing more of one requires producing less of the other. An example is producing butter and milk or cheese. If the price of butter rises, then the supply curve for cheese must shift to the left. In order for the producer to meet the higher demand they must supply less cheese at any given price. Substitutes have a negative cross elasticity of supply – as the price of butter rises the supply of cheese falls.

$$CX\varepsilon_S = \frac{\%\Delta Q_S^A}{\%\Delta P^B}$$

Complements in production are pairs of goods that are by-produced, such as mutton and wool. If the price of wool rises, to produce more wool, the number of sheep needs to be increased - hence the supply curve for mutton shifts to the right. Complements have a positive cross elasticity of supply – as the price of wool rises so does the supply of mutton.

To summarise, the sign tells you whether the two goods are complements or substitutes and the value indicates whether the goods have a weak or strong relationship. For example, mutton and wool are complements so their $CX\varepsilon S$ will be positive. As they are strong complements, the numerical value will be high. Butter and cheese will have a negative $CX\varepsilon S$. As they are strong substitutes, the numerical value will be high.

substitutes	0	>	−1	>	−∞
complements	0	<	+1	<	+∞

Cross elasticity of demand

Cross elasticity of demand measures responsiveness of quantity demanded of one good to a change in price of another. If the two goods are unrelated, there will be no response. However, if they are related, the change in the price of the other good will *shift* the demand curve under consideration. If the two goods are **substitutes**, they will

$$CX\varepsilon_D = \frac{\%\Delta Q_D^A}{\%\Delta P^B}$$

have a positive cross elasticity of demand. As the price of good B increases, consumers switch from purchasing good *B* to good *A*. This shifts the demand curve for good A to the right. If the two are **complementary** goods, they will have a negative cross elasticity of demand. As the price of good *B* increases, consumers reduce their demand for good *B*. As good *A* is purchased in combination with good *B*, this shifts the demand curve for good *A* to the left.

Butter and margarine are substitutes so their CXεD will be positive. As they are strong or close substitutes, the numerical value will be high. Shoes and shoe-laces will have a negative CXεD. As they are strong complements, the numerical value will be high.

complements	0	>	−1	>	−∞
substitutes	0	<	+1	<	+∞

Income Elasticity of Demand
If the good is not affected by the income of consumers, the good have a zero income elasticity of demand. However, if the consumers' income does affect their demand for the good, the demand curve will *shift.*

$$Y\varepsilon_D = \frac{\%\Delta Q_D}{\%\Delta Y}$$

If the good is classified as inferior, it suggests that as consumers' income grows, their demand for this good falls; they purchase a more expensive version, perhaps. As income rises, the demand curve for this good shifts to the left. YεD is negative.

If the good is classified as normal, it suggests that as consumers' income grows, their demand for this good increases. As income rises, the demand curve for this good shifts to the right. YεD is between 0 and 1. If the good is classified as luxury or superior, it suggests that as consumers' income grows, their demand for this good increases as above but the response is disproportionally high. As income rises, the demand curve for this good shifts to the right. YεD is greater than 1.

We could use elasticity as an indicator: shoppers are getting richer. At a time of a price war, sales of supermarket own-label budget goods fell by 24.5% in 2016Q1 relative to 2015Q1. Premium foods, such as taste the difference, rose 4.4%. Indeed, the ONS found that household expenditure in 2014 was 5% greater in real terms than in 2012; £547/wk vs. £507.

In September 2017, the EU was apologising for a dual food quality issue. With lower incomes, Eastern European consumers cannot afford the same quality foods. In response manufacturers cater for this. The Tulip Food Company sells luncheon meet in Germany and the Czech Rep. The former bought a pork meat version whereas the latter were sold mechanically separated poultry meat instead. This was just one of 15 brands sold in the Republic with a differential quality. Inferior versions are sold in low income countries and normal, in high.

Stirring Coffee

Volatility in the coffee market is leading to a crisis in production. Nestlé is using coffee as one of four priority growth areas. However, falling benchmark prices over four years for Arabica coffee is making production uneconomic. An ICE futures price of $2.05/kg is below the $2.65-3.31/kg Central American growers need.

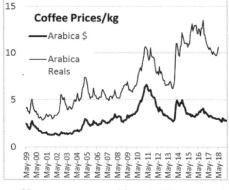

Grower	1p
Processor	0.4p
Transport	0.3p
Exporter	0.2p
Roaster/margin	8p
Milk	10p
Cup&napkins	18p
Staff	63p
Shop/Rent	88p
Tax&small costs	38p
Profit	25p
Total	£2.49

A fall in the Real against the Dollar makes Brazilian coffee more competitive. With a record harvest of 62m bags, the world's supply curve shifts right, depressing world prices. The flooding of the market with low grade coffee is causing Colombian coffee growers are shifting to coca. A £2.49 cup of coffee contains only 9.9p in actual coffee, so we would hardly notice that; and only 1p goes to the grower.

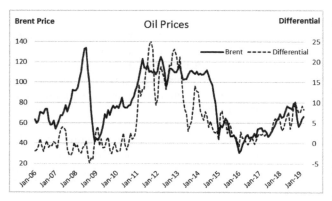

A Gap in the Oil Price

In June 2018, a new constraint depressed West Texas Intermediate crude (WTI) relative to benchmark Brent. Infrastructure constraints in the shale-rich Permian basin have kept WTI below Brent crude. Pipelines were overwhelmed as production continued to hit new highs of 10.9mb/d. Typically, Permian barrels go to the Gulf Coast for refining or export, but those pipelines were at full capacity. More oil has started to flow to the storage hub of Cushing, Oklahoma, where US futures are priced. For the week ending June 1st 2018, pipeline utilization from Cushing to the Gulf Coast was about 92%, up by 3% and 4% on April and May, respectively. The price differential hit $11.57, the largest since March 2015. The bottlenecks will likely remain until the end of 2019 or early 2020, when about 2.4m bpd of Permian-to-Gulf pipeline capacity is added. The average monthly price differential can be seen in the graph above. The differential grew over the rest of the year.

Oil as an Input
Miners use heavy fuel oil to generate electricity at remote sites; they also use it for transport, with large trucks and other equipment it uses millions of gallons each day across industry. For underground miners, wages and power comprise ⅔ of their expenses. With gold down 6% in 2017/18, copper down 3% silver down 8% and cobalt down 30%, rising costs would offset two years' worth of efficiency gains.

To reduce the exposure to diesel and greenhouse gas emissions issues, Goldcorp is building the world's first new all-electric mine in Canada. The gold mine in Borden will save about $9m/ yr on diesel, propane and electricity. Productivity gains are also possible, from equipment that can keep working while gas from dynamite blasting clears. Electric equipment should help keep mine workers healthier. WHO find that an elevated cancer risk for underground miners exposed to diesel exhaust. Although they will have lower maintenance costs and halve ventilation costs, typically pieces of equipment are 25-30% more expensive.

Goldcorp still needs to truck material to its processing plant, two hours away, and diesel vehicles are preferred. Even within the mine complex there are challenges, including a long, steep road that will extend 4km into the mine. The 40 ton electric trucks cannot run a full shift hauling ore out of the mine. But then as the world's near-surface mines are depleted, production is moving deeper underground, where high temperatures and ventilation costs make diesel impractical, so recharging will have to be accommodated.

Segmenting the Market
Elasticity is associated with price discrimination. The necessary conditions for price discrimination are:
- The firm is a price maker – this would exclude small (perfectly competitive) firms;
- Markets can be separated – the firm can prevent reselling or arbitrage between the high and low priced markets;
- Customers in each segment have different price elasticities – the higher price is charged to the customers with the least price sensitivity.

In effect, price discrimination is designed for the firm to extract some, or the entire consumer surplus available.

There are three types of price discrimination
- First Degree: is where the firm sells to customers the same good at different prices. The price reflects what that someone is willing to pay, such as individual haggling or an auction. In June 2016, the exploitation of personalising product was reported in the FT. Digitised Printing allows Heinz to sell a 50p tin of tomatoes for £2 or £3 as a 'get well soon' can.
- Second Degree: is where the price per unit varies with volume. The lower price is a 'reward' for greater the volume (bulk purchase discount). Here, one should keep in mind the supersized food portions, such as popcorn cartons in cinemas. This

value-for-money larger unit is responsible, in part, for the obesity crisis in the western world. In the diagram right P_1 stands for the price of a normal portion. This is the profit maximising quantity ($MC = MR$ at Q_1). However, assuming constant average costs, the food monopolist, by offering a larger version, the supersize, can increase profit by area D, at Q_2, which is a lower price per unit but requires a larger volume to be purchased/ consumed.

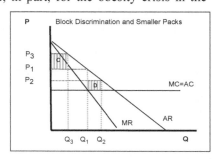

An alternative analysis focuses on the impecunious. P_1 may be prohibitive for some poorer consumers. To lower the outlay, a price discriminator may offer smaller unit to sell, Q_3, charging price P_3. It also appropriates more consumer surplus (area C). An example of this is the pack of 10. As they made smoking more affordable for young smokers, in October 2013 Euro MPs voted to prohibit the sale of packs of 10 cigarettes. Also, smaller packs provide an easier route for a lapsing person to return to smoking. In May 2016, this became EU law.

The Sunday Times found that some groceries sold in smaller sizes in Poundland were more expensive per unit than in supermarkets. Kellogg's cornflakes sold at 40p/100g whereas a full sized box in Sainsbury's cost 26.7/100g. Milk available in 2litres for £1 was sold in 4pint units in Asda for 89p. Perhaps this is an economy of scale or perhaps it is price discrimination. But this penalizes the poor.

❑ Third Degree: is where the market is segmented by some characteristic and a different price is charged in each segment. For example, there may be some cosmetic repackaging of the product. 1st and Standard class rail tickets or air flights fit into this category. The train or plane arrives no quicker for both groups, but the 1st class passenger is granted special privileges or superior conditions of passage. Other forms of segmentation include peak and off peak (mobile) phone with free minutes per month. Euro Disney was revealed in July 2016 to be engaging in geographical discrimination, charging French customers €1,346 when UK (€1,870) and German (€2,447) visitors were paying more for the same services. This charging is possible as most French visitors' book through Google.fr.

Today, large on-line retailers, such as Amazon and Walmart, go as far as intra-day price changes on the most popular items. The discrimination can depend on shopping habits by country. Borderfree finds that Canadians tend to shop in the evening after work, Australians tend to shop in their lunch hour, and Russians tend to shop all day long.

A long standing form of third degree price discrimination hit the headlines in 2016 – gender discrimination. Cases revealed included:

- Bic at tesco.com: a pack of 10 twin-bladed men's razors on offer at £1 Or pack of 8 twin-bladed lady razors at £2.
- Levi's original version started at £75 for men in a mid-blue wash, and £85 for women.
- Clarins cream for men £29/50ml and £44/50ml for women.
- M&S plain 100% cotton vests (pack of 3) for men £12.50 or £6 for a single female one.
- Nike's football studs for men £29.99 but for women from £125.
- Argos blue scooter was £5 cheaper than a pink one.

Following the Times report in January 2016, Boots, Argos and Superdrug vowed to review sexist pricing. Bic though was saying that pricing was a retailers' issue. Tesco argued there are 'additional design and performance features.' But is this just too simple? This occurs in the US, so not a UK repressed cultural issue. The New York Department of Consumer Affairs found that female versions were, on average, 7% more expensive than male. This was over 800 products. Women are much more careful shoppers than men, better able to scrutinise adverts and pricing gimmicks. It may be that there is a Veblen dimension; women perceive more value in the more expensive products

In the table, below, are relative costs of haircuts in US$. Female haircuts are not universally more expensive. The UK has similar prices to Ireland. Chinese women face similar costs to Indian. But Indian men pay less than all the others. Is this discrimination, or a reflection of value? How does that operate in China?

One would expect that DVD sales would decline, as storage and players become issues for the next generation. Economies of scale would be lost and the actual physical cost would make DVDs just a high priced alternative for the oldies, but they ae not. A new release digital film can be as little as £3.49.

$	Women	Men	Ratio
USA	73.33	17.5	4.19
UK	49.34	18.5	2.67
Ireland	43.25	15	2.88
China	13.1	14.4	0.91
India	13.5	2.72	4.96

The pricing of individual titles and formats varies according to retailers' trading and licensing deals with content owners. One explanation is the need to shift the stock out of a warehouse. If it has not sold as well as they had hoped, a film studio may have done a deal with Amazon to shift the physical stock at a discount.

	DVD	Download
Blue Jasmine	£4.92	£7.99
House of Cards series 1-3	£16.99	£44.97
Breaking Bad series 1-5	£28.71	£53.94
The West Wing series 1-7	£39.99	£104.93
Friends series 1-10	£45	£129.99

Impatience coupled with price discrimination could be another. Young adults not used to owning a physical copy are more interested in instant gratification; they want to see the next episode now and are willing to pay the price. This does not work so well with bundled episodes or seasons. The packaging or storage costs make a DVD an expensive option. Here, the higher price is either a two part tariff, in that you need to buy a DVD player. Alternatively, it is 3rd degree price discrimination; segregating the market on those who prefer digital delivery. BPI reported that physical music consumption was down 9.3% in 2016 when streaming was up 67% by volume with similar market share (41% vs 36%).

Unfair Competition
The FA cup games between Manchester United (MU) and Cambridge United (CU) highlighted strange finances and something not quite right about an essay title.

'Assess the contention that Cambridge United, when visited by Manchester United in the FA cup, should raise the gate price.'

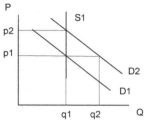

The basis of the essay is the notion that, in the very short run, there is a fixed capacity. This price elasticity of supply is then zero. CU has a capacity of 9,000. Also, the two clubs have a different following. CU has annual turnover in 2013/14 of £1.6m and MU earned £433m. So, the travelling fans could dwarf the normal number through the turnstiles.

We expect that CU would price to fill the stadium. With a vertical supply curve, a shift in the demand curve to the right, should lead to a higher ticket price. One would expect the larger MU travelling fan base would increase the demand for tickets at CU above the normal home game. The diagram above illustrates what one would expect.

If the ticket prices do not rise to p_2, as some might view this as exploitative, undermining the loyalty that CU may be relying upon, there would be excess demand for tickets (q_2–q_1). This could be resolved by ticket touts, extracting consumer surplus, or by a queue. Here, we are assuming a market determination. If we view CU as a monopoly, pricing may be based on revenue maximization. This may not lead to pricing to fill the stadium.

The reality about the visit is actually counterintuitive. CU is better off playing away. Under FA cup rules 45% of gate receipts should go to the opposition. Cambridge would receive £1.25m when they played away. The home game though, after they had passed over the 45%, would leave them with less than a normal home game against Stevenage. Fewer local consumers than normal could see the adverts around the ground. Anyway, national advertisers keen to take advantage of the 7m TV viewers would replace many.

Peak Load Pricing[1]
In April 2016, Delhi banned the use of 'surge pricing.' This is where the Uber and local taxi apps manage excess demand by raising price when demand for services outstrips supply. This rise in price may be six or seven time the base price. The licences issued by the Local Authority control the number of standard taxis and autorickshaws. The LA also regulates fares. The number of private taxis has surged.

In an effort to reduce the amount of pollution emitted by vehicles, private vehicles can only use the road every alternate day depending on the licence plate of the vehicle. This should boost demand for taxis. Let us again consider this case using microeconomics.

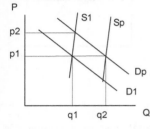

'Should taxi drivers raise price at peak time'

The basis of the essay is the notion that, in the very short run, there is almost fixed capacity. This price elasticity of supply is low. It is not vertical, rather than taxis, the taxi services can increase: they could travel more quickly to their destination. Having said that, because peak times may correspond with peak traffic, slowing services down, it could more than off-setting this. Ignoring that congestion element, normal demand = D1. At peak times (say the school run) the demand curve shifts right to Dp. Through the app, knowing both the demand and supply, Uber respond to this increase by pushing up price from base at p_1 to p_2. If services could be scheduled to reflect the peak load, price need not rise. This requires more taxis to be on the road, shifting the supply to the right (Sp).

If the taxi fare did not rise to p_2, as some might view this as exploitative, there would be excess demand taxi services (q_2–q_1). This could be resolved by a queue.

Upon it emerging that Tottenham would meet Liverpool in the Champions League final on 1st June 2019, return tickets on budget airlines, normally available for around £100 pounds, rose to as much as £1,500, while nightly hotel rates in Madrid soared from €100-150 euros to over €1,000. Unlike the taxi issue, travellers juggled two inflated prices.

In the World Cup match between England and Colombia in July 2018 pub chains took advantage of the increase in demand. Stonegate Pubs charged up to 50p more for a pint in some of its 690 pubs; Yates in Manchester charged an extra 20p on drinks; Walkabout in Colchester added 25p; and the Clock House in Harlow, 50p. Let's analyse this with a question. 'Should Pubs Raise Prices when England Pay?' Using our supply and demand analysis we have two elasticity issues and two shifts. First, once

[1] FT 22 4 16 Delhi puts brake on 'surge pricing' among taxi apps p19

supplied to the pub, the cost of each pint of beer remains the same but that additional bar and door staff are needed. To make life easy, it will be assumed that the additional costs are paid for by the additional charge – the gap between P_2 and P_1. Price elasticity of demand is treated as high under normal conditions. The quantity consumed over the evening is q_1. The British Beer and Pub Association expected England fans could consume an extra 6m pint during the evening, suggesting the demand curve would shift to the right. However, overcome by the urge not to miss too much, fans are less likely to worry about the price and shift pub, so the demand curve D_M would be steeper. If price does not increase, consumption rises to q_3. The price hike shifts the supply curve from S to $S+P$. If the elasticity is less than unity, $(P_2 - P_1)q_2 > (q_3 - q_2)P_1$, so revenue increases. This may tick off the regulars, but the revenue bump may be worth it. In effect, this looks like a tariff diagram with a branded product that is advertised.

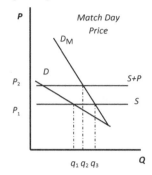

Economies of Scope

The theory of economies of scope states the average total cost of a company's production decreases when there is an increasing variety of goods produced. Economies of scope relate to complementary products while focusing on core competencies. For example, a taxi can carry both passengers and goods more cheaply than having separate vehicles, one for passengers and another for goods. In this case, joint production reduces total input costs.

The ONS estimated that in 2015, 76% of adults bought goods or services online, up from 53% in 2008. Light goods vehicles, many delivering items ordered online, have seen a 20% increase in miles covered in 10 years (DoT). IBISWorld estimate the same-day courier service sector is worth £7bn a year in the UK and the global courier and parcels delivery market is $246bn. Global annual revenue from taxi operations of all types is estimated to be 10% of that at $22bn.

Take Uber. The Licensed Taxi Drivers Association reported that at least 500 taxis have disappeared from London's 25,000-strong fleet alone due to Uber. In October 2015, it unveiled its same-day delivery service, UberRush. ParcelHero predicted UberRush would capture 10% of the global market, disrupting the FedEx /DHL market. By March 2017, UberRush was still only in New York, Chicago, and San Francisco, the three US cities it initially launched it in. By 8th May 2017, Uber switched UberRush, from deliver-me-anything platform, to UberEats, a delivery service with restaurants in mind. The company collects a delivery fee ($5 in most cities), a cut of around 30% from the restaurant, and a cut of 25% to 30% from the courier on each order, rather than the flat mileage-based fees on Rush.

Supply and Demand using Equations
Let's begin with two expressions, one for each schedule. Supply could be expressed as $Q_S = c_S + \beta_S P$ and demand could be written as $Q_D = c_D - \beta_D P$. Putting values to coefficients we could generate for demand and supply as $Q_D = 92 - P$ $Q_S = -12 + P$. Equilibrium is found at p = 52, q = 40. We could impose a tax on this diagram.

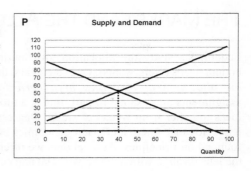

The choices are ad valorem and the lump sum tax. The lump sum is a fixed amount whatever the initial price. An ad valorem tax will increase price in proportion to the initial price. For example, the price before tax is £1. The lump sum adds 10p and the ad valorem adds 10%. Both push price up to £1.10. However, if the initial price was £2, the corresponding final prices would be £2.10 and £2.20 respectively.

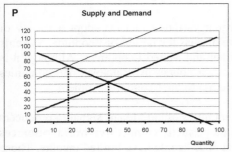

The lump sum shifts the supply curve upwards in parallel like the shifts we normally display. Assume the size of the tax = 44p, so that the new supply curve is expressed as $Q_S = -56 + P$. The new equilibrium p = 74 q = 18. The tax is worth 44p but the price change is 22p. The price elasticity of demand is = −1.3.

If the demand curve was less elastic, the changes would be different. Assume the demand curve is $Q_D = 69.7 - 0.57P$. The new equilibrium occurs where p = 80 q = 24. The tax is worth 44p but the price change is 28p. The price elasticity of demand is = −0.743.

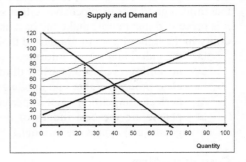

THE MARKET AND THE ALLOCATION OF RESOURCES

Economists study the allocation, distribution and utilisation of resources to meet human needs (well, wants). Over the years, the question *what role profit might have in the allocation of resources in a perfectly competitive world* has been set for assignments and exams. In part, this is a tool for assessing how well students can tie ideas together from weeks of study. Degrees such as Economics build a knowledge base. Advance micro and macroeconomics builds on Intermediate, and Intermediate is founded on Principles. At level one, we offer the tool kit you need. We also construct the lens through which we view social and economic problems. We begin by outlining what we regard as the resources and their factor returns:

Land (rent) Labour (wages) Capital (interest) Entrepreneurship (profit)

The *Economic Problem* and the questions of:
1. what and how much is produced;
2. how it is produced;
3. whom should consume it.

Through history and possibly general consent various countries adopt a variety of means of addressing this problem. Here, we discuss the notion of Economic Systems outlining three archetypes: Command, Market and Mixed Economies. Although it is recognised that the market is a poor master, a course in Principles of Economics outlines how the market mechanism is a solution to the Economic Problem.

The market both signals and rations. Large numbers of individuals signal to producers what they want: through price and profit in a perfectly competitive world, resources are allocated and reallocated to achieve that end. People have limited income. Those that think a good is 'too expensive' either seek a substitute or buy less. In other words, it is presumed that people make the best use of their limited income to maximise their utility in the light of a set of goods and their prices. Here, we are assuming that:

- ❑ the individual is well informed - there is perfect knowledge;
- ❑ no spillovers exist that affect third parties – no externalities;
- ❑ clear property rights - no public goods;
- ❑ perfect competition – not imperfect competition;
- ❑ people are the best judges of their own well-being – no merit or demerit goods/ consumers are rational.

Costs of the Firm

Total Cost = FC+VC

Average Total Cost=AFC+AVC;

ATC = TC÷Q

Marginal Cost = ΔTC÷ΔQ

Total Profit = TR–TC

Total Revenue =P×Q

Average Revenue = TR÷Q

AVC=VC÷Q; AFC=FC÷Q

Marginal Revenue = ΔTR÷ΔQ

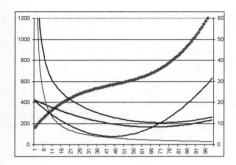

In order are the TC (left-hand scale), MC, AC, AVC, AFC (from the top and on the right-hand scale).

At zero output, VC = 0 so TC = FC. The AFC declines with volume. When drawing, the AVC and AC are at a minimum when cut by the MC (at q = 66 and 71).

In order are the TC (left hand scale), MC, AC, AVC, AFC (from the top and on the right-hand scale).

At zero output, VC = 0 so TC = FC. The AFC declines with volume. When drawing, the AVC and AC are at a minimum when cut by the MC (at q = 66 and 71).

Q	TR	AR	MR	TC	MC	AC	Profit
10	220	22	20	318	14.4	31.8	-98
11	240	21.8	19.6	332.1	13.8	30.19	-92.293

Profit Maximisation

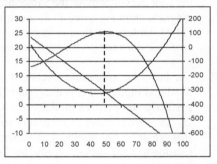

In expanding output from q = 10 to q = 11, ΔTR> ΔTC. At q = 11 MR was greater than MC, so there was a marginal profit but overall (Total) profit was negative. The figure right shows three lines: Total profit Π, MC and MR. The peak of the total profit curve Π occurs where q = 50. In the table above when q = 49 MR > MC, expanding output increases profit and when q = 51, MC>MR so profit is lower than when q = 50. We conclude that profit is maximised when MC=MR.

The construction of these diagrams follows two simple rules.

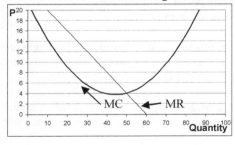

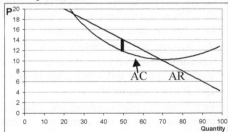

1) Find the quantity where MC=MR, the level of output where profits are maximised or losses minimised. We have discussed this already above. In this case the

quantity to operate at, regardless of the profit or less situation is at $q =$ 50.

2) AT THAT QUANTITY ($q =$ 50) find the difference between the AR curve and the AC curve. If AR > AC, the firm is making Supernormal Profit (SNP). If AR = AC, the firm is making Normal Profit. If AR < AC, the firm is making a Loss.

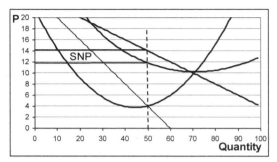

Note: SNP = (AR − AC)×q. SNP = (14 − 11.8)×50 = 110. The price will always be taken from the demand curve (which is the AR curve) given the profit maximising quantity q. Price = 14. These rules can be followed for all market structures. In effect, the cost curves remain the same and the shape of the demand curve alters. Above is a diagram showing price (14) quantity (50) and the cost associated with that quantity (11.8). Unless the firm is in perfect competition making only normal profit the lower cost line does not go through the lowest point of the AC curve.

So, how are economic decisions taken through the workings of the market? Our idealised model for this analysis is Perfect Competition. Necessary conditions for the perfectly competitive model:-
❑ A large number of relatively small buyers and sellers all of no economic power.
If there are large numbers of sellers, then any one seller's supply will be so small in relation to total market supply that increasing or decreasing his/her output will not have any effect on the price. This implies that the firm is a PRICE TAKER. We use the small ≡ price taker in trade diagrams. Similarly, buyers are so small in relation to total market demand that again no one buyer can influence the price. This forms the basis of the perfectly elastic demand curve of the firm.
❑ Buyers and sellers are perfectly mobile and perfectly informed.
❑ There are no barriers to firms entering or leaving the market.
❑ The product is homogenous.
We assume these to ensure uniformity of the market. Given that all the products are the same and everyone is aware of where the good is sold and at what price, any increase in price will encourage buyers to look elsewhere.
❑ Profit Maximisation.
Profit and the profit motive are central to the allocation of resources. It is the financial incentive given to the entrepreneur that drives them to innovate, minimise costs and prices, and be efficient.

Advantages of the perfectly competitive environment

❑ Price = marginal cost i.e. this is the optimum position and suggests that resources are being *allocated efficiently*. The marginal benefit from consumption = the cost to society of its production

❑ Competition acts as a spur to efficiency. If a firm becomes less efficient than other firms, it will make less than normal profits and go out of business. If it is more efficient, it will make super normal profits until firms copy its more efficient methods. All firms have access to the same knowledge. Any firm not incorporating the most effective technology will collapse. Customers will pay only the lowest price.

❑ Competitive situation will encourage new technology as firms try to make super normal profits.

❑ Because the product is homogeneous there is no point in advertising, which can be seen as a waste of resources.

❑ The firm in the long-run will produce at the lowest point on the AC curve – is cost efficient – *productive efficiency*

❑ The consumer gains from low prices, since not only are costs kept low but also there are no super normal profits to add to prices.

The price observed by the consumer is determined by the interaction of TOTAL INDUSTRY or MARKET SUPPLY and DEMAND. The [representative] firm takes the market price so the demand curve of the firm is perfectly elastic. Observe that the market price determines the position of the firms' [horizontal] demand curve.

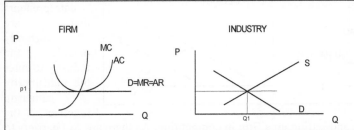

Our initial position entails the PC firm making only normal profit. This is an equilibrium position: there is no tendency for firms to enter or leave the industry.

Equilibrium is disturbed by some news - a change in demand conditions. Assume the good becomes more fashionable. If the market demand curve shifts from D to D', the market price rises to p_2 and market quantity to Q_2. Remembering that MR=AR and AR=D and the firm's demand curve is linked to the market price, the demand curve of the firm shifts upwards (D to D'). The firms currently in the industry work their way up their MC curves. At the new MR, the firms produce more output, at q_2 where MR' = MC (hence the supply of produce) and this output is sold at the higher market price, p_2. The firms now make supernormal profit (SNP).

Note that the firm diagram should display the right information – do not guess – know what you are doing. When going through the diagram, it should look like the one right. If the market price is p_1 – the firm operates at q_1 and makes normal profit. If the price is p_2, it makes SNP and the output is q_2 – to the right of q_1. Moreover, there should be three horizontal parallel lines: the original demand curve D,

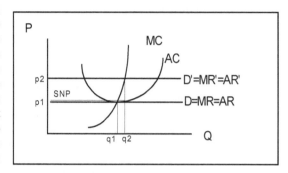

the new demand curve D' and the third line associated with the costs when operating at q_2. If the first line is not distinguished from the third, you have *not* completed the diagram correctly.

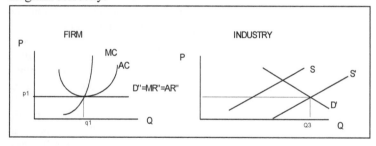

SNP is the signal to other entrepreneurs that are currently outside the industry to enter the industry by gathering together the factors of production and setting up a firm in competition. As there are NO barriers to entry, there is market access. Firms can break in. This increases the number of firms in the industry. The industry's scope for production is enhanced so the industry supply curve shifts to the right (S to S'), leading to a fall in market price. Whilst SNP is being made in the industry, firms will continue to enter the industry. So this process will continue until all SNP is eroded. The representative firm is back at square one (well p_1, q_1 long run equilibrium) but the industry has moved from Q_1 to Q_3.

So what has occurred here? Why is this process important? Perfect competition leads to CONSUMER SOVEREIGNTY. Consumers, through the market, determine what and how much is to be produced. Firms have no power to manipulate the market - the only thing they can do is to increase their efficiency for short-term super normal profits but in the long run the consumer will benefit from lower prices. There was a change in tastes. Consumers collectively wanted to consume more of the good. This information was signalled to produces through price to producers. Those in the market place responded by expanding output but they also made SNP. This profit was the signal to entrepreneurs to shift resources from one use to another. Because there is an absence of barriers to market entry, these itinerant profit seekers acted as a counterweight, driving price down. What the consumer wanted – the consumer got. Through price and profit resources were drawn into the industry.

In one sense, this is unlikely to be entirely true. Unless the industry is small, the price of materials and labour could have gone up.

Note that the entrepreneurs are acting in their own self-interest, pursuing profit. Indeed, it is this drive to maximise profit that benefits consumers. Profits come from making things that consumers wish to buy. Thus, profit motive (inadvertently) drives firms to facilitate the maximisation of well-being. Friedman (1970) and Hayek (1967) argue that:- so long as it plays by the rules *a business has one social responsibility: increasing profits and, hence, enhancing shareholder value.*

However, there are two main problems with perfect competition that can be overcome by other forms of market structure.
- ❑ Because firms in the long run do not make super normal profits they may not be able to afford large research and development (R&D) budgets to make themselves more efficient and create new products.
- ❑ Also, there is no consumer choice in that the product is not branded or differentiated in any way, therefore other models may be seen as more relevant to real world conditions.

Let us examine the obverse. Again, our initial position entails the PC firm making only normal 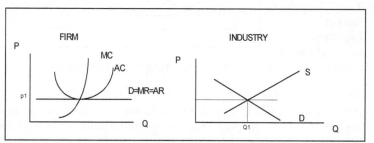 profit. This is an equilibrium position: there is no tendency for firms to enter or leave the industry.

Equilibrium is disturbed by some news, a change in demand conditions. Assume the good becomes less fashionable. If the market demand curve shifts from D to D', the market price falls to p_2 and market quantity to Q_2. Remembering that MR=AR and AR=D and the firm's demand curve is linked to the market price, the demand curve of the firm shifts downwards (D to D'). The firms currently in the industry work their way down their MC curves (above the AVC). At the new MR the firms produce less output, at q_2 where MR' = MC (hence the supply of produce) and this output is sold at the lower market price p_2. The firms now make a loss.

A loss cannot be made for ever so this is the signal to entrepreneurs that are currently inside the industry to leave, releasing resources to be used elsewhere. As there are NO barriers to exit, there is market egress.

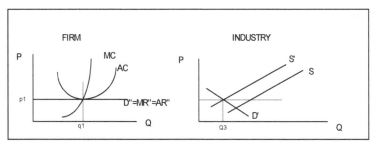

This decreases the number of firms in the industry. The industry's scope for production is diminished so the industry supply curve shifts to the left (S to S'), leading to a rise in market price. Whilst losses are being made in the industry, firms will continue to leave the industry. So this process will continue until all loss is eroded. The representative firm is back at square one (well p_1, q_1 long run equilibrium) but the industry has moved from Q_1 to Q_3. This time, a loss of interest in the product, through price and profit, leads to resources being released for better uses.

The efficient market hypothesis uses this vehicle to explain why an asset's price should reflect all information.

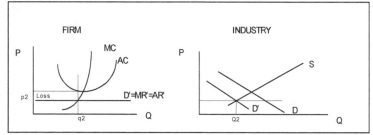

The Small Trucker

Perfect Competition is often criticised by the new economist as an irrelevance as there are no real world examples. This may not be the point... however, the trucking industry does come quite close. Obviously, one barrier to entry is the capital needed to buy a truck, but after this the industry has favourable characteristics. Most of the market is dominated by small providers (Eddie Stobart has only 10% of the market). The 33,000 UK truckers make around 1.5-2% profit – more or less breaking even. Fuel makes up 50% of the running costs.

Ethics Inherent in the Demand Curve

Edelman's Earned Brand survey suggests something akin to Friedman's defence of corporates social responsibility. Of the 14,000 respondents in 14 countries, 57% buy or boycott products because of a brand's stance on political or social issues; 27% more than three years ago. Almost a quarter of consumers are willing to pay more for those products where brands share their values. Indeed, 67% will try a brand for the first time because of its position on a controversial issue. By contrast, WGSN the trend forecaster, suggests increasingly, people are looking to companies to fill the void around social problems as a tribal mentality and public mistrust in governmental institutions grow.

COMPETITION AND CONTESTABILITY

Competition is viewed as desirable. Through rivalry among competing firms, technologies and processes, members of society are free to choose from a set of options that, whilst maximising consumers' well-being, results in making the best use of a set of resources. Beneficial outcomes include low price, low cost and the incentive to be efficient. In the real world, (i.e. not restricted to Perfect Competition) competition also drives firms to be innovative and provide the consumer with a variation of product as well as provider. By operating at a larger scale and investing in innovative products and processes, large firms can lower unit cost.

In neoclassical theory of the firm, the Monopoly is the *sole* supplier in the industry. Monopoly power may not be in the public's interest because:
- There could be a higher price and lower output than under perfect competition;
- Of a lack of competition that may lead to higher cost curves, X-inefficiency;
- There is a lack of a drive to be innovative;
- Monopoly profits are an exploitation of the consumer;
- It may exert undesirable political pressure on governments.

In practice the monopoly is replaced by the oligopoly. Thus, market imperfections associated with a small number of providers include the exploitation of the consumer, slack financial control, consumer insensitivity, relatively poor innovation, collusion and predatory behaviour. We consider three perspectives or theories of competition:-.
- Structure Conduct Performance
- The Austrian School of competition
- Contestable Market Theory

Two of these suggest the monopoly/oligopoly can still serve the public interest.

Structure-Conduct-Performance
The Structure-Conduct-Performance (SCP) is defined as the relationship between market structure, firm conduct and firm performance. SCP was based on the following causation:
1. that structure of the industry influences managerial conduct. Lower concentration leads to more rivalrous competitive behaviour;
2. that conduct influences performance. Less market power leads to more competitive behaviour, which produces greater social well-being.

Structure

Structure: refers to market structure defined mainly by the concentration of market shares in the market. This will include:

- Size and number of firms. From PC vs Monopoly analysis (see Monopoly Power), the monopoly extracts 'monopoly profits' by charging too much for the product. The market share of the largest businesses (measured by the concentration ratio) is a measure of the market power (see Herfindahl Index).

- Barriers to market entry. This element can be tied to the above point, so that with an open market the number of firms and the extent of overseas competition is a constraint on price. However, this also relates to how firms from outside the industry can break in. In practice, major firms can inject competition by switching focus from one market to another. Despite low running costs, one major barrier could be the short run high set-up costs. The degree to which an industry is vertically integrated, either forward or backward integration, can also act as a barrier. Buyers or suppliers are already tied in to formal arrangements that are difficult to breach.

- Independence. In theory of the firm a separate entity competes with another with an identical set of resources. In reality, firms are not identical. Some may achieve competitive advantage, not through their own devices but through their relationships with other firms. Thus, network economies are a difficult area to assess. A variation of this was the Keiretsu. Informal relations between families of Japanese companies would appear like a restrictive practice to the Americans.

- Barriers to market exit. Switching costs from one provider to another could act as a disincentive to change and so an exit barrier. This may include finding an alternative provider or source, or breaking a contract. A sunk cost is an incurred, irretrievable cost. It can be a past or future cost, either fixed or variable. For example, a factory could be 'sunk' fixed cost because it was a one-time expense and cannot be recovered, or a regular payment on a contract to lease this building. A variable sunk cost could be the power usage for this factory. Once incurred the sunk costs do affect future decisions but would be a disincentive to enter into arrangements where they can occur.

- Homogeneous product. One of the problems for the consumer is choice; are they equipped to make a good, informed choice? Asymmetric information and bounded rationality limit the buyer's ability to identify the best price from several million, in the case of mobile phones. So that the consumer has but one decision to make, and that is on the basis of price alone - perfect competition assumes away alternatives. In reality, there is price discrimination and a hierarchy of variations that serve differentiated markets. A branded good can act as a barrier to entry.

- From a Porter-like perspective, the relative power of the buyers or suppliers is important. If industry is dominated by a small number of firms but their buyer or supplier industries exerted sufficient power to maintain pressure to keep price low, the structure may not be deemed problematic.

- Porter also identifies the threat of substitutes as price/profit limiters. Here, we are looking at the scope for the consumer to switch to alternative products. For example, cable linked *or* mobile devices can provide telecommunications.

Conduct / Behaviour of Firms

How does market structure affect pricing, output and other decisions of businesses within the market?

❑ There may be anti-competitive behaviour. For example, with large firms there might be predatory pricing, which acts as a barrier to entry.

❑ How might independence manifest itself?

  o Long-term arrangements that could make sense for planning purposes could appear as restrictive practices.

  o Are the firms agreeing price and output levels collectively to boost profits? Collusion among oligopoly firms is not that rare and generally not in the interests of the consumer.

❑ How important is non-price competition in the market? Heavy advertising can act as a barrier to entry and, in a Baumol model sense, is characteristic of an oligopoly market.

❑ Merger activity, particularly horizontal mergers, makes a poor structure worse. Mergers are not always problematic. With the *Market Power Hypotheses* a horizontal merger can be justified for the social good or for the national interest. If profits are negative collectively and the industry has high costs, a merger and a managed reduction of capacity make more sense than a protracted price war.

❑ A key measure of monopoly power relates to the scope for raising price above marginal cost. So pricing and, hence, monopoly profit are key measures of nefarious activities.

❑ Innovation, and the measure, R&D, are indicative of activities good for society. One would expect that, more economic progress would result from a more innovative industry, which is facilitated by R&D. There would be a better allocation of the resources that the economy can command. In general, the larger R&D budgets are commonly found with larger firms.

❑ With asymmetric information, the seller can baffle the buyer with excess information or choice. Utility companies, for example, would offer two systems; one with and one without a standing charge. However, the second was more or less the same as the first for all but the most frugal users. This choice could lead to the consumer choosing the wrong product or service – the adverse selection. Government sought to address this with utility tariffs by limiting the number of tariffs.

❑ A variant of this is misselling. Banks in particular have been fined heavily for selling inappropriate products to unsophisticated, ill-informed customers.

❑ Without having the opportunity to choose between providers, consumers cannot impose any pressure on firms. Having a selection is not sufficient. Poor conduct from firms has entailed bombarding the consumer with choices so that they are disinclined to switch or if they do, they switch to a worse contract. Overall, a key measure of a competitive environment is customers *switching providers*. Switching could be a sign of dissatisfaction so a lack of switching may point to the reverse. The banking sector has been reviewed several times. In 2002, the Competition Commission investigated the supply of banking services to small businesses by clearing bank. In 2008, the Office of Fair Trading investigated the provision of personal current accounts. In 2011, the Independent Commission on Banking recommend promoting financial stability and competition. However, they have always stopped short of restructuring the industry. It was the European Competition Commissioner that forced Lloyds to sell off TSB. In October 2015, the Competition and Markets Authority (CMA) reported that switching could save £70/year. Those who regularly utilise an overdraft facility could save as much as £260/year.

❑ Just 57,779 used the 7 day switching service to move accounts in September 2017, was less than half of the 120,774 of March 2016 and the lowest number since the scheme was launched in 2013. Banks were offering account holders financial incentives to stay (HSBC) or shift (Halifax, Clydesdale and Yorkshire), so something had changed.

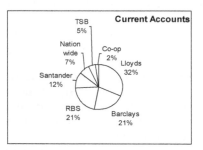

❑ The 4 big Australian banks, treated as arms of the state are worse, prioritising profit over customer welfare. In May 2018, a report found that they lied to the regulator on a regular basis. AMP, a financial advisor, lied 20 times. CBA was investigated for 50,000 breaches of money laundering

❑ In April 2014, Ofgem found that between 2007 and 2012, 5.6% of objections made by British Gas to business-to-business customers who wished to switch suppliers were invalid, so incorrectly blocking them from going elsewhere. British Gas also failed to give some businesses notice that their contract was due to end. Fining it £1.3m for the affected businesses, a further £3.45m into an energy efficiency fund; and a £800,000 penalty, the total came to £5.6m. This covers two issues of competition. Blocking a switch would lower the competitive pressure. Also, with a limited time to make an informed choice, customers will be deterred from switching.

❑ In December 2017, Apple admitted that it deliberately made changes to iOS to slow down some models of the iPhone. The practice was confirmed after a customer shared performance tests on Reddit, suggesting their iPhone 6S had slowed down considerably as it had aged but had suddenly sped up again after the battery had been replaced. Apple charged £79 to replace iPhone batteries, and also covers the work under its AppleCare policies. Some believe that Apple slows down older iPhones to encourage people to upgrade. Apple pointed out that as the lithium-ion battery ages, devices unexpectedly shut down. When in cold conditions, batteries become less capable of supplying peak current demands when they have a low battery charge. French prosecutors in January 2018 were investigating whether the quasi planned obsolescence, which is illegal in France, warrants a fine of up to 5% of turnover. The US began investigations in February 2018.

❑ Predatory or limit pricing is a problem for both CMT and SCP. Here, the price is set by the large firm to prevent market entry or drive out a competitor – much like the aim in a price war.

❑ A most unusual case, creating not a national but a super-national champion Siemens-Alstom, mooted in 2017 to compete with CRRC of China. In December, the German independent competition monitor, Bundeskartellamt, reported to the European Commission that Siemens-Alstom merger presented major concerns that were not allayed a month later. The national champion argument was not supported by Vestager.

Performance

Performance: social efficiency - mainly defined by extent of market power. The notions are that the monopoly is sloth-like and inefficient, whilst exploiting the consumer. Indicators:

❑ Size of business profits. In SCP, evidence of excess profits rates is indicative of exploiting the consumer. Trends in real price levels over time can indicate whether prices and hence profits are suitably modest, e.g. BG and wholesale gas prices.

❑ Efficiency is a major outcome of the competitive process. Allocative efficiency concerns allocating resources to maximise well-being. Productive efficiency relates to achieve the maximum feasible output from a given set of inputs.

❑ Technical progress is an outcome of investment decisions; possibly in R&D; possibly on human capital. A more technically advanced society has a higher standard of living. Investment in these areas is key indicators of future growth.

❑ Growth in output and productivity are the sources of rising incomes. Does it lead to rising labour productivity in the industry?

❑ Quality of the output or service can rise or fall depending on the state of the economy. Better quality goods would last longer, leading hopefully to less waste.

Unfortunately, SCP tells us that socially desirable corporate performance can only be achieved by a 'good' market structure comprising many equally-sized, small firms. In the neo-classical world, this would involve rivalrous rather than collusive price setting, little rather than a great deal of advertising and a great deal of innovation, although small firms may find this difficult to fund. If you like, competition is the spur that keeps the firm running just to stand still. The threat is always there that without the drive to be competitive rivals will steal market share. To a great extent it posits that the greater cost of market entry makes it easier for existing firms to maintain SNP. Market concentration decreases the cost of collusion between firms and results in SNP. The theoretical predictions of SCP appear to be difficult to reconcile with the reality of the evolution of some market structures. It could be that conduct affects structure, through merger activity. Indeed, with the most efficient firms taking market share from rivals, performance can affect structure also. This gives them more market power. The fine line between market dominance and economic efficiency comes with the 'abuse of dominant position.' The EC focuses on evidence of abuse rather than market dominance.

Post 2000 Performance

Robert Gordon finds that American companies are looking weak when it comes to technological innovation. The fifth long wave is waning. There is a decrease in the productivity of research spending. Comparing US spending on research and development with increases in reported labour productivity, the system needs a lot more R&D spending to keep improving at the same pace. More precisely, it would take a doubling of research effort every 13 years just to avoid a productivity slowdown. McKinsey Global Institute in 2017 reported that average annual US productivity growth was 2.1% between 1987 and 2004 but only 1.2% in the subsequent decade.

If the stream of innovation is thinner, fewer companies should be able to enjoy entrepreneurial profits and durable competitive advantages, so lead to a narrowing profit margins. However, Gutierrez and Philippon measured the contribution to annual national productivity growth of the four largest US companies by market capitalisation in 62 industries (= 248). The companies at the top shifted over the years, so the list always included the winners of the period. From 1960 to 2000, the annual average contribution to productivity growth of companies was 72bps. From 2001 to 2016, the average was 43bps. The pattern is similar for market shares. In 1980 domestic sales of the 248 = 29% of GDP, but by 2016 = 25%.

Corporate profit/GDP between 1991 and 2000 was 5% but for the following decade it was 10%. Profit did not feed capital spending. Private investment declined in the same periods (17.6% to 16.2% of GDP). The IMF found the same but across 27 countries two-thirds of them in developed economies. Examining detailed financial statements for 900,000 firms from 2000 to 2015, 'mark-ups' increase by 6% overall, but by 30% in the firms which already had the highest 10% of mark-ups. Once corporates have significant market power, they slow down their pace of technical improvement, particularly digital technology industries. In sophisticated and highly specialised industries, the market leaders benefit from network effects and economies of scale, which squeeze smaller rivals. With few constraints on pricing, market winners are also profit winners. This trend to higher profitability and market dominance can cause problems.

Despite what claims are made at the outset, *mergers* increase size which often brings higher mark-ups. However, more rapid increases in market share also accelerate the arrival of the technological tipping point, when companies have more to lose from disrupting their own technology than they can gain from adding new customers.

Google –FANGS and Regulation

Concern for innovation or non-price effects rarely animates or drives investigations or enforcement actions, especially outside of the merger context. Economic factors that are easier to measure, such as impacts on price, output, or productive efficiency in narrowly defined markets, have become disproportionately important. One of the problems with SCP in pegging competition to short-term price and profit outcomes is these are not consistent with the architecture of market power in the modern IT economy. Static competition underappreciates the risk of predatory pricing and how integration across distinct business lines may prove anti-competitive. The economics of platform markets create incentives for a company to pursue growth over profits. Under these conditions, predatory pricing becomes highly likely and which down plays profit as an indicator of monopoly practice. Because online platforms serve as both market-maker and supplier they to control the essential infrastructure on which their rivals depend - information. This dual role also enables a platform to exploit information collected on companies using its services to undermine them as competitors. Take the EC antitrust investigation into Amazon to establish whether it maintained barriers to market entry into the ebooks market through clauses in contracts with publishers. There are two types:

1. it requires to be informed of more favourable or alternative terms offered to competitors;
2. it seeks the right to terms and conditions at least as good as those of its competitors.

It has 90% market share of the UK market, one of the two largest markets in Europe. In September, without a complaint, it launched an investigation into this dual role over Marketplace. Like Tesco et al, it has its own-brand products, worth possibly $7.5bn in 2018.

The European Commission in April 2013 found Google results were favouring its in-house services to the detriment of consumers in areas such as maps, finance or weather. In February 2018, Google was fined 1.36bn Rupees (£15.2m; $21.2m = 5% of Google's average annual revenues in India) by India's competition regulator CCI for abusing its dominance in the country. Users searching flight details were directed to Google's own flight search page, disadvantaging rival businesses. The complainants, Bharat Matrimony and a consumer protection group, filed in 2012. In June 2017, Google was fined €2.42bn euros by the European Commission after it ruled the company had abused its power by promoting its own shopping comparison service at the top of search results. In July 2018, Google's fine was €4.34bn (2 weeks of revenues, below the 5 weeks max). It was ordered it to stop using its Android mobile operating system to block rivals. With the free Android system running on 80% of the world's smartphones, it is a virtual monopoly. As they cost more and require users to exert significant effort to adopt, Vestager argued that competition from Apple iPhones was not a sufficient check on Google's dominance. Moreover, although phone owners could download alternative web browsers or using other search engines, only 1% used an alternative search app, and 10% a different browser. In March, another record €1.49bn fine for abuse of dominant position stopping publishers from placing any search ads from competitors on their search results pages, forcing them to reserve the most profitable space on these pages for Google's ads, and a requirement to seek written approval from Google before making changes to how rival ads were displayed. Google put its own shopping links at the top of the list of results, with rivals' elsewhere. The smaller mobile phone screen accentuated the advantage denying other companies the chance to compete on their merits and to innovate. It denied European consumers the benefits of competition, genuine choice and innovation. The European

Commission has been investigating Google Shopping since late 2010, based on complainants such as Microsoft and Foundem.

Amazon launched an Australian site in December 2017, and its Prime service for faster delivery, in June 2018. In response to a sales tax on internet purchases, in July Amazon excluded Australians from their overseas sites. The Australian government extended its 10% percent goods and services tax (GST) to all goods bought online from overseas, effective July 1st, requiring online retailers to collect the tax. This could constitute third degree (geographical) price discrimination. The alternative explanation is in the tax collection system. Ebay's decision to build the new tax collection and payment system had paid off with early figures suggesting Australian shoppers were not swayed by the new tax.

The Importance of the Click Monopoly
The Australian Competition and Consumer Commission launched an investigation into Google and Facebook in December over the bundling of Chrome, creating a near monopoly position on internet search. The top three in any search get 35%+17%+11% of the clicks. The top 10 on page 1 get 95% of clicks; the top of page 2 gets 1%, so controlling page 1 matters. The ACCC believes that for every A$100 spent on digital advertising in Australia, A$47 goes to Google and A$21 to Facebook. Procter & Gamble's chief brand officer, told the Association of National Advertisers' media conference in March 2018 that the average view time for an ad on a mobile news feed is 1.7 seconds. Consumer data company, Dunnhumby, find that the average time that an ad is viewable on retailer sites is about 16 seconds, where 'viewable' is when at least half of the ad is on the screen. Dunnhumby estimated that almost £100,000 of sales of a leading brand of dishwasher tablets came from customers exposed to a banner advert on Tesco website, with 6% of the sales occurring in a store, and 2,200 new customers had added the brand to their online favourites list as a result of the campaign. This translated into a return on advertising spending of £11.34 for every £1 invested, far more than an average return on ad spend of £2.62 for every £1 invested across all media types (Nielsen, 2016).

Retailers like Tesco and Walmart are aggressively attracting big advertisers like Kraft Heinz and Procter & Gamble to their websites. Specifically, they are selling more ad space, pop-up banners and search-bar keywords to consumer goods companies. What they are offering is guided buying. The target consumer has a revealed preference to buy; using their individual shopping habits, they are guided to specific products. This online ad revenue offers significantly higher margins for retailers than selling goods in stores. Retailers are offering pop-ups, banner ads, and money-off deals which, in return earn the advertiser pay anything from 25¢ to $2 each time a shopper clicks on a sponsored search item, depending on the product being sold.

Google - Another Microsoft SCP view
The list of innovative products that Microsoft is associated with, but, in fact copied, is noteworthy. The icon-based operating system was an innovation on the Apple Mac but

copied by Windows. Wordperfect and Lotus 123 were market leaders in word processing and spreadsheets until Word and Excel swept them away. Pegasus email was trounced by Outlook and Netscape fell to Internet Explorer. However, this was not necessarily because their products were better. Microsoft's facilities are bundled. Why buy a package when MS provides it free with the bundle. In 2009, the EC required Microsoft to offer customers choice. The operating system would be required to present a list of browsers, such as Firefox, Opera with IE. In response, Microsoft stripped out Internet Explorer from the Windows bundle.

Margrethe Vestager, the EU Competition Commissioner, in April 2016, accused Google of bundling. By June 2018, she was to instigate formal proceedings. That is restricting users of Android in a similar way that Microsoft had constrained users to utilising Explorer and media player. Android accounts for 80% of mobile devices, but it is given away. Earnings come from complementary sales and advertising. In February 2014, it was shown that Google's contracts suppressed competition. A contract with HTC to distribute Google products, such as Gmail or search, was contingent on all Google applications being pre-installed onto the smartphone with Google search as the default. At its peak in 2000, Windows controlled 97% of the world market. However, by 2016, on all computing devices it was down to 26% of the operating system market.

In April 2016, Getty Images, in effect, claimed that Google was doing to it what Microsoft did to Pegasus email – giving a rival service away free. Getty claimed that, from January 2013 when high resolution, large images were presented during searches on Google.com and Google.co.uk, Getty's revenues dropped propitiously. They did not see a revenue drop on French and German versions of Google where these images were not available.

Advertising Revenues
The German advert blocker, Eyeo, developer of Adblocks Plus, was paid by Amazon, Google, Microsoft and Taboola to 'white-list' their adverts. As a free addition to Firefox and Chrome, an advert blocker would undermine the business model of these internet-based companies. The unknown fee was estimated at 30% of the ad revenue that would be unblocked. On-line advertising revenue is estimated at $120bn, $69bn on mobiles. From June 2015, iOS 9, the Apple operating system included ad-blocker. This can be seen as part of a privacy and security theme that differentiates iOS from Android.

Digital advertising, a rising market is under threat. In May 2015, Facebook signed a content and an ad revenue sharing agreement with nine organisations including BBC News, the Guardian and NYT. Social media now controls access to news. This agreement reflects its power in the market over the ad revenues upon which news outlets would rely. It also gives Facebook editorial control over what has prominence – a Google problem.

In April 2016, this was made more evident when its CEO, David Pemsel, threatened to ban readers that used adblockers. This followed a warning from CityAM and Incisive Media in the UK. In Germany, Bild's owner Axel Springer in 2015 forced readers to choose between a subscription and advertising, which shifted at least 14% to switch off their ad-blocker. A further battle is being fought over web revenues. From June 2016, Tesco Mobile was offering customers a discount of £3/month on their bills if they use the app, Unlockd, which displays adverts and offers from companies including BA, McDonald's and the Sun.

In effect targeting Google and other advert revenue dependent, data-heavy users, network providers were offering ad-blockers. This would provide some leverage to get Google et al to share some of the pain of the network providers. From September 2015, Digicel became the first mobile operator to block adverts. The most exposed are those that rely on the open web. The costs to the industry range from $1bn (UPS) to $22bn (PageFair and Adobe). Interestingly, it is Google that is the most exposed of all. It is likely that without adverts the free rider generation will lose services.

Facebook members outside the US and Canada, are governed by terms of service agreed with the company's international HQ in Ireland. In May 2018, the EU's General Data Protection Regulation permitted regulators to fine companies of up to 4% of global annual revenue for infractions for collecting or using personal data without users' consent. Of the 1.9bn Facebook users potentially protected, 1.5bn were in Africa, Asia, Australia and Latin America. Facebook shifted this latter group to fall under the corresponding but more lenient US legal framework.

Hirchman-Herfindahl Index

As discussed numerous times in various *Updates*, Structure-Conduct-Performance emphasizes structure as a means of assessing the likely conduct and hence performance of companies. An assessment of changing structure, where barriers are high (and the market is not that contestable) is necessary. One measure of market concentration is the Hirchman-Herfindahl index. The formula $\sum_{i=1}^{n} S_i^2$ is based on market share (S) of the n firms in the industry. The US Dept. of Justice posts the following:

❑　　　HHI of 1,500 to 2,500 points is considered moderately concentrated;

❑　　　HHI in excess of 2,500 points is highly concentrated;

❑　　　Mergers that increase the HHI by more than 200 points in highly concentrated markets are presumed likely to enhance market power.

	MS	MS²	MS²
Aldi	7.50%	56.25	56.25
Asda	15.30%	234.09	
Co-Op	5.90%	34.81	34.81
Iceland	2.30%	5.29	5.29
Lidl	5.30%	28.09	28.09
Morrisons	10.60%	112.36	112.36
Ocado	1.10%	1.21	1.21
Other Outlets	1.60%	2.56	2.56
Sainsbury's	15.90%	252.81	973.44
Symbols & Independent	1.70%	2.89	2.89
Tesco	27.70%	767.29	767.29
Waitrose	5.10%	26.01	26.01
Total	100.00%	1523.66	2010.20

If there were 6 firms having equal market share, the HHI would be 1,667. If two of them merged, the index would rise to 2,222, clearly over a 200-point change. Notice that with similar market shares, the HHI is lower. If one of the 6 collapsed and the remaining 5 attained shares so that each controlled 20% of the market, the HHI would rise to 2,000. Thus, a measure of market dominance is captured here.

UK mergers are exempt from scrutiny if the turnover of the firm being taken over is £70m or less and the combined firms will have no more than 25% market share. In April 2018, Sainsbury's announced a £7.3bn takeover of Asda. The combined revenues were £51bn. Despite the claim that none of its 2,800 stores would close, it was estimated that there were synergies of at least £500m, and interestingly, enabling prices to be lowered by about 10% on many products. It was blocked by the CMA a year later on the basis of price rises in local markets. HHI would have jumped from 1,524 to 2010 and market share would be 31.2%. That said, over that period market Sainsbury's and Asda's share dropped by 0.3% each.

Tesco's March 2018 purchase of the wholesale group Booker supplying 5,000 outlets, was cleared unconditionally, when the regulator accepted that the presence of Aldi and Lidl deterred the merging parties from raising prices. Discounters account for 22% market share in Europe, up from 17% a decade ago. Moreover, September saw joint venture between Carrefour and Tesco on global purchasing and expanding their own-label ranges, tightening a squeeze on major brand producers, such as Nestlé and Kraft Heinz.

Oligopoly (the focus of SCP)
In practice, the monopoly is far less common than its close companion, the oligopoly. Oligopoly market is defined as small number of firms sharing a large proportion of an industry or market, such as firms producing an almost identical product, e.g. metals, chemicals, sugar, petrol. Alternatively, oligopoly firms produce differentiated products, e.g. cars, soap powder, cigarettes, electrical appliances, that are quite similar. Because there are only a few firms in the industry each firm's decisions will depend on the perceptions of the potential behaviour of rivals. Therefore, firms are mutually dependant – they price interdependently.

Either explicitly or implicitly, if they act as one (so like a monopoly), oligopolists may find long run profit are maximised jointly. Acting as one when either coordinated or uncoordinated, implies less rivalry. Cartels comprise coordinated oligopolists that agree price or output quotas among themselves. Based on oil, perhaps OPEC is the most famous inter-State cartel. Colombo, Sri Lanka, India, Kenya, Indonesia, Malawi and Rwanda formed the International Tea Producer's Forum. Collectively, they control more than 50% of global production. Note, there is an incentive to renege on the agreement, which could undermine the cartel.

In August 2016, four of the 6 largest European truck makers were fined collectively €2.93bn for jointly manipulating price and delaying emissions reductions measures in diesel trucks. This would include MAN and Scania, both Volkswagen marques. They had been collaborating from 1997 to 2011. MAN was exempt as it whistle-blew. The Road Haulage Association began preparing legal action seeking damages of £6,000×650,000 trucks = £3.9bn. Scania denied any wrongdoing but in the end was fined €880m in September. Commissioner Vestager pointed out that the EC had uncovered nine cartels in the automotive sector and fined companies more than €6bn for their illegal behaviour in the past decade.

Following the emissions scandal, it emerged in July that Volkswagen and Daimler being investigated for collusion in fixing the price of diesel emissions treatment systems. BMW was being investigated in October. Bosch agreed to pay $327.5m in colluding with VW, installing the software, which itself was fined €1bn. In January, Ford was being sued for using similar software in trucks. Daimler car engines in June 2018 were found to have five "illegal switch-off devices" possibly used by the bulk of Daimler's new Euro 6 diesel car fleet (1m vehicles).

A letter to the Telegraph in 2014 from the CEO of First Utility claimed two issues of interest. First, Ian McCaig asserted that the big six energy companies were engaged in **limit pricing**. They were setting tariffs so low as to attract customers from new rivals to quash competition. Second, the costs of this policy were being borne by those on standard tariffs. This is at odds with the claim that tariffs in 2018 were 'rip-offs.' Legislation was proposed to allow Ofgem to limit how much companies can charge their 11m standard variable tariffs (SVT) customers. Ofgem estimated the price difference between the average SVT default deal and the cheapest rate in the market was £308 (December 2017). One way around this is to scrap SVT – the regulated bit. Of course customers are still likely to be better off by searching and switching themselves (see Competition Thoughts). Between April 2016 and May 2017 the large and medium-sized suppliers charged consumers on SVTs a similar amount (£1,074 and £1,082 respectively). Over the same period, on average, consumers on fixed tariffs were charged £116 less by the six large suppliers, and £165 less by medium-sized.

Citizens Advice central estimated in July 2018 that there was £7.5bn of excess profits[2]. The average company rate of profit was running at 10% and none earn less than 7%. The big six made £54 of profit per dual fuel customer in 2016.

You become weary of the lame debate. Firstly, the government claimed that domestic customers of the big six energy companies were paying on average £1.4bn a year more than they would in a truly competitive market. The government knows that this claim is costless to make to them. Secondly, Lawrence Slade, CEO of the industry body, argued a cap would damage investment and competition. The industry knows that can still make large profits. Centrica raised its electricity charges by 12.5% in August 2017, claiming it made a loss on electricity supply. E.On in March 2018, in effect, raised

---

[2] https://www.citizensadvice.org.uk/Global/CitizensAdvice/Energy/EnergyConsumersMissingBillions.pdf

SVT rate by £22/year. It removed various discounts for paperless billing and using both electricity and gas, making it 'easier for customers to understand its tariffs and to compare them with competitors.' Paperless and double tariffs are standard! Moreover, blaming the cap, Centrica added an extra 4,000 jobs to be shed by 2020, saving £500m/yr. This takes the total to be made redundant to 9,500, and a saving of £1.25m/yr.

The industry and the government know that competition is skewed. In 2011 there were 14 energy providers. By June 2018 reached 70. In 2018Q4, small and medium suppliers grew to a market share of 26% and 27% in electricity and gas. Moreover, those with less than 250,000 customers do not pay certain environmental charges. Government policies add £165 to a bill, up from £81 in 2014. This threshold could drop to 100,000. But these can fail. By March, 10 new entrants into the energy market had failed, Brilliant Energy - which supplied energy to 17,000 households failed. This followed National Gas and Power, Iresa, Gen4u, Usio Energy, Extra Energy, Spark Energy Supply Limited, OneSelect, Economy Energy and Our Power. Customers are commonly shifted to another small provider. Economy Energy and Our Power customers have been automatically switched to Ovo and Utilita, both of which were under investigation. Many of the customers of failed firms have faced difficulties owing to poor customer service. This puts into sharp relief whether this is a good thing. From a CMT basis, these firms act as a threat, forcing the incumbents to behave well. But this might be stressful for subscribers.

Ofgem calculated the HHI for various sections of the electricity and gas wholesale markets for small and large energy buyers. Here, the market dominance of the largest suppliers is not so great and getting smaller. The wholesale market is becoming volatile. PwC estimate that 17% of industrial companies are looking to generate some electricity, particularly on site. Carriage for domestic suppliers makes up 26% of the bill. Northumbrian Water saved £12,500 using the Bran Sands solar scheme. The cost/unit is half that off the grid. Lightsource Renewable Energy suggests that even

HHI	2016	2017
E small	1.276	1.200
E large	1.112	1.017
G<73,200 kWh	1.544	1.320
G>73,200 kWh	1.115	1.270

without subsidies businesses could save 15-25% of their electricity bill using solar. Hanson built a £13m 12MW solar farm in its abandoned Ketton Cement works, saving £7-8m over 22 years = 5% of its total energy bill.

Ofgem recognises that the grid charges will have to be reviewed with this trend. Indeed, Citizens Advice highlight that National Grid, across gas and electricity in 2016/17 made an operating profit of £2.1bn in their UK network business.

Airline Income Issues
Periodically an airline admits where its real profit strategy is aimed. 60% of United Airlines' $5.8bn revenue in 2017 were additional charges or optional extras. Half of Sprint Airlines' $657bn revenue was not ticket and 28% ($2bn) of Ryanair's was not ticket. Indeed, over 10 years the top 10 airlines saw a rise in revenue from $2.1bn to

$29.7bn. Ryanair take a stepped approach to customers so that they can sell more to their existing group. The lowest level involves the ticket, then car hire, booking a hotel room and buying tickets for activities such as tour guide. The top level is the opportunity in the airline's one-stop shop.

In the 10 years from 2007 the number of people flying internationally from Britain grew 43% to 229m/yr. By contrast internal, domestic flights fell by 10% to 22.8m. The fall has seen the number of routes with more the 1,000 passengers/yr from by 40 to 188. A key driver is tax. As £13/passenger. For a small airline, such as Flybe, it is 20% of the average fair, possibly 50% with promotional fares. Long haul rail transport grew by 40% over a similar period to 145m suggesting that the closure of routes benefits alternative transports. Budget airline continue to collapse as the European airline sector grapples with over-capacity and high fuel costs. Recent failures include Britain's Flybmi, Iceland's Wow, Germany's Germania, Nordic budget airline Primera Air and Cypriot counterpart Cobalt.

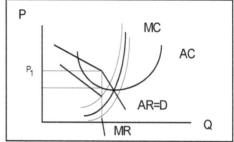

A non-collusive oligopoly is associated with the kinked demand curve. The kink can be explained in terms of its inelastic and elastic portions. Revenue increases if price rises on the inelastic portion but falls on the elastic. As a result, in the figure right, the oligopolists choose to operate at the kink at P_1; any movement away from that point will lead to a reduction in revenue. Alternatively, the kinked demand curve of Sweezy carries the presumption that if an oligopolist cuts its price, to avoid losing customers/market share, its rivals will be forced to follow suit, whereas if an oligopolist raises its price, because they can gain extra custom from not doing so, its rivals will not follow suit.

	Dec-17	May-19
Lloyds	1.96	1.43
RBS	1.71	1.67
Tesco	1.52	1.43
Nwide	1.38	1.37
HSBC	1.32	1.16
Sector	1.6	1.43

A Price War in Mortgages
In May, Tesco announced it was withdrawing from the UK mortgage market. Entering the fray in 2012, it got its mortgage book up to £3.7bn. It was squeeze out by a price war sparked by an aggressive HSBC which increased its book by 10% in 2018 to £94.2bn holding a market share of 6.6%. Two yr fixed mortgage rates fell from 4.79% in 2009Q1 to 2.49% in 2019Q1. The spread over swap rates fell from 1.6 to 1.43bps from the end of 2017 to May 2019. Nationwide reported the net interest rate (lending–deposit rate) fell from 1.31% in 2018 to 1.22% in 2019. The price war meant costs were not covered.

Because the oligopolist will lose revenue if they change price in either direction, rising costs may not alter price. The MC curve moves anywhere in the gap (indicated by the dashed MC curves) in the MR and the firm will not change its price. Practically, what we see is an alteration of the product. Possibly as a result of the falling value of Sterling, Toblerone, choosing to change the shape of the bar, and *not* raising the price, elected to put bigger spaces between the segments. The move resulted in the weight of the 400g bars being reduced to 360g and the 170g bars to 150g, while the size of the packaging remained the same. Perhaps a fine example of this backfiring was the 2015 decision by Mondelez to change the recipe for Cadbury's Creme Eggs using cheaper chocolate. The product was the same for 45 years. Research by IRI for The Grocer found that it lost more than £6m in sales revenue in 2016. A recent examination of chocky activities can be seen left. Comparing 2014 with 2018, Hobnobs appear cheaper, reduced from £1.90 to £1.83, a 3.68% reduction. However, less well observed, due to the reduction is size, the unit cost rose by 17%.

	Weight Grms		Price £		Unit cost £/g	
	2014	2018	2014	2018	2014	2018
Hobnobs	250	205	1.9	1.83	0.76	0.89
Jaffa Cakes 2p	150	122	0.84	0.87	0.56	0.71
Jaffa Cakes 3p	450	467	2.35	1.55	0.52	0.33
Snickers 4p	136	119	1.58	1.33	1.16	1.12
Snickers 7p	232	167	2.38	1.9	1.03	1.14
Toblerone	400	360	3.5	4	0.88	1.11
Twix	58	50	0.45	0.6	0.78	1.20
Twix 4p	200	160	1.2	1.38	0.60	0.86
Yorkie	55	46	0.59	0.62	1.07	1.35
Yorkie 3p	160	132	1.57	1.25	0.98	0.95

The Jaffa cakes two pack was not much worse value than the 3 pack at 52p/g in 2014. However, the three pack saw a reduction in price and increase in weight, whilst the two pack saw the reverse. This could in part be linked to second degree price discrimination. However, that does not work with Snickers, which despite the extra volume, unit cost for the 7 pack is greater than the four pack.

Although we are discussing Oligopoly, the monopoly is the standard unit for discussing whether the market is efficient or not. Or whether there is a market failure where a suboptimal level of output is produced. From this, the profit maximising firm with market power and the **cartel** draw a criticism.

The diagram below shows the standard comparisons. Under Perfect Competition, the market price is determined by the interplay of Supply and Demand. Market price would be P_1 and market quantity Q_1. The industry supply is based on the Marginal Cost curves of the firms in the industry.

The formation of a cartel or a monopoly from these providers changes the analysis. The supply curve is now the MC curve of the cartel. As the cartel is large relative to the market, to sell more it must lower price. The marginal revenue from selling the additional unit should be no less than the MC. It is in the cartel's interest to restrict supply to Q_2 and charge the monopoly price P_2. As a result of this action: price rises from P_1 to P_2, reducing consumer surplus; output is lowered from Q_1 to Q_2, reducing producer surplus; but the cartel's marginal cost per unit C is less than the price P_2 (The gap is not total SNP).

At price P_1 a competitive market can be analysed as:

Consumer surplus   A+B+F
Producer surplus   C+D+G

At price P_2 a monopoly produces less - Q_1 to Q_2 and can be analysed as:

Consumer surplus   A;
Deadweight loss   F+G;
Input cost   E;
Reallocated resources   H.

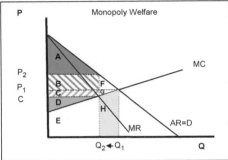

Hence, there could be a higher price and lower output than under perfect competition.

But Monopoly can benefit the community due to:

- Economies of scale - larger plant, centralised administration. These benefits may be passed on to consumers in lower prices;
- More large scale investment, such as the HS2 project can only be delivered by a large firm;
- More R&D - innovation and new products – the promise of entrepreneurial profits may encourage new (monopoly) industries producing new products;
- Natural monopolies - where it only makes sense to have one firm (only one provider of pipes to your door);
- Greater stability – Monopolist can provide steady employment.

In neo-classical economics, we assume monopoly profits are protected by insuperable barriers to market entry. Barriers to entry may take the form of:

- Natural monopolies - only one provider of pipes to your door so you cannot switch providers;
- Advertising and branding - where a market is dominated by one seller it would be difficult for a new firm to break into the market i.e. to attract customers away from a familiar brand;
- Lower costs for an established firm - will have specialist production and marketing skills, likely to have cheaper suppliers and access to cheaper finance;
- Monopolists could use limit-pricing to reduce access to the market. Price is set so low to deter entrants (is this bad?);
- Aggressive tactics - can sustain losses for longer than a new entrant e.g. engage in a price war (retaliatory price cutting);
- Legal protection, such as copyright, patents;
- Control over key factors of production;
- Control over wholesale or retail outlets.

Austrian Perspective

The Austrian School of thought, inspired by Schumpeter, proposes that profit of itself is not evidence of nefarious practices nor is a monopoly necessarily a source of market failure. Rather than the static view of competition whereby a stable economic environment is populated by established firms producing a well-known product using techniques that are known by all, competition is dynamic and subject to imperfect information.

Relaxing the assumptions of a homogeneous product and perfect knowledge, competition, according to Schumpeter, is driven by innovation. The firm exploiting new products processes and markets serves the consumer. The entrepreneur utilises new technologies, driving forward technical progress. Profit is the incentive for this innovation and the reward for taking risk.

Assume all parties have only impacted (asymmetric) knowledge. That is, the customers, suppliers of resources and entrepreneurs are aware partly of each other's capabilities and needs. The actor that responds most quickly to new information is the entrepreneur. Others may copy but the entrepreneur leads the way. This information may be freely available to everyone or, possibly in world of constantly changing taste, only revealed when the consumer can see what is on offer. To acquire information about consumer tastes the entrepreneur presents something new to the market. If this product is not to the consumer's taste, sales will be modest and losses may lead to the product being dropped. However, considerable profits may follow the launch of a product that consumers find highly desirable. This new product is distinct, produced by a single firm and generates significant profits, not directly related to the marginal cost. From a SCP perceptive, this is problematic.

Depending on whom you read, one can suggest that entrepreneur has two roles: opportunity spotter and a risk bearer. For Schumpeter, only a small number of people can be entrepreneurs who can bear the risk of losing their shirt on an investment of sizeable proportions. They are risk-neutral whereas we are risk-averse – that's what makes them different. The scope to spot opportunities though could be in all of us. The basis for profit could be the reward for identifying gaps in the market and getting a product there before others. Alternatively, realising that a process can be improved, someone being entrepreneurial but not risking their own money could initiate this.

In this world there are three type of profit: Monopoly, Windfall, and Entrepreneurial. The monopoly profits are those that are generated by the restrictive or collusive activates that SCP focuses on. The windfall profits are those that are not related to barriers or investment. The entrepreneur just has good fortune. It is more like gambling than investing. The entrepreneurial profit is the reward for spotting the opportunity and taking the risk. In a sense, the fruits of investment follow after years of research in the area. Without the reward, the risk may not have been taken and hence, the innovation would not have occurred.

The process that the Austrians envisage is that once the entrepreneur succeeds their monopoly position is only temporary. As with perfect competition, once the creator is rewarded with high profits, others see these profits. In perfect competition, using the freely available information, they break into the market. With this Austrian school this could include mimicking, so driving price downward. However, the pioneering work may drive others to innovate in the same area to improve existing products and so they then become temporary monopolists. The process entails a succession of temporary monopolists developing better more powerful products for the consumer. How long this process might take is open to question. Holding a patent acts as a barrier to entry and yet the income stream from this patent is what drove the entrepreneur to innovate in the first place. Today, technology companies squabble over patents. Patent laws may be a help in certain industries but be a hindrance in others. From an Austrian perspective, a patent restricts a potential monopolist from emerging from that pack of innovators desperate to improve on the existing model. From the pharmaceuticals industry's perspective, copycats steal some profits but are not innovating. Mainly because of the need for large clinical trials, bringing a new drug to market is inordinately expensive. To amortise these costs, monopoly rights over what has been produced are spur to future invention: without them the risk-reward ratio will deter the exploitation of new drugs.

Should mobile phones and the like be granted the same protection as a drugs company? Drugs companies may need 20 years' worth of protection. It is suggested that, with the Hi-Tec electrical products, the patent protection inhibits innovation and should be removed. The iPhone and the iPad sold many millions of units within their first years. With the latter, Apple has been rewarded by the first-mover advantage. Perhaps we could view these two cases by examining monopoly vs. entrepreneurial profit. Buying a patent just to extract rent is a case of monopoly profit. Holding a patent to amortise the costs of development is entrepreneurial profiting.

There is a new form of behaviour where an 'entrepreneur' holds patents with no intention of using them to fabricate products. They wait for a major corporation to use them so that the entrepreneur can then sue. This is much like companies buying up ip-addresses, parts of the broadcast spectrum or telephone numbers they suspect will be useful in the near future. Moreover, control of intellectual property is becoming the driver behind mergers. Google, in May 2015, was accused by the EC of 'abusive enforcement' of its intellectual property rights over a technology vital to the smartphone, acquired from Motorola. The action was to thwart Google from preventing innovation by Apple. The technology, which should become an industry standard, should be licensed on a non-discriminatory basis.

Monopoly Patent
An exploitative industry where patents act as barriers to entry is the pharmaceutical industry. The FT noted that the pharmaceutical industry's most common exploitative pricing strategies:

- Raise price annually – the new normal from 2017. Some, under pressure, have promised to keep them to single figures but this turns out to be 9%, or 7% above the cost of living rise. Humira rose from $792.14 in 2007 to $2923.22 for 40mgs. The best example is an Aids medicine that was increased in price by 5,000%.
- Raise price twice a year – the old normal. Pfizer's Viagra rose from $12.03 in 2007 to $88.45 in July 2018.
- Being the sole producer (even without a current patent) – the classic example of finding a medicine without rival producers and bump the price. Cerecor, the only maker of 5mg pills of Millipred, off-patent for years, rose from ¢40 in 2008 to $16.87 in 2017.
- Stymie the competition – formularies drugs are lists of drugs that insurers and employers are willing to allow doctors to prescribe. In effect, they exclude very expensive ones. However, access to these lists can be purchased, keeping cheaper alternatives off the list. This purchase is through the rebates given to pharmacy benefit managers.

Eli Lily Pfizer and the like extracted over $1bn in 2016H1 selling branded drugs to consumers rather than generics. Prozac was on the market at $11.39/pill when the generic costs 3¢. Lipitor costs $10.59 when the generic costs 13¢. The EpiPen was increased in price by 500% in 6 years. When under pressure during the presidential election the EpiPen price was reduced. Casper Pharma raised the price of a bladder infection antibiotic to $2800. Later Nostrum Labs raised the price of their version from $474.75 to $2,392. This treatment has been around since 1953. The CEO, Nirmal Mulye, implied it was a moral imperative to maximise profits. These were the liquid forms which were more difficult to produce. In the UK, the price was £446.95.

In 2019Q1, almost 3000 drug prices were increased in the US. Greed trumps social responsibility. But in May, 44 US states filed a lawsuit accusing 20 drug companies of a sweeping scheme to inflate drug prices and stifle competition for more than 100 generic drugs.

In May, the Competition and Markets Authority (CMA) alleged that, between 2013 and 2018, the price of Prochlorperazine rose from £6.49/ pack to £51.68, increasing the cost to the NHS from £2.7m to £7.5m, even though it dispensed fewer packs. Four suppliers colluded. Alliance supplied exclusively to Focus, which paid Lexon which shared payments with Medreich.

Contestable Market Theory
Where it is unlikely that the firms in the industry can be anything other than large, the consumer can still be served if the market is 'contestable.' Contestable Market Theory (CMT) has similarities with SCP. As with any perspective of competition, the threat of greater rivalry requires low barriers to market entry. Indeed, implicitly, the market should be mature and the product well understood so that the consumer is not subject to exploitation of an asymmetry of information. The key difference between SCP and CMT is in the number of competitors. A contestable market only requires a threat of

competition, not actual competition. The threat of market entry should force the incumbent [possibly a monopoly provider] to keep the customer happy by maintaining a good service, and prices and profits are modest. This means that the large firm can be limited to a range of activities that are socially desirable: there is an incentive to be innovative and to exploit economies of scale.

Contestable Market Theory focuses on exit costs. A deterrent to market entry is the assets that the firm is left with if it is squeezed out of the market. If the assets are market specific and the costs of such investment are irretrievable, these are called sunk costs. Crucially, the definition of a 'market' is rather specific. If we were analysing bus deregulation, a market could be a specific bus route. Is a bus limited to that route? As it can be transferred almost costlessly to another route, it is not a sunk cost.

Other pre-conditions for a contestable market are that new entrants face no additional costs or retaliatory price-cutting from the incumbents. By assumption, new small players not squeezed out by monopoly practices or by significant cost disadvantages. Like Perfect Competition, this is a standard. The model predicts that a monopoly will behave in a socially desirable way if it could be subject to hit-and-run competition. Thus, for there to be potential rivalry, the new entrant needs to have access to the market relatively costlessly, with low set-up costs.

By developing a second hand market for the assets necessary for market entry, contestability can be fostered by the State. Where the market is regulated, market access can be promoted by partial deregulation. Controls on retaliatory activities are needed and subsidies for set-up cost.

If a firm is protected from competition due to the ownership of a resource or patent needed to enter the industry, the same outcome could result – one monopolist player. However, this monopoly can be overcome by innovation. This is not a feature of CMT.

The Neworked Industry
We have stated the consumer can still be served if the market is 'contestable.' A contestable market requires only a threat of competition, not actual competition. A market without any competitors could still serve the public. One would have thought that a natural monopoly, such as a utility, would pose major problems. The theory of natural monopoly is an extreme case where the economies of scale are such that an industry may only be in equilibrium when there is one producer. With utilities, such as gas and electricity, it only makes sense to have one pipe or cable running to the house. The LRAC would be such that a second player in the market, taking some (equal) market share, could result in both firms making a loss.

A close examination reveals the natural monopoly element is the grid. Separating the grid or network from the service provider can make the market contestable. The customer selects from a number of competing service providers, each of whom can send the same product along the grid. Thus, a consumer can select from a list of 20+

electricity or gas providers, each of whom can use the same cable or pipe to the consumer's accommodation. If a rival is willing to offer electricity or gas at a lower cost, the consumer can switch. This threat of switching keeps the current provider on their toes.

In an effort to improve contestability Ofcom forced Openreach to extend access to rivals to BT. Before, rival accessed telegraph poles and underground ducts to lay their own fibre networks to reach residential and small-business customers. In May, this was extended to rivals serving large businesses as well. This also encouraged a faster roll-out of high-speed fibre cables.

Watering Down
In April 2017, the water market in England and Wales for 1.2m businesses, charities and public sector bodies was made contestable in that they were able to choose their supplier. Ofwat estimated that a net benefit of £200m. The next stage is deregulating the market for domestic customers. The benefit for this is up to £2.3bn. In June 2017, the lack of competition was estimated by Greenwich University to cost each HH £100/yr (£2.3bn). This is based on comparing the situation at privatisation in 1989 with the following era. Over 10 years to 2016 dividends of £18.1bn were paid out of £18.8bn post tax profit – almost all. Investment, funded by borrowing, resulted in £500m in interest payments. Water bills grew 40% faster than inflation over the 28 years. Investment declined by 10% to £4.56bn/yr in the decade to March 2018. Companies might prefer being fined to investing in waste disposal.

Open Access
Both sides of the Atlantic are tackling the issue of broadband and access. A concern regularly raised is the increasing demand placed on network providers by bandwidth hungry services like Facebook. With postal services, some customers pay for a faster service (1st class). If one looked at email, being delivered by the web, 'net neutrality' would imply all post would be treated equally and there would be no discrimination based on speed. However, internet service providers (ISPs) want to charge on the basis of the user's willingness to pay for speed, particularly with data-heavy applications. If there is pay for content, there will be a two-speed approach: some providers will pay for favourable treatment.

Network neutrality is, to some extent, based on a sharing of pain. The proprietary network (dumb-tube) provider is unwilling to bear the heavy cost of investment alone. Since 2008, YouTube video traffic from Google is flooding networks, leading to an imbalance in cost and benefits. Until they can amortize their investment costs, charging will be high on their agendas. It wants to shift from charging access to the internet to charging for heavy use: move from delivery to weight. This must be resolved otherwise the EU's hope of a significant investment in network infrastructure of possibly €300bn will not result. The House of Lords reported in February 2014 that to drive the economy forward, broadband and the digital revolution would be front and centre: broadband should be treated as a utility. This was mirrored in February 2015 by the

US Federal Communications Commission, which decided to treat broadband as a public utility. In June 2016, the US Court of Appeals for the District of Columbia Circuit ruled that broadband providers must act as "neutral, indiscriminate platforms for transmission of speech". The Federal Communication Commission switched US policy in December 2017. Although this may prevent start-ups from succeeding, the big winners from the neutrality were the FANGs, so their profits/power may be changing the policy landscape.

The current system in the US allows local cable companies to act as local monopolies, which is credited with generating the highest cable charges in any developed country bar Mexico, Chile and Turkey, combined with speeds only one tenth as fast as those in Singapore. The implication was that users would have received a bill that reflects their usage. Now that's not the case. There remains a problem of investment. The claim is that this would reduce the rate at which the infrastructure would improve.

Regulatory Capture
Regulation is an alternative means of addressing monopoly. Regulation entails a quasi-government body imposing on the industry the incentives and disincentives that competition should provide. This commonly involves setting price (for UK utilities) or rate of return (for US utilities) targets. 'Effective' regulation, though, is based on full information. The regulator is reliant on the information that the firms whom they regulate provide to them. The firm has an incentive to provide the regulator with a view of the business that best suits the corporation, not society. Thus, it has an incentive to boost its cost base or play down any likely benefits from innovations. For example, Severn Trent was accused of manipulating its accounts to underestimate its profits to the water industry regulator, OfWat, in 2004. Perhaps a worse accusation is that the Chief Regulator and the minister to whom they reported might have had an eye on the future. When they retire, these people may find that the firms that they were regulating are interested in hiring them. The likelihood of this may be inversely related to the harshness of the imposed regulatory regime. In October, the House of Commons criticised the OfWat for favouring the investor.

A variant of this is the advising minister. The Liberal Democrat, Steve Webb, who was a pensions minister joined the board of Royal London. He was in post during the largest pension reform of recent decades. Gregg McClymont, Webb's Labour shadow, joined Aberdeen Asset Management. Both lost their seats in the 2015 election. One could argue that this is the usual reward for regulatory leniency. However, the reforms were opposed by the industry. These appointments could be about contacts and influence as the policy is implemented, and how future changes can be moulded.

Mergers in Telecoms
In January 2015, BT agreed a £12.5bn takeover of EE. The estimated £360m a year in savings in operating costs and capital investment should emerge within four years, with an additional £1.6bn/yr in sales. The plan was to become a digital publisher along the lines of Netflix, Amazon and Sky, not just a network (dumb-tube) provider. This

precipitated a bid in March 2016 from Hutchinson Whampoa's 3 for O_2. This latter £9.25bn bid, it is suggested, would force the regulator, Ofcom, to investigate the competition issues for that merger and then for BT-EE. Without it, BT-EE merger may have avoided an investigation.

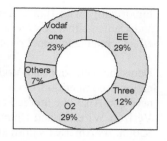

Irish telecoms in 2013 saw a merger bid by 3 for O_2's Irish subsidiary, which would reduce the number of mobile operators from 4 to 3. The merger was approved provided that a package was offered aimed at ensuring the short-term entry of two mobile virtual network operators (MVNOs), with an option for one of them to become a full mobile network operator by acquiring spectrum at a later stage. This involved releasing 30% of the merged company's network capacity. Second, the merged company offered a package aimed at ensuring that Eircom stays a competitive mobile network operator in Ireland.

In September 2015, Margrethe Vestager, the EU's Competition Commissioner blocked a merger between two Danish operators, Telenor and TeliaSonera, which would have reduce the number of telecoms groups in Denmark from four to three. This had implications for Hutchison's £10bn acquisition of O_2 from Telefónica, which would also cut the number of big operators in the UK market from four to three. This marked a shift. Perhaps it represents a concern that industry consolidation leads to higher prices, not more investment.

Although it appeared that the UK was heading for the standard number in the industry, the CMA recommended that the 3 - O_2 merger be blocked: the EU agreed in May 2016. Creating a group of 31m subscribers or 41% of the mobile phone market and having 45% of mobile infrastructure (spectrum) passed what appears to be a magic 40% threshold. EE would have 29% and Vodafone 23% of the mobile phone market. The Competition and Markets Authority approved the BT-EE merger without remedy. This could be used as a basis for a challenge.

To achieve economies players have been sharing masts and cables. O_2 shares with Vodafone and EE shares with 3. The merger would disrupt competition over coverage and quality to the detriment of the retail consumer. Investment is often the justification for consolidation. Ofcom believed that it would stifle investment in speed, coverage and reliability. Moreover, independent retail outlets on the high street take a large share of that market. The 3 - O_2 merger would shift power to the networks with implications for price of phones and bills. Hutchinson responded to the claim by pledging to hold prices fixed for 5 years. To what extent this is reliable is a good question.

In September 2016, Vestager approved a €20bn merger between 3-Italia and Wind Telecomunicazioni. With 31m customers, this created the largest supplier of mobile phone services in Italy. The Commission requires some spectrum to be sold to Illiad.

Importantly, with Illiad, there would be four players in the market. The Italian, Irish and Danish situations are instructive. The remedies would require incumbents to, in effect, create additional rivals in the market.

Deutsche Telekom and Vodafone proposed a merger in April 2018. This will have national competition issues but could facilitate the development of a pan-European network. Also, the merged company would be a European champion rivalling AT&T, Verizon Wireless and China Mobile. At the same time, T-Mobile bought Sprint for $26bn. As America's third and fourth largest mobile broadband carriers, it would have 127m customers. Verizon has 116m and AT&T has 93m. Both Sprint and T-Mobile are far behind Verizon and AT&T in upgrading their network to accommodate next generation 5G wireless technology, required for self-driving cars. Even after their merger, the combined company's budget to invest in 5G will be smaller than Verizon or AT&T's. In May 2018, Vodafone agreed to pay $21.8bn for Liberty Global's assets in Germany and eastern Europe to take the fight to rivals with a broader range of superfast cable TV, broadband and mobile services. Liberty is the world's second-largest mobile operator. This would compete with Deutsche Telekom. As this is not a horizontal merger, it will target revenue synergies of more than $1.8bn by cross-selling multiple services to the combined customer base. In May 2019, Vodafone attempted this again with Liberty Global in Germany. Telefonica Deutschland has 6% of the local market, Liberty Global 34% and Deutsche Telekom 40% so granting wholesale access to Telefonica may improve the competitive environment. All of these required approval.

AT&T and Time Warner
The US DoJ filed an antitrust lawsuit in November 2017 to block the merger, a deal valued at $108.7bn, including debt. The merger is a vertical merger. AT&T distributes TV and movie content. Time Warner's networks, like HBO and CNN, create it. As with previous similar mergers, it was approved but then challenged. The power of firms in sectors that are linked with the FANGs need to increase to present real competition for them. They control algorithms and can change what content people see.

Combining AT&T and Time Warner would also create competition problems. AT&T as the largest pay-TV provider in the country that now owns HBO's Game of Thrones NBA Games etc.. AT&T would also sell that programming to competitors like Comcast. With its new ownership of content, it has the incentive to extract monopoly rent, estimated at $580m/yr. Moreover, it could price rivals out of the market – akin to a price war. Moreover, the merger could inhibit innovation and alternative emerging rival TV shows or networks. For example, after the merger of NBCUniversal and Comcast, Bloomberg's financial news TV channel limited to cable. Bloomberg had to lobby the FCC for two years before it ruled in its favour.

In June 2018, a federal judge rejected claims from the US Justice Dept. that the merger would lead to less competition and higher consumer prices, only for the US government to appeal. It lost the appeal in February. The logic behind the AT&T-Time Warner merger is interesting. It perhaps reflects a 19th vs 21st Century business model. The former is about control whereas the latter is about renting. Marketing might have shifted from 4Ps to data to find value for the company. Personal preferences including style, timing, cost and externality can focus the market down to a very narrow market, possibly one. This is *bundling* but in a different way. Firms could become even smaller with a smaller set of managers and a looser set of freelance workers.

Competition Policy Thoughts

In a sense, the large firm cannot be *expected* to behave in a socially desirable way. The profit motive only produces favourable outcomes if its less desirable behavioural traits are limited. One approach, if you like, the backstop approach, entails legal constraints. To maximise their profit, businesses may drive hard bargains and even mislead or bluff their customers /suppliers so that they pay over-the-odds. As such, the market place is not necessarily fair and businesses are morally ambiguous. The law may require a given set of information be made available to buyers or a good last a minimum period of time. But this does not limit the price to be 'fair.'

One of the tests of competitive pressure is the ease with which one can switch providers. If switching costs (barriers to exit) are high, this would lower the pressure to keep the customer happy. Also, if there are no real alternatives, because of the limited number of competitors or that the industry has a common rather undesirable way of treating customers, what can you switch to? Having a variety of providers with distinctive products is OK if they are simple. Complex products, such as pensions, require considerable time and some guidance to avoid an adverse selection. Here, a skilled technician that is not a tied agent should advise. Pension advisors that are paid commission are incentivised, perhaps inappropriately. In May 2017, the Conservative party announced it would put a cap on energy prices. As noted above, legislation was introduced in February 2018. This is a sign that reliance on switching to force good behaviour DOES NOT WORK. Lethargy was estimated in January to cost 12.4m HH £709m in excess fees for home insurance. The Citizens Advice Bureau suggested that those that do not shop around paid more than they should. Overall, insurance, mobile phone and other broadband services added £4bn/yr in excess charges. Hitting a 6 year high, 15.8% of customers switched energy provider in 2016. The CMA reported in 2016 that over a 3 year period, 35% of HHs with earnings over £36,000 switched but for those with under £18,000 the rate was 20%. Ofgem finds that ⅔ of the 17m HH are on the SVR. Which? argued that customers were confused by the choice of tariff.

CSR and Enlightened Self Interest

The coal industry may have thought that Donald Trump would save it in the US. However, it might be the CSR of another industry, insurance, will kill it off. 25 of the world's largest insurers are refusing to cover miners and power generators that use coal. Global warming would directly affect their profitability. Examples include Axa and Zurich. That said, 54% of coal-fired power stations in Europe are loss making. This will rise to 97% by 2030 if climate change targets are to be met. The costs of exit (shutting) though are high. Redundancies and clean-up are expensive… so investment may be driven by profit rather than CSR.

In March 2018, BlackRock, the largest shareholder in Sturm, Ruger & Co and American Outdoor Brands (formerly Smith & Wesson) was considering offering investors the chance not to invest in gun firms. It also called for those firms to explain how they monitor safe use of weapons. Online lender Kabbage withdrew funding for the manufacturing of assault rifles and for the purchase of guns for under 21s. United and Delta airlines and rental giants Hertz and Enterprise, have stopped offering discounts to NRA members. First National Bank of Omaha did not renew NRA-branded credit cards. Chubb stopped underwriting an NRA-branded insurance policy. Insurer MetLife Inc also cut ties. Dick's Sporting Goods, no longer sell assault-style rifles. Walmart raised the minimum age for anyone buying guns or ammunition to 21 years.

The Bank of England concluded that financial scandals can be categorised in to seven groups: price manipulation; inside information; reference price influence; circular trading; collusion and information sharing; improper order handling; and misleading the customer. Compared with 200 years ago price manipulation techniques have changed but one can see the similarities. For example, fabricated twitter accounts were set up to spread fake negative news about Audience, a tech company and Sarepta Therapeutics, a biotech company. Misleading the customer was evident in The British Steel pension scandal. Members of the £15bn pension fund were given the option to shift their assured benefits to a new fund linked to Tata or to the Pension Protection Fund in August 2017. Of the 130,000 members, 11,000 asked for quotes on the value of their pension by December 2017 1,700 had left. Funds worth between £300,000 and £500,000 were being transferred in to vehicles that were unsuitable or with unhealthy charges. There is an accusation of misselling. Advisors were offering little advice other than to transfer, prompting a description of a feeding frenzy, particularly at the Port Talbot plant. This could be an ethical stance or possibly a commercial one. There could be major claims following this misselling.

Follows the FCA investigation of the role of financial advisors and the Tata Steel pension arrangements agreed with the pension fund and the regulator, Personal Financial Society for financial advisors highlighted that, when specialising in pension transfer advice, its 37,000 members were increasingly finding it difficult to get insurance.

In February 2018, Unilever added to the pressure on Google and Facebook to exercise greater responsibility on postings or they would refocus some of the €7.7bn marketing budget. This could be about something else. P&G spent $100m on digital marketing in one quarter in 2017 but saw no impact on sales. Are ads being viewed by people?

NATIONAL INCOME ACCOUNTING

National Income (NY) is defined as an estimate of the value of the goods and services made available as a result of a country's economic activity over a given period of time (usually one year) and reduced to a common basis by being measured in monetary terms. In attempting to measure the national income of a country for a particular year we are assessing the *flow* of goods or wealth produced in that particular year: we are *not* concerned with the *stock* of goods or wealth produced in the past.

We can learn about the measurement of National Income by looking at a Primitive Economy. The first settlers come to Lincolnshire and during the course of the first year produce 3 types of goods.

i.   wheat   - to stand for consumer goods
ii.   huts   - to stand for consumer durable goods
iii. tools   - to stand for capital goods

If we assume the primitive economy has no money and all goods produced must be handed in to a central authority for distribution, then we can measure the total amount produced in that economy in its final year in three ways:-

i.   At the OUTPUT stage: we could add up the total amount produced and handed to the Central Authority.

ii.   At the INCOME stage: we could add up the shares of the product handed to each family

iii.   At the CONSUMPTION and SAVING stage: we could add up the total amount of these goods that the families had in the course of the year either consumed or saved i.e. how they disposed of their income. We can conclude that

TOTAL OUTPUT = TOTAL INCOME = TOTAL CONSUMPTION and SAVING

In a modern economy the measurement is done through the medium of money and over 1 year. Thus, in the same way using money as our measure the total value of the output that is produced (TOTAL PRODUCT) will be equal to the total amount that is available to share out in wages, salaries, rent and profit (TOTAL INCOME) which again must be equal to the total amount which consumers can spend (TOTAL EXPENDITURE). In the following example, a bushel of wheat is sold for £1000. This production might involve the payment of £600 wages and salaries, £200 rent, £100 interest charges, £100 profit. The recipients of these incomes will have £1000 to spend or save. If this is carried out for the economy as a whole, then the same principle can be represented in a diagram illustrating the circular flow of income.

The households that provide the factors of production for firms do so in exchange for money. Firms use these factors to produce goods and services upon which the public spend their incomes. These incomes will be spent on those goods that households have thus helped to produce. We can measure national income at three points in the circular flow of income.

Firms produce that output

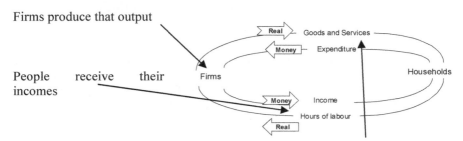

People   receive   their

incomes

These incomes are spent on goods and services produced.

Thus, total or *national output* will *equal* total or *national income* will *equal* total or *national expenditure*. All three totals are usually referred to as NATIONAL INCOME of the country for a year. Each method of income accounting faces certain problems

The **output** or **product method** attempts to measure the total value of goods and services produced by all sectors of the economy (public and private) during the course of a year. Essentially, we are seeking to measure *work done*. A good guide to work done is work paid for.

There should be an inclusion of goods and services that do not change hands against money. Examples include:

❑ Goods consumed by those that produce them, e.g. farm produce consumed on a farm. In less developed countries this problem has to be allowed for otherwise figures for output and income can appear unrealistically small.

❑ Unpaid services, such as household duties. A value for the work done should be imputed and included.

❑ Government services must be valued at cost of providing them. If £1bn is spent on education, then this is regarded as the total income generated.

❑ Rented houses provide an income in the form of rent. An amount must be included for living in owner-occupied house according to their current rental value.

❑ Double Counting - care must be taken to include only the value added at each stage of production process e.g. value of flour must not be included in value of bread.

The **total domestic product at factor cost** is essentially the sum of value of all goods and services produced in a year. The following adjustments must then be made:

❑ Deduct Stock appreciation. Allowance has to be made for the fact that this value of output may rise because of a rise in price of work in progress and goods held in stock.

❑ Residual error. This allows for statistical discrepancies in collection of data usually added by different means and from different sources for income, output and expenditure.

After these adjustments, the total becomes **gross domestic product at factor cost**. The following adjustments must then be made:

Net property income from abroad is where UK property owned abroad such as subsidiaries yield incomes in the form of interest, rent, profits etc. is included as part of output. Foreign property held in UK will cause income to flow abroad. Add this.

After these adjustments the total becomes **gross national product at factor cost**. Capital consumption or depreciation entails replacing worn out obsolete capital equipment. This output does not represent an addition to the capital stock.

Gross Capital Formation – Depreciation = Net Capital Formation

After these adjustments, the total becomes **net national product at factor cost (NNP) or national income**.

The **income method** is calculated as the total value of all incomes received by individuals and enterprises in the economy during the year. Incomes are in the form of wages, salaries, rent, and profits. The criterion is 'is the income the payment rendered by a person or his/her property?' Or is the income the result of output? The sort of difficulties one might face include:

□ Transfer incomes and payments are incomes received unrelated to any economic activity. They represent a redistribution of income e.g. student grants, pensions etc.. They must be removed unless they are provided by the private sector.
□ Taxation: include gross incomes as these are generated from output. They must be added in.
□ Profits of companies: whether distributed or undistributed, must be included as they are incomes generate from output. Also, include trading surpluses of public corporations, nationalised industries and Local Authorities.

After these adjustments, the total becomes **total domestic income at factor cost**. Stock appreciation (revaluation of stock) must be removed, as should residual error. The total becomes **gross domestic income at factor** cost. Removing net property income, the total becomes **gross national income at factor cost**. Adjusting for capital consumption or depreciation, the total becomes **net national income at factor cost**.

The **expenditure method** measures total amount spent on consumer goods and services and net additions to capital good and stocks in the course of the year. These include:

□ Current personal spending by private individuals on goods and services.
□ All government-spending central and local government spending except transfer payments.
□ All investment spending (Gross domestic capital formation).
□ Saving provides funds for investment, spent on capital good and for private consumers, such as their investment in house purchase.

Also included are stocks of goods not sold and goods but still on assembly line as these are outputs that have yielded an income. It must be included in expenditure and may be regarded as involuntary investment.

After these adjustments, the total becomes **total domestic expenditures at market prices**. Adjusting for foreign transactions (add export spending subtract import spending), the total becomes **gross domestic expenditures at market prices**. Subtracting taxes and adding subsidies produces **gross domestic expenditures at factor cost**. Then, adding net property income results in **gross national expenditures at factor cost**. Subtract capital consumption to produce **net national expenditures at factor cost**. O=E=Y.

Gross measures (GDP, GDI, GNP and GNI) reflect work done or wealth generated. Net measures (NDP, NDI, NNP and NNI) subtract capital consumption from the gross measures. The consumption of fixed capital or depreciation relates to an allowance for replacing the buildings and equipment that is gradually wearing out. As it shows output accounting for the state of the productive capacity, in a sense, the net figure is the more useful.

As part of a quinquennial revision of the national accounts, the US Bureau of Economic Analysis, in the summer of 2013, changed the composition of NDP. One notable variation in the composition of capital in recent years is the increased importance of information and communications technology. This is a fast depreciating asset sector. This would increase total capital consumption, *ceteris paribus*. Moreover, GDP will be 3% larger because corporate expenditures for intellectual property will be classified as 'capital investment.' Previously, they were an 'input cost.' All costs of buying a house are now seen as an investment. Before, just estate agents' commission was included. R&D is now part of capital investment. A taxi firm's purchase of a vehicle is viewed as a 'capital investment.' As this wears out, there is consumption of fixed capital, but this is disregarded entirely in the GDP number. The value above the labour time and the fuel is summed to form value-added in GVA, which ignores input costs. Thus, reclassifying corporate purchases as 'investment' rather than 'input' inflates value added or GDP but not NDP.

As measures of well-being, NDP and GDP/head are imperfect. Kenyan real GDP/head grew by 10% over 1993-2009 but the number with electricity doubled, the proportion with a phone went from almost zero to 60% and the proportion with a flushing toilet tripled. These changes in well-being are not captured by the GDP values.

Using UN standards for compiling national income, Japan's 2015 GDP was reevaluated from ¥499tn to ¥531tn. This was, in part, boosted by R&D spending, patents and copyrights. Potential growth is estimated at 0.5%. Given discussions elsewhere about full employment in Japan and upward revisions of growth and GDP, Japan appears to growth at full employment without inflationary or wage pressures.

Happiness

The French government, in 2009, appeared to be leading the way in incorporating unfashionable but logical economic policy ideas into their armoury. Stiglitz and his International Commission on the Measurement of Economic Performance and Social Progress considered how to assess well-being and the use of GDP as a proxy for this. At a basic level, GDP measures output – what is produced. For this to be a measure of well-being, income would have to be closely associated with utility – the homo economicus' acquisitiveness predominates. However, in this era of greater social and environmental concerns, is more consumption enhancing utility? The human costs of production are not measured. Working longer hours may boost income but it comes at the cost of leisure, perhaps more stress, and a less fulfilling family life. Investment requires a temporal shift of resources: less consumption now for more in the future.

The Commission proposed adjustments to the way GDP is calculated; new measures of well-being and happiness; and new metrics for environmental and financial sustainability. By taking into account its high-quality health service, expensive welfare system and long holidays, one consequence of these changes, is to improve France's measured economic performance.

The founder of Enlightenment Economics, Diane Coyle, suggested that happiness is not a 'policy useful' measure; policy levers cannot affect it easily. Rather, good health and type of employment, which are strongly linked to well-being, can be affected by government nudging.

The ONS reported[3] that the likelihood of reporting very high life satisfaction as a result of doubling of the share of spending on a particular category, April 2016 to March 2017, showed people do not like paying for communications. Take two people with the same level of household spending for example: the one who spends double the share of their spending on communication is 38 % points less likely to report very high life satisfaction than the other spending less in this way.

	Likelihood of very high	Income	Odds ratio	Age	Odds ratio
Miscellaneous*	-14.5	£18k <	1	70+	1.74
Household furnishings	9.3	£18k up to £24k	1.0	60-69	1.79
Recreation	8.0	£24k up to £32k*	1.3	50-59	1.13
Hotels and restaurants*	18.2	£32k up to £44k*	1.1	40-49	1
Food*	-18.2	> £44k	1.0	30-39	1.25
Communication*	-38.4			16-29	1.36

There is a schism between income and expenditure. There is evidence that respondents were more likely to report higher life satisfaction if they have higher household expenditure but *not* income. However, breaking down income into quintiles, those whose household income was between £24,000 and £44,000 are significantly

3 ONS 15 May 2019 Personal and economic well-being: what matters most to our life satisfaction?

more likely to report higher life satisfaction with increasing income. The odds ratios of higher life satisfaction associated with 10% higher household disposable income is 1.3. Age is another key variable. Happiness is U shaped. Using 40-49 as a benchmark, all other age groups are happier.

GNP or GDP – Does it Matter?
GDP covers wealth generated within the borders of the country or region concerned. GNP measures wealth generated by the citizens/ corporates of the country or region. GNP = GDP + incomes (remittances), dividends and profits earned outside the country or region – incomes, dividends and profits earned inside the country or region but not by its citizens.

Ireland is an example of a country where the distinction matters. The cornerstone of Irish industrial policy is low corporate taxes (12.5% of profits). In effect, it is a tax haven. It has attracted FDI especially regional HQs from the US and Europe, such as Google, Yahoo and Forest Labs. 20% of Irish GDP being profit must be both taxed lightly and remitted overseas. Any attempt to boost the tax-take from this quarter would be self-defeating. The footloose investment would relocate. In 2009, a deficit ratio based on GDP of 12% would become 17.9% based on GNP. Ireland, a county that requests regional assistance, has a higher GDP/head than the UK.

PPP
We use GDP/head as a measure of the relative standard of living. In an important sense, the measure is based on relative income per head. If priced in different currencies, the data needs to be converted. Exchange rates, if allowed to move freely and with perfect capital movements (freely convertible), should reflect relative costs. So, a basket of goods should cost the same in both countries. However, this should be adjusted for purchasing power in the local currency. In the chart right, Ireland had the highest income per head at $76,889.

PPP theory states that the relative exchange rates between two countries should equal the relative price levels in the two countries concerned. In the chart right, OECD estimated GDP per head in dollars for 2017 for a variety of countries. The UK value $44,909 at current prices. China was at $16,762 in 2016.

The Economist's Big Mac is a variant on PPP. The notion that one could find a collection of goods common to both countries is central to PPP. The Big Mac is a standard product found in a range of countries. The relative costs of a Big Mac in both countries could be a proxy for relative general costs of living.

Problems
GDP is a product of the mass production era, measuring quantity rather than quality. Having four memory sticks is better than three. Having four spoons is better than three but is it better than a knife, fork and spoon?: in output terms, no, but in terms of eating a meal, yes. Products, like computers and, latterly, mobile phones, are problematic for national income accounting. Normally, a higher price not associated with inflationary pressures, implies the product is of a higher quality. But the price of computers tends to fall whilst their power rises. In particular, Moore's law saw the price of computer power fall 70%/yr for 3 years, now that decline is 3-4%. The consumer is better off, whilst the assessment using GDP by the expenditure method would have them as worse off. Interestingly, the reverse is not true. There is no downgrading of GDP because of goods becoming shoddier. As reported above, shrinkflation is not uncommon. Goods can be priced the same but fall in unit size. Thus, there is an upward bias in its estimate. Given that the definition of a recession rests on GDP estimates, this can provide a politician with an incentive to time the introduction of changes to estimates.

The number of hours worked to generate that GDP is also important. If two countries generate the same GDP from the same population, but one does it using fewer worker-hours, does this mean they are equally well-off? In GDP terms yes, but in leisure time, not.

GDP/capita is an average and may not reflect the well-being of the median income group or those at the bottom of the income hierarchy. Adjustments need to be made for the distribution of income.

Excessive consumption in one era, which would boost GDP, could compromise the productive capacity in a later one. Depreciation of productive capacity is accounted for with NNP but does that include a degradation of the environment? No account is taken of depleted resources. With finite resources an over-consumption, which lowers current cost would add to well-being today whilst worsening it tomorrow. With open access, 'tipping points' may be passed, leading to a sudden collapse of fishing stocks, or worse, irreversible global warming.

Externalities, such as pollution, are not included in GDP unless expenditure is allocated to cleaning up the mess. The consumption of bads is treated in the same way as goods. Heroin and cigarette consumption are just as good as green vegetables. They hold a value in GDP terms based on the expenditure made on them.

If there is a catastrophe, capacity loss is a NDP issue but not for GDP. However, the reconstruction effort is a GDP issue. This, through a multiplier effect, can stimulate further growth. Energy Saving Trust reported in July 2013, from a survey of 86,000 British households, that the average shower lasts 7½ minutes. If this was reduced to 6½ minutes, £215m would be saved on utility bills. 95% of people boiled the kettle every day with 40% using one over four times a day. ¾ of households overfill their kettles, wasting £68m/ year. Although these are unproductive uses of water, they count towards GDP.

When calculating GDP how does one account for home ownership? If I pay for work to be done on my house, money changes hands and that work is included in the GDP estimate. Although increasing the value of my property, DIY work does not enter the GDP estimates, but it should (as work is done), hence a value needs to be imputed. The third party criterion states that if an activity were both productive and could (under usual circumstances) be contracted out to a third party, then it would be included in an extended boundary of production.

Similarly, rented houses provide an income in the form of rent, but a home that is occupied by its owner, does not. GDP would be higher if two neighbouring owners that swapped houses and paid rent to each other compared with them living in their own houses. Again, a value needs to be imputed.

Yet another problem area is the consumption of something below the price the consumer is willing to pay. Consumer surplus provides utility/happiness that is not priced. This is made all the worse with internet services provided free of charge. These services are very valuable to many. To value this is difficult. If forced to pay for news, people avoid it so the Independent and Guardian say are vulnerable and the New Day failed. Maps and Images are offered free destroying companies that sell those services. Again, time using the service multiplied by a utility value may be a way forward. US GDP between 2007 and 2011 could have been 3% higher because of the free service consumption. Measuring internet traffic might present a more rapid growth rate.

In the ONS' *Household satellite accounts: 2005 to 2014*, it attempts to measure non-market work done.

Total Output = CoE + IC + GoS + Imputed Rentals

CoE = Compensation of Employees is the equivalent labour costs that would normally have been paid to maintain the housing services using market sources

IC = Intermediate Consumption are goods and services (resources) used up by housing such as utilities as electricity or water

Intermediate Consumption	£222,692m
Input of household production of housing services	£116,639m
Input of household production of transport services	£21,658m
Input of Housing services produced by owner occupiers	£166,386m
Total	£527,375m

GoS = Gross Operating Surplus is the market equivalent profit which a third party contracted in to provide some of the household upkeep activities could reasonably expect to generate in any given year.

GVA = CoE + GoS

GVA excludes imputed rentals for housing as this is already accounted for elsewhere.

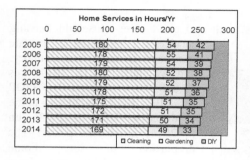

Left are examples of hours of labour used for imputing GDP. Here, average annual hours carrying out household upkeep tasks per person, 2005 to 2014. There was a general decline in the time spent cleaning, doing DIY, and gardening/person but the imputed value of the work increased, resulting in the growth of GVA of household housing services at an average of 1.4%/yr.

GVA of informal childcare was £320.6bn in 2014 making it the largest component of home production (31% of the total). Private household transport (£235.8bn = 23%). This value is approximately 6.5 × total household expenditure on publicly provided transport.

Nutrition services of households is a term that covers home catering. This includes all activities related to the provision of food and drink, such as cooking, shopping, setting the table, and washing up.

Output = total number of calories consumed in the home × cost per calorie eaten out.

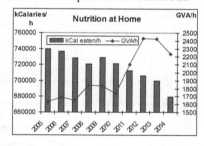

The value of home nutrition services was £144.3bn or £2234/h, up from £1632 (37%). The number of calories eaten per person declined by 8.1%. The price of food and drink eaten out (in restaurants, cafes, and pubs) is used as the monetary value.

The number of adults receiving informal adult care remained largely static between 2005 and 2014. However, there has been an increase in the number of hours per cared-for person, leading to 4.2% average annual growth in the GVA of informal adult care.

Gross value added of volunteering activities = total number of hours by type of voluntary activity × an appropriate wage rate to estimate output of frequent formal volunteering.

There has been a general downwards trend in the total number of volunteered hrs (2.28bn to 1.97bn) when the population grew 6.9%, implying the average number fell by 19.3%.

GVA of clothing and laundry services was £88.4bn in 2014, growing by an average of 4.3% per year.

The GVA of home production includes adult and child care; household housing

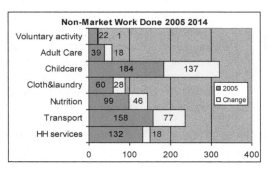

services; nutrition; private transport; clothing and laundry; and volunteering in 2014 was £1,018.9bn. Extended GDP (EGDP) which includes home produced services was £2,836.2bn in 2014, in current prices. The proportion of total home production to GDP grew from 52.2% to 56.1%. ONS provides current prices. Prices rose by 38% between 2005 and 2014. The largest component by value, childcare, increase from £184bn to £321bn. There was a 2.9% increase in the total number of hours of formal childcare, when the average hourly cost of a child minder increased by 61.1% from £2.52 per hour in 2005 to £4.06 in 2014.

OUTPUT GAP

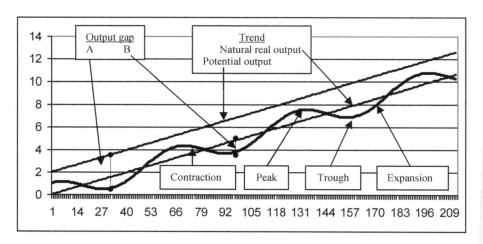

The standard theory of the inflation, used by all the major central banks, assumes that the rate of inflation is driven by the size of the output gap in the economy (i.e. the extent of spare capacity) and by expected inflation. As such, the notion and the assessment of the gap are important to economic policy. The output gap is a measure of lost production. It is based on two notions, both of which are complex and difficult to assess. Potential output provides a view of what could be produced; what could be the level of income at a time. Actual output is what is produced. The gap is forgone production/wealth generation.

The time path of the actual level of production is commonly characterised as a business cycle. A cycle has a sequence of four phases: trough, expansion, peak and contraction. Underlying that cycle is a trend. The trend could be measured by assessing the gradient from peak-to-peak or trough-to-trough. It is common to find that quarterly change data is assessed either by comparing the period's value with an earlier one, i.e $\Delta x_t = x_t - x_{t-p}$. If $p = 1$, it could provide a 'lumpy' picture of a quarterly change. If $p = 4$, the comparison is an annual one, which should provide a smoother time-profile. For monthly data, $p = 1$ or 12.

One way of viewing potential and actual output over time is illustrated in the diagram above. The trend's slope represents potential growth rate. The actual growth rate is captured by the business cycle. Various authors interpret the trend slightly differently. In Sloman, the trend is positioned above the cycle and represents potential output. The gap between John Sloman's trend line and output, as measured by gross domestic product (GDP), represents the output gap (A). If GDP growth is above trend, the output gap closes. However, actual output is never greater than potential. Robert Gordon draws the trend line through the cycle and it represents natural real output. The natural real GDP is a level of output consistent with zero change in inflation. If GDP is above trend, actual unemployment rate is below the natural rate in an Expectations Augmented Phillips Curve (EAPC) model, and greater inflation ensues. Gordon also defined the output gap as the percentage difference between actual and natural real GDP (B). He also defined the output ratio as the ratio of natural to actual GDP. A figure over 100% implies inflation would be accelerating.

Okun's Law

There are two versions of Okun's law: the static and dynamic. The static or gap version: is $Q = Q_n - \delta(u_n - u)$, where Q is actual and Q_n potential or natural output. Krugman restructures the gap expression as $u = u_n - \lambda(Q - Q_n)$. As these natural rates are difficult to assess, we use the dynamic. $\dot{Q} = \dot{Q}_n - \gamma(\Delta u_n - \Delta u)$ (dot indicates growth rate of). Here, the actual growth rate is related to the gap between the change in the natural and actual rates of unemployment. Assuming the change in the natural rate of unemployment is approximately equal to 0 and that potential growth is α, the expression becomes $\dot{Q} = \alpha - \gamma(\Delta u)$. With potential growth of ($\alpha =$) 3%, and $\gamma = 2$, a 2% fall in unemployment leads to a rise in actual output by 7%, 4% higher than the potential rate.

If the trend in Q_n falls, output growth will so do. This is a secular as opposed to a cyclical recession. Credit cycles have been with us for as long as there has been credit. However, some prove remarkably damaging. In a sense, one has to distinguish between a trend and a cycle. There are three types:

1. Output is permanently lost but the trend remains. The example is Sweden in the 1990s;
2. The trend is lower. An example is Japan since the 1990s where there is a productivity puzzle and a secular recession;
3. Output is lost permanently and the trend is lower trend (see PLOG and secular stagnation).

The third being the most damaging and encompassing the two others is worthy of comment. Over indebtedness, when the crunch comes, leads to mass defaults. As firms fail and make workers redundant this causes a loss of output. Moreover, if banks are more cautious, this could stifle growth further down the line.

Larry Summers proposed four reasons for believing in a secular stagnation thesis:-
1. Even though financial repair had largely taken place several years ago, recovery has only kept up with population growth and normal productivity growth in the US, and has been worse elsewhere in the industrial world;
2. Despite ultra-loose credit in the run up to the crash, only moderate economic growth emerged;
3. Short-term interest rates were severely constrained by the zero lower bound: real rates may not be able to fall far enough to spur enough investment to lead to full employment. Of course, now governments utilise negative interest rates, this implies there is no longer a clear lower bound.
4. Deflation and falling wages nominal wages are likely to worsen performance by encouraging consumers and investors to delay spending. More interestingly, deleveraging and the lack of borrowing redistributes spending to high income and wealthy but low spending creditors from high-spending debtors.

In November 2013, some awful realisations were arrived at. The PLOG acronym emerged; the *p*ersistent *l*arge *o*utput *g*ap. It will be presumed by the OBR that output will be below capacity for possibly 7 years, suggesting that monetary policy, QE and low interest rates, will not move [equilibrium] economic output to full employment. Across the Atlantic, Summers and Krugman suggested that the RR* in the global economy had been around −2 to −3% since at least the mid 2000s, but that the actual real rate (at least on bonds) had been positive. The level of spending at any given set of interest rates is likely to have declined (the demand for money has shifted left).

The definition of RR* *equilibrium real rate of interest or* the neutral rate is that rate consistent with full employment and stable inflation (or zero output gap or full employment). In March 2015, Yellen was saying that the US RR* was close to zero but rising, with a long-term rate of 1.75%. The *Taylor rule* is $R_t = RR^* + \pi_t + 0.5(\pi_t - 2) + 0.5Y_t$, where R denotes the federal funds rate, π is the current inflation rate, and Y is the output gap $Q - Q_n$. If RR* is assumed to equal 2% (roughly the average historical value of the real federal funds rate) and the natural rate of unemployment is assumed $= 5\frac{1}{2}\%$, given that core inflation in April 2015 was running close to $1\frac{1}{4}\%$ and the unemployment rate was 5.5%, then the Taylor rule would call for the nominal funds rate to be set a bit below 3%. But if RR* is instead assumed to equal 0% and $u_n = 5\%$, the rate should be less than ½%. In April 2016, core inflation was up to 2.1% suggesting a rate of 2.3%. In June 2018, RR* was 0 < 1.5% with a 0.9% median. HSBC, JP Morgan and Heteronomics in July were more pessimistic putting it at -0.5 to 0% so that R of 1.5-2% ultimately would be needed to keep inflation steady at around 2%.

With actual > equilibrium output there has been a prolonged period of under-investment in the developed economies, with GDP falling further and further behind its underlying long run potential, leading to a PLOG or secular stagnation. The actual output does not wrap around the old trend, but a lower path reflecting the damage done to the capital stock and the effective supply of labour by the recession. Investment demand may have been reduced due to slower growth of the labour force and slower productivity growth. Risk aversion following the crisis and has led deleveraging by both States and consumers and more precautionary holdings. The costs of financial intermediation (banking) have risen.

Adjustments rely on cuts in interest rates and wages, but although nominal interest rates can fall below zero, can they fall sufficiently to find equilibrium? Also, monetary policy will not encourage current against future consumption. Due to a redistribution of wealth to the very wealthy, this lowers MPCs and APCs so that consumption may be lower. Declines in the cost of durable goods, especially those associated with information technology, mean that the same level of saving purchases more capital every year. Therefore, none of the normal forces for restoring equilibrium apply.

Extrapolating IMF/OECD estimates of potential GDP output from before the 2008 crash, Lawrence Ball from Johns Hopkins University estimated the loss of potential output in 2013 across 7 developed countries was 7.18% plus a 2.56% output gap. Potential growth had dropped from 2.39% to 1.68%. The corresponding figures for the UK are 10.98, 2.14, 2.66 and 1.85.

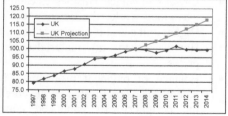

Productivity
Productivity quantifies how an economy uses its resources, by relating the quantity of output to inputs. In the graphic right, using index numbers with 2007=100, GDP Output/hour is displayed. We see uninterrupted growth in productivity until 2007; then it stagnates.

The productivity puzzle is illustrated with UK figures when compared with other OECD benchmarks for 2014.

It was estimated by the ONS that, of the 4.3% UK productivity drop, oil and financial services explained 1.3% each and utilities a further 0.65%. In other words, three industries accounted for ¾ of the decline in long-term productivity growth.

In April 2015, poor growth was ascribed to lawyers, accountants and management consultants, whose output had grown by 2% after, when before 2008 they had grown at 3.8%/yr. Telecommunications, banking and finance had a similar tale. Recruitment grew at the same rate as before when output growth did not. The new steady state growth of output per worker is 1.75%. By February 2018, the BoE was suggesting that workers had shifted from high to low productivity sectors. From 2002Q2 to 2007Q3 output per man-hour increase by 9.6%. From then to 2017Q3 it increased by 2.5%, a 7.1 point decline. Of this, 5 points are explained by shifts from sectors such as aviation and mining to health and hospitality. The collapse of finance is still in evidence. Over 2002-07 it contributed 1.6 percentage points. Over 2012-17, it contributed 0.2 percentage growth.

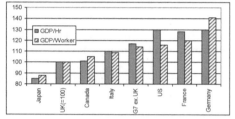

In December, Britain's productivity gap with France was reduced when adjustments were made for hours of work. As Brits work fewer hours than thought, they have more leisure time and greater productivity per hour; both boosting well-being.

A recession, as defined as two consecutive quarters of negative growth is problematic with differing potential growth rates. The US trend of 2% would fall into a recession less often than Japan with a trend of 0.5%. It is proposed that rather than zero, use a fixed number, such as two consecutive quarters of growth 200bps below trend. So the US it would be below zero but for Japan, it would require shrinking by 1.5%.

This sluggish productivity growth rate can lead to:
- Lower real wages: Businesses cannot afford to maintain wages in line with prices when their workers' efficiency levels are sluggish;
- Higher unit costs: If running at about the same level, pay increases can be afforded. However, rising raw material costs might be passed onto consumers in higher prices;
- Balance of payment problems: Thirlwall's Balance of Payments Constraint Hypothesis is predicated on the core having a faster productivity growth rate than the periphery. Its enhanced competitiveness leads to a favourable trade performance. Thus, export growth is related to relative productivity growth and lower unit costs;
- Lower profits: The periphery is trapped in a cycle of lower productivity leading to lower profits for companies, which affects re-investment to support the long-term growth of local businesses;
- Lower economic growth: A sluggish potential growth rate will constrain the growth of actual output. For any given level of output growth, the output gap will be narrower, implying demand pull inflation will be higher.

The issue of a secular recession is interesting. In the graph right, we can see GDP/quarter at factor cost (ABMI). The annual growth rate from 2000 to 2008 was 2.50%. The trend following the crash from 2009 to 2018 the annual growth rate was 1.3%. However, from 2000 to 2018 the annual rate stands at 1.86%. Since 2011, the rate has sat at a steady rate of around 1.93%. Of course this reversion does not have to be related to productivity.

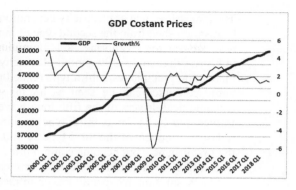

Adair Turner has, over some years, discussed the restructuring of the economy. The productivity paradox is in large part due to a shift in employment from high productivity sectors to slow with the corresponding wage divide. Of the 10 sectors forecast to provide 29% of all new jobs in the US over the 10 years from 2014, 8 have below median wages. Some jobs generates are socially useless, zero-sum, rentiers. Including arbitragers, tax lawyers, marketers, lobbyists, these contribute little to actual output/ social well-being. Worryingly, even higher education can be zero-sum (just reshuffling the rank order for jobs). The new economy extracts monopoly rent through the patents on the technology we all use. Previously, he criticised socially useless lending. A key example is housing – more lending for the same dwelling. This is compounded by the rise in land values, the classic area of economic rent. Over the medium term, this rent needs to be taxed more to offset the lower level of employment and wage.

INDUSTRIAL STRUCTURE

Technology destroys old jobs and creates new ones. It is a key source of productivity growth. There are several relevant notions about technological progress:
- The great waves of development in the industrialised world have been analysed by many authors. Some have described Kondratiev or Long Waves. Long waves do not fit within broad macroeconomics as macro is essentially industry-neutral and makes no value-judgement about investment appraisal. Building on the work of Perez (1983), Tylecote (1991) distinguishes three types of innovation:-
  1. First, enabling technologies present new factors of production that are clearly cheap by existing standards, and are likely to become pervasive. These enabling technologies or *styles* are water, steam transport, steel and electricity, the Fordist style, and microelectronics and biotechnology. When the potential for further productivity growth is exhausted, each is superseded by the next, which Tylecote argued, took around 50 years. The innovation in enabling technologies provides the basis for developments in the other two.

2. The industries, such as electricity generation, that *make* the new factor should be distinguished from the second type of innovation. These industries *use* the new key factors. Chlorine and aluminium production are examples of industries that could ably exploit electricity generation. This second type of innovation precipitates a third type related to 'new' goods and services. The home computer can be seen as an innovation that exploits one of the technological drivers of the fifth long wave, microelectronics. This, in turn, formed the basis for a third type of innovation, the computer software industry. Products of the third type should have a high-income elasticity in the first instance, but become commodities as their life cycles mature.

3. The diffusion of a new style is characterised by new labour skills; new products; substantial expenditures on infrastructure projects and, importantly, new patterns of spatial exploitation and hence, competitive advantage. By implication, the competitive advantage of a company or region may be undermined by a change in *technological style* that could lead to the obsolescence of key products and processes.

The Small-Big Beast: Apple
As with the computer, the mobile phone is embedded in the fifth long wave. Although it began life literally as a phone that was portable as opposed to fixed wire, today, with innovation, the mobile smartphone is a minicomputer. It is a second type of innovation, whilst the enabling technology, microelectronics, drove companies to put down fibre-optic cable or mobile phone masts and substations.

In July 2009, the number of mobile phone connections reached 5bn: there were 3.3bn connections (½ the world) in November 2007. This astonishing growth has change the world's capacity connects to each other and to the internet. In 2009, there were 1.73bn with access to the internet. By 2017, 3.59bn (½ the world) were linked. There are places in Africa where you cannot get running water but you can stream a video. With its computers, by licence agreement, Apple software is only permitted to run on its hardware. The smartphone market, though, was dominated by Nokia (39%) but was destroyed by the Apple iPhone.

*   The iPhone spawned the Apps industry. There are now 20m software developers. A further industry followed, based on location. The driverless car will be dependent on the technology the mobile phone generated.
*   The climax of the computer age, the peak of the dotcom bubble in the 1990s (March 2000) saw Tech companies worth 33% of all publicly traded companies. In 2018 we were back to 25%.

3D printing is thought to offer a major reduction is design and development costs. Take the example of a Ford engineer designing an intake manifold engine part. Using software, they could take 4 months at a cost of $500,000. 3D printing technology could reduce that to 4 days and $3,000. GKN is developing a metal printer that can reduce machining time for a titanium bracket from 4 hours to 40 minutes and cut material usage by 30%. Siemens predict that spare parts industry will change. Rather than storing parts, they can be made to order, close to the customer. Using conventional technology, a GM stainless steel seat bracket would require eight components and several suppliers. With 3D, it is 40% lighter and 20% stronger.

➤ In the NIDL, the machine replicated much of what the skilled worker offered the capitalist, freeing it from the city and high cost regions.

➤ In the neoclassical world, an enhancement of labour productivity would shift the demand curve for labour to the right. However, a fall in the cost of capital relative to labour would lead to a substitution of capital for labour.

➤ In the world of the Austrian economics, technological improvements enhance the well-being of the consumers and the entrepreneur is rewarded with profits. The nature of deindustrialisation is evolving and accelerating (see Changing Vehicles).

The 5th Long Wave is associated with nanotechnology and biotechnology increasing the productivity of resources and energy. However, robots will feature strongly. The *second machine* age and thinking robots are about to make the future worse for many workers whose work is routine. This shift is permanent and will be divisive, further separating the high from the low paid worker.

A Stitch in Time
Little has changed in the manufacture of T-shirts since the invention of the sewing machine. Mechanisation of the process can be seen in four stages: picking up the cloth; aligning it; sewing it; and disposing of the garment. Three of the four are not yet automated because of the flexible fabric with numerous tiny processes in their implementation.

The motivation for pushing for a sewbot - a robot sewing machine - relates to politics, logistics and just-in-time. Fashions are ephemeral; reducing lead times can provide a competitive advantage. Producing in the US, not only placates Donald Trump, but shortens delivery distances and time.

Levi Strauss is accelerating its use of lasers to automate the way its jeans are made. By 2020, lasers will finish a pair of jeans every 90 seconds, rather than two to three pairs an hour, currently. Levi uses overseas contractors to make the vast majority of its products. Reshoring is related, in part, to the faster fashion cycle utilised by low-cost, fast-fashion brands such as Zara and H&M. Akin to the lean/JIT seen in the car industry the combination of flexible machines and software the time-to-market will drop from six months from the start of the design cycle to weeks - even days in some cases. The number of steps involved in the finishing process - which used to involve hand sponging and sand papering wear patterns and other details onto the denim - will drop from 18 to 20 steps to around three.

Drones and Crawlers
Poland and South Africa to have fully developed regulations and laws permitting both unfettered commercial drone flights and flights that go beyond a visual line of sight. Non-military drones have enormous potential to both enhance and replace labour. A key area is height. Ladder climbing or dangling from ropes has risk implications. Also

hard-to-reach locations, such as oil rigs, offshore wind farms or gas pipelines, involves time getting to the problem. The cost of a drone inspection of a wind turbine is roughly half the $1,500 cost of a human doing the same job. In 2017, BP, the largest operator in the US Gulf of Mexico, piloted Maggie, a magnetic crawler, which can move across rigs, platforms, and pipelines above and below water using ultrasonic test devices and high-definition cameras. A crawler can cost $60,000 or $600 to $1,000/ day, plus the operating technician to rent. Drones and crawlers can do inspections in about half the time of rope access technicians, while placing fewer workers in harm's way. The 2010 Deepwater Horizon rig explosion killed 11 people. Warehousing is further area of innovation. They are now the workhorses online that retailers rely on. Today's inventory management requires workers to scan items manually. A key area of improvement is in the misplaced items or faulty inventory records. Pinc, one of the firms offering aerial robots, claims almost 100% accuracy. For a warehouse that is 95% accurate, it means that 5% is ambiguous. So if the warehouse is storing $100m worth of inventory, $5m is uncertain.

A further factor is productivity. Argon Consulting argues that two drones can do the work of 100 humans over the same time period. Of course, they don't need the tea breaks and can work a 3 shift day. Whilst creating 10% more jobs in the field, automation technologies, including artificial intelligence, will replace 17% of US jobs by 2027 – a net loss of 7%. Automation reduces the demand for lesser qualified jobs whilst boosting the need for specialised skills within the logistics sector. Between October and April 2017, 89,000 shop workers were laid off.

The Internet and Disintermediation
Technology is leading to disintermediation that is the merchant traders that buy from farmers and sell to retailers. Archer Daniels Midland, Bunge, Cargill, and Louise Dreyfus (ABCD) had an information advantage which is waning. Market traders have access to satellites that can see crops. Farmers can observe market prices from the cabs of the self-driving tractors.

Estate agents are also information conduits that will be subject to disintermediation. To find a new markets agents in the UK (Gerald Eve) and (Cushman and Wakeman) the US are looking to long term advisory roles, moving from one-off fees. Large landlords such as British Land, do what agents used to do. For example, marketing campaigns, attend meetings with lawyers, and agree terms with tenants are now undertaken by in-house leasing teams. Agents must deliver complex transactions that are difficult to duplicate, including financial advice.

Nike in June 2017 announced a 1400 (2%) cut in jobs as part of a refocused strategy away from physical outlets to direct online sales. In part, this reflects a just in time approach, chasing fashions particularly in 12 global cities where 80% of sales growth is expected to come. Then again, it also will reduce its range by 25%. Ikea, like Nike, also announced that sales will shift more to online and away from out-of-town outlets.

Fisher/Clark

The Fisher/Clark thesis posits that manufactures can grow independently of agriculture, and services can grow independently of manufactures. Hence, the decline of manufacturing (deindustrialisation) may not be that significant. Historically, deindustrialisation or at least the movement of resources from one

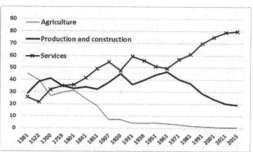

sector to another is linked to rising prosperity rather than mass unemployment. The story of technological change is usually short-term pain for long-term gain at least for the economy overall. Take farming. Over the past 150 years the UK has lost 1.5m farming jobs while agricultural output has grown by about 400%. From the figure above you can see the decline in the proportion of those that worked in farming from the 1841 Census in GB (22.35%) to 0.9% in England and Wales in 2011.

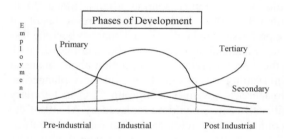

The Fisher/Clark is becoming problematic. Peak industry is occurring at lower per capital incomes and lower shares of total employment. Peak years are: Mexico, 1980; Brazil, 1986; India, 2002; UK, 1961; and US, 1953. The IMF noted that productivity growth linked to manufacturing, could be duplicated by the service sector. Globally, the share of manufacturing employment and output was stable for 50 years implying productivity improvements are not automatic. Performance in advanced economies was not improved by a shift from the secondary to tertiary sectors. Industrialisation was the route out of poverty for the developing nations, absorbing the great unskilled. This forms the basis for the creation of a middle class that values education. There needs to be a sector for these to join otherwise there will be very many well-educated disappointed young people. For example, with industrialisation, the first sector normally a country develops is textiles. Bangladesh's exports are made up of 82% clothes: this is generated by 2.5% of the population. Indeed 27m in the Indian subcontinent make textiles. Chinese factory wages in 2017 stood at $3.60/hr, similar to Portugal and South Africa. It was 5 × Indian wages. Although jobs are to be lost in the developed, it is the developing world that will be the big loser. Recently, 400 robots have replaced car workers in Chennai, in a labour abundant country. This could mean that the peak in manufacturing employment is much lower than ever before.

Bank of American Merrill Lynch estimated that 45% of all manufacturing jobs over the next 10 years would be replaced. UK employees on £30,000 or less are five times more likely to be replaced by artificial intelligence in the next 20 years than those paid in excess of £100,000. Take the IKEA flat pack chair. Nanyang Technological University showed in 2018 that robots could assembled the frame of a dining chair in around 20 minutes. You could say it took three years designing and programming the robot (made of arms, grippers, sensors and 3D cameras). However, soon robots will fully assemble a piece of furniture from a manual, verbal instruction or by just looking at an image of the finished item.

Deindustrialisation also hits the service sector. In June 2016, Bank of America announced that up to 8,000 jobs out of 68,400 were to go from its back-office staff. In the previous 7 years 1,400 retail branch staff had gone. As this represented a quarter of the establishment, this was a significant shift.

The call centre can add to the productivity of the service sector. The standardisation of service sector jobs could reduce the costs of provision. This though does not resonate with all customers, who like the human touch. Another productivity increase in banking is the total mechanisation of a branch. As around 95% of branch activities could be mechanised, banks would become rather spartan affairs. Since 2010, transactions at branches have fallen by 30%. Both changes were a result of technological advances. Back-office processes can be digitised. Branches become less populated as banking goes mobile. Financial advice could be automated, with sophisticated decision-trees giving the customer relevant information about financial products. Indeed, this overcomes misselling incentives. That said BoA planned to increase sales and advisory staff to increase revenues. Citigroup CEO in February suggested possibly 10,000 jobs in its call centres could be replaced by AI. 30 of the most common customer journeys could be easily automated. That represents half of the jobs in that realm. Indeed, Citi suggested that route was better than joining with SunTrust-BB&T in a merger. In October 2017, the National Australia Bank announced 6,000 jobs were to go by 2020. This represented 18% of its full-time equivalent workforce. As with manufacturing the services sector is subject to productivity enhancing developments that costs jobs. In the eighties the ATM was introduced. This was followed by mass branch closures over the next three decades. Offshoring some functions led to more job losses as well as the rise of the apps and mobile banking. At the same time as these jobs are to go, NAB is to hire 2000 new people with digital skills: AI; robotics; and automation technologies.

Software robots will replace 4m back office jobs in the US by 2021. Forrester Research argued that routine work done by humans in front of computer screens, filling the gaps between fragmented systems, is more cost effectively done by computers themselves. Licence agreements costing $8-9,000/yr are cheaper than the equivalent 3-4 full time staff.

The Estimated Effect
In March 2017, PwC reported that around 10.4m jobs in the UK could be replaced by robots over the next 15 years. This is equivalent to 30% of those currently employed.

With the advent of driverless vehicles Transportation and Storage is one of the most vulnerable sector where 56.4% of current jobs are soon to be replaced. This makes up 4.9% of all the jobs to go. Manufacturing will lose a further 1.22m jobs, comprising 7.6% of all jobs to be lost. 2.25m jobs will disappear in retail and wholesale as shops could become more like 'showrooms', where customers look at goods before buying them online. This would lead to more giant warehouses, such as Amazon's. The skill factor as ever is important. 12% of graduate degrees or higher are at risk whereas those with only GCSEs face a 46% chance of losing their jobs.

Frey and Osborne (2013) suggest the *safest jobs*: Recreational therapist; Healthcare social workers; Surgeons; Athletic trainers; Clergy; Foresters; Audiologists; Choreographers; Dentists; Farmers. *Most vulnerable*: Library technicians; Accounts clerks; Insurance underwriters; Maths technicians; Sewer workers; Telemarketers; Title examiners; Tax preparers; Cargo handlers; Watch repairers.

		% of Industry Jobs	Jobs
Domestic personnel and self-subsistence	0.3%	8.1%	0.01m
Education	8.7%	8.5%	0.26
Human health and social work	12.4%	17.0%	0.73
Other services	2.7%	18.6%	0.17
Agriculture, forestry and fishing	1.1%	18.7%	0.07
Arts and entertainment	2.9%	22.3%	0.22
Mining and quarrying	0.2%	23.1%	0.01
Construction	6.4%	23.7%	0.52
Accommodation and food service	6.7%	25.5%	0.59
Professional, scientific and technical	8.8%	25.6%	0.78
Information and communication	4.1%	27.3%	0.39
Real estate	1.7%	28.2%	0.16
Electricity and gas supply	0.4%	31.8%	0.05
Public administration and defence	4.3%	32.1%	0.47
Financial and insurance	3.2%	32.2%	0.35
Administrative and support services	8.4%	37.4%	1.09
Retail and Wholesale	14.8%	44.0%	2.25
Manufacturing	7.6%	46.4%	1.22
Transportation and storage	4.9%	56.4%	0.95
Water, sewage and waste management	0.6%	62.6%	0.13
Total for all sectors	100%	30%	10.4m

In Australia, a 2015 study from the Office of the Chief Economist found that 44% of Australian jobs were highly susceptible to automation, with telemarketers and bank workers at the top of the list. By contrast, the Asian Development Bank estimated that across 12 developing countries over 10 years to 2015, technology had destroyed 101m jobs whilst creating 134m.

In 2015, 38% of robots are found in the car industry (103,000 in 2016); 20% were in electronics (91,300); with chemicals plastics and metals making up a further 19%. Small firms are not well placed to use robots. Currently, it takes a lot of man-hours and money to service robots: the engineering can cost 3 to 8 times the hardware. Boston Consulting Group estimates that a human welder costs $25/hr. A robot has operating cost/hr $8. The extra cost of maintaining a robotics system be amortised over a five-year period.

In January, Walmart announced that it would raise its starting wage to $11/hr, up by $2. As a result someone would be earning $22,000/yr. There will also be 10 weeks of maternity paid leave. The expected additional costs amounted to $700m/yr. As with the raising of minimum wage in the UK much of the benefit is likely to be lost as it would increase the incentive to automate.

Deindustrialisation: The Adjustment Cost
IPPR suggested that the closure of a steel works will be similar to the collapse of employment in the pits. Tata employed 15,000 directly and a further 25,000 elsewhere. IPPR estimated that the cost to the exchequer in lost VAT, income tax and a rise in benefit payments would be £4.6bn. Tata was not the first collapse. In October 2015, 2,200 Sahsviriya Steel Industry UK employees and 1,000 contractors at the Redcar blast furnace and its steel slab-making plants lost their jobs. These were supported by a £80m government package: £30m for redundancy payments and £50m for retraining, business start-up grants, wage subsidies for employers taking on former steelworkers and support for Teesside businesses.

The decline in steel in Teesside is rapid. From 33,000 employed in 1980 what was left after Redcar was around 1,200. The task force managing the support had committed £14.5m to training and support for businesses and jobs. It had agreed 10,855 training courses for nearly 3,000 people and says 1,342 former SSI and supply chain workers have moved off benefits into full-time work or training. Also, 71 businesses started by former steelworkers. The number unemployed locally before the closure was 5,600; the collapse added a further 900. The wage that those employed earn is lower. Manual workers were on £33,000, plus overtime. An electrician could have been on twice the £20,000 a year for a current vacancy.

The Work Foundation and Birmingham Business School found that, following the collapse of MG Rover, 90% of the 200 people surveyed were in some form of employment within three years. Of the 6,300, about ⅓ of the workers had found new roles in manufacturing and were earning roughly the same as they had at MG Rover's Longbridge plant in Birmingham. But ⅔ were earning less, with the falls averaging £5,640 a year. Of the 60% that shifted from manufacturing to the service sector, most had suffered a pay fall, averaging over £6,000 a year. Almost one in four of the 200 interviewees then said they were currently in debt or drawing on their savings.

Fort, Pierce and Schott argued that Trump may be defending the wrong bit of manufacturing. Between 1977 and 2012 the number of US manufacturing jobs halved from 20m to 10m, but non-manufacturing plants that were owned by manufacturing firms increase employment from 13m to 25m. These jobs were IT and design. In other words, deindustrialisation occurred but within manufacturing firms.

The Spatial Dimension Analysed
In the Centre for Cities' Cities Outlook 2018 it suggests that automation and globalisation generate and destroy jobs in different parts of the country. It estimates that 20% of existing jobs in British cities are likely to be displaced by 2030 (3.6m jobs). In conjunction with Nesta, a consultancy, it projects that 53% of all jobs at risk in cities are just in five occupations, with Sales Assistance and Retail Cashiers making

up a fifth of the total.

Share of jobs at risk in Cities	
Sales Assistance and retail cashiers	19.5%
Other Administrative Occupations	11%
Customer Service Occupations	9%
Administrative Occupations: finance	7%
Elementary Storage Occupations	6.6%

Significantly, however, this risk is not spread evenly across the country, with peripheral cities/regions in the North and Midlands more exposed to job losses than the more affluent cities in the South. Around 18% of jobs are under threat in Southern cities, compared to 23% in cities elsewhere in the country. It considered the political dissatisfaction and divisions highlighted by the outcome of the EU referendum in 2016 that automation and globalisation would exacerbate. Top 3 British cities most at risk of job losses resulting from automation and globalisation are Sunderland, Wakefield and Mansfield. These were firmly Brexit cities. The least threatened were Hi-Tec and University cities.

THE LOCATIONAL CONVEYOR BELT

City	Share of jobs to be lost by 2030	Vote for Brexit %	Workplace ave week income
Huddersfield	25%	55%	£424
Doncaster	27	69	447
Stoke	28	67	455
Worthing	16	53	455
Mansfield	**29**	70	472
Wakefield	**29**	66	483
Sunderland	**29**	61	484
Blackburn	26	56	488
Brighton	19	36	496
Telford	25	63	497
Blackpool	19	63	500
Dundee	25	40	503
Northampton	26	58	508
Portsmouth	19	59	520
York	19	42	520
GB	21	52	539
Edinburgh	18	26	598
Oxford	**13**	30	600
Cambridge	**13**	26	609
Reading	15	43	655
London	16	42	727

Echoing this divide are two reports. The Centre for Towns added yet more colour to the future of places debate. It reported in November 2017 that from 1981 to 2011 large towns and cities were in receipt of 3m of working age whilst medium towns and smaller settlements attracted 2.75m plus a further 2m over 64s. Only 30 years ago inner city populations that had grown rapidly in the late 19th and early 20th Centuries had dwindled. With a 10% increase on overage and some city centres doubling in size since the start of the 21st Century, the reversal that has taken place especially in the north of England and the Midlands. Centre for Cities reported in November that mapping from a notional city CBD centre Liverpool grew by 181% (9,100 to 25,600 people) between 2002 and 2015; Birmingham 163% (9,800 to 25,800); Leeds 150% (12,900 to 32,300), Bradford 146% (1,300 to 3,200); Manchester 149% (14,300 to 35,600) and London 22% (268,700 to 327,200).

The analysis in McCann (p.125) suggests both denesters and young people should be dominant. The number of 20 to 29-year-olds in the centre of large cities (those with 550,000 people or more) tripled over 2001 to 2011, to comprise half of the population. Some are students, whose numbers grew with the expansion of university education, but the draw is high-skilled professional occupations, reflecting the growing importance of sectors like financial and legal services to the UK economy, supplying half of the cities' work and the short commute: 32% of city centre residents walk to work.

Housing, Communities and Local Government Committee found in February that as shopping habits change, city centres are in danger of becoming ghost towns. In 2018, the High Street lost 22,000 jobs. A fifth of UK retail sales now occur online with that proportion likely to grow. Amazon UK's rates, are about 0.7% of its UK turnover, while most High Street retailers pay 1.5-6.5%. The retail industry, the UK's largest private sector employer, makes up 5% of the economy and pays nearly 25% of the overall business rates bill, over £7bn/yr. To 'level the playing field' for High Street retailers taxes on online giants should be increased. This is not so far-fetched. In June 2018, the US Supreme court ruled that online retailers could have levies imposed on their sales even if they did not have a store in the jurisdiction of the tax-imposing body. This aligns the bricks and mortar with the virtual retailer reducing the cost advantage of the latter. That said, Core Insight reported 5730 stored closed in the US in 2018; but 5480 in 2019Q1 – perhaps a bit late.

Bill Grimsey in his second report into the future of town centres and High Streets in July made a different claim. 'Forget retail for town centres, they need to become community hubs based on health, education, entertainment, leisure and arts and crafts.' So much like the growth in cities, together with housing and some independent shops, facilities such as libraries and digital and health hubs should be part of the offering to bring back people to town centres. However, towns do not provide the same amenities or jobs as cities.

In fact there is a spatial conveyor belt. The young move to the cities in search of work, later, seeking a pleasant environment, they move out to commuter land and then retirement, possibly downsizing and extracting capital from their property but move to villages. The Centre for Towns argues that in 1981 the proportion of 65+ was similar at 23-26.3 per 100 of working age and was around that in 1991. From then on Core Cities have seen old age *dependency* ratios drop to below 20 with Large Towns at 22.5. Villages saw an increase to 35.6.

Change 1981-2011	Under 16	16 to 24	25 to 44	45 to 64	65 plus	Total	OAP/100	Dependency
Village	-172855	-145953	-123044	804394	566301	928843	61.0	73.5%
Community	-71209	-43335	63789	512481	389797	851523	45.8	59.8%
Small town	-171743	-90720	177206	763196	566096	1244035	45.5	46.4%
Medium town	-166440	-133746	333016	658180	445432	1136442	39.2	32.5%
Large town	-116690	48731	681024	538985	236534	1388584	17.0	9.4%
Core City	185053	120179	1461593	241939	-183048	1825716	-10.0	0.1%
Overall	513884	244844	2593584	3519175	2021112	7375143	22.7	39.9%

Of the 929,000 population increase in population in Villages, 61% was attributable to OAPs. The dependency on a working population that grew by 535,000 was partially offset by the decline in the number of school children. That said, the *change* in dependence divided by the *change* in the workforce =73.5%. In other words, for every 100 new residents 73 were not of working age. Core Cities gained youngsters as quickly as they lost OAPs.

CONSUMPTION AND DEBT

The ONS reported that UK households are more likely to be borrowers than savers. The savings ratio in 2017Q1 at 3.7% was at its lowest annual level since 1963. Explanations include expectations of future interest rate rises; low time preference of money; and HH financial distress. Alternatively, one could suggest consumption smoothing.

Forward-Looking Consumption
The simple Keynesian consumption function links consumption expenditure with current disposable income. Forward-looking expectations models of income posit that consumers maintain a stable consumption pattern, altering expenditure not with transitory income changes, but if they are viewed as being permanent. Friedman's *permanent income* and Modigliani's *life cycle hypotheses* posit that consumption is smoothed relative to income. Gordon defines permanent income as the average annual income that is expected to be received over a period of years in the future. Consumption is a function of permanent income $C = kY^P$, where C is consumption and Y^P is permanent income. With a permanent income hypothesis there is no explicit horizon to this forward planning: the horizon is beyond the current. Modigliani's life-cycle model posits consumption is based on the present value of total resources that the household accrues over a lifetime, suggesting a life time budget constraint and that the value of assets directly affect consumption behaviour.

A Perfect Capital Market
Means emerge, such as hire-purchase arrangements and mortgages, of facilitating the inter-temporal mismatch between accumulating the necessary funds, and purchases. A perfect capital market permits the borrower to borrow against the future value of their income or property, negating the need to forego current consumption to accumulate wealth prior to purchase.

Life Cycle Consumption Smoothing
Adair Turner estimates that only 15% of bank lending is for entrepreneurial projects where wealth is created. The remaining 85% goes towards smoothing lifestyle consumption funding (corporate assets, real estate or unsecured personal finance). This is consistent with the above. Campbell and Mankiw argue that a relaxation of financial constraints allows consumers to behave as the permanent income hypothesis suggests. With the abandoning of the special deposit scheme in 1980 and the Building Society Act 1985 plus banks entering the mortgage market in a major way in mid-1981, there was a massive restructuring of the character of debt. Debt became far more commonplace. Over the past 50 years, private credit/GDP has doubled to 200%. More

rapidly, household debt in China, Turkey, Singapore, Thailand and Brazil has increased by more than 40% since 2008. Institute of International Finance estimated that as of September 2008 global debt ratio was 214%; by June 2014 it was 245%; and 325% in 2016).Total debt grew by $70tn in the 10 years to 2016 to $215tn.

Turner, though, makes a fair point with house purchases. The funding of house purchase can be associated with construction, but commonly is not. He concludes that the productivity of money has fallen. Increasing money supply has not led to an increase in total productivity.

Life cycle effects concern such phenomena as expenditure related to family composition, where more is spent on a larger membership and maturing children. An employment career captures the notion of a progression, where seniority, responsibilities and salary rise with time. Thus, as the household [head] ages, income rises. However, income peaks when the head is in their fifties and sixties. Following this there is a decline in income, which, perhaps, coincides with retirement. Fernández-Villaverde and Krueger plot the lifetime profile of expenditure, which turns out to be an inverted-U shape.

Income, consumption and wealth over a life time are modelled right. The wobble represents the business cycle over which consumption can be smoothed. The current arrangement shows someone that earns over a 40-year career and dissaves from the assets when they

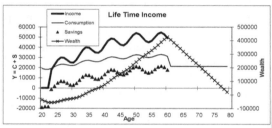

retire until they die at 80. Income rises and then falls. The sum of all saving equals wealth. Notice:

❑ so that consumption at aged 70 could be broadly in line with that at 40, the enormous stock of wealth that must be accumulated. The longer people live, the more they MUST save (or pay higher taxes);
❑ if there is any smoothing the MPC is possibly tiny, so Keynes' multiplier falls apart;
❑ a change in government expenditure could results in changes in savings only;
❑ if the income profile is as shown, why not borrow from your future income?

The IFS reported in June 2018 that, contrary to fears and theory pensions were too caution about their wealth. Rather than depleting their wealth to zero (the LCH view), those between 70 and 90 had 69% of their wealth intact. The wealthier half of that group used only 61%. Pension freedoms, like pensions themselves, may only be a stark problem for a minority.

As a debt, student loans should be included in BoE data for all credit. In July 2012, because the demand for this sort of credit is not subject to the same sort of forces as other credit, it was dropped from some data series.

Debt is an emotive subject. Krugman disparages those who claim that, in future we are impoverished by the need to pay back money we've been borrowing. He suggests that using a family finance analogy where the mortgage must be paid in good and bad times otherwise the family home will be repossessed is poor in at least two ways.

1. Families have to pay back their debt. Governments do not. They just need to be able to services the debt ensuring it grows more slowly than the tax base to service it. Taxes are a lot less dramatic than the interest payment analogy;

2. An over-borrowed family owes money to someone else, whereas sovereign debt is, to a large extent, money the State owes its citizens. He concedes that foreigners now hold large claims on the US, including sovereign debt. But there are US claims on overseas assets that almost off-set this, with higher yields.

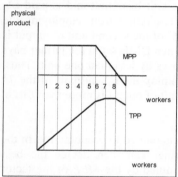

LABOUR DEMAND

A profit maximising firm will, using marginal analysis, employ someone when the marginal benefits are greater than or equal to the marginal costs.

Let us then consider what will determine the amount that increased employment of labour adds to a firm's total revenue. Labour has a derived demand, therefore labour will only be demanded to produce extra output. The marginal product (marginal physical product MPP_L) is the physical additional to total output that results from employment an extra unit of labour. The value of this additional output is the marginal revenue the output sold × the amount produced. In a perfect market, this marginal revenue is the price. The extra revenue generated following the employment of marginal unit of labour is the marginal revenue product of labour (MRP_L). This is the demand for labour.

MRP_L or the value of the marginal product $= MPP_L \times MR\ (P)$

In the case on the below, worker 2 contributes the same amount to output as worker 1. So does 3, 4, and 5. Worker 6 adds less to total output than worker 5. Worker 7 adds less than worker 6 and employing worker 8 leads to a reduction of total output.

More formally, if one combines an increasing greater quantity of factors together, with at least one of them being fixed, then after a certain point, diminishing marginal returns will set in.

The firm's short run marginal cost curve will follow directly from the Law of Diminishing Marginal Returns. Taking the farm example, assume that labour is the only variable input and that each unit receives the same wage. The first unit receives his/her wage in return for his/her unit of output. This wage is the marginal cost of production. We have assumed that so long as each unit of labour has enough room they will be equally productive. Each unit of production will have a marginal cost of one wage. The next unit of labour will not produce the much as the previous one, but s/he will still receive the same wage. Thus, that will mean that whereas previously the entrepreneur paid a wage for a unit of output, now s/he pays a wage and his/her return is less than a unit of output. The full cost of that unit of output will be more than a wage i.e. the marginal cost has increased. The next unit of labour employed will also produce a lower return for his/her wage than the last. The equivalent marginal cost will be even higher. Thus, it is clear that the LDMR directly leads to the firms marginal cost curve.

In the diagram right, assume worker 1 produces one unit of output and is paid £1. Therefore the cost of the first unit of output is £1. The return from employing the second worker is also 1 unit, s/he is paid £1 so the MC of the second unit of output is £1. This applies to the 3rd, 4th and 5th unit of output. When DMR set in the farmer pays the 6th worker £1 but in return the total output increases by less than one unit. Thus, to produce the 6th unit of output the farmer has to employ the 6th and part of the 7th worker's time. As both receive £1 the MC of the 6th unit of output is more than £1 i.e. the MC curve is upward sloping.

With $= W = MPP_L \times P$, $MPP_L = W \div P$ The real wage is related to productivity. In the long run the farmer can vary all inputs. The farmer can then decide the best combination of factors to suit. This decision is determined by the MPP of the factor and its price relative to other factors. Thus, the following holds:-

$$MPP_L \div P_L = MPP_{Cap} \div P_{Cap} = MPP_{Land} \div P_{Land}$$

If factor A's price increased, say the price of labour, the farmer could do two things: 1) Produce less; 2) Substitute more of factors B and C for A. That is, use more land and or capital. As s/he brings in extra units of B and C s/he finds that each will add less to total product or output than before i.e. MPP falls and as the farmer employs less labour s/he moves back up the MPP_L curve of A, i.e. MPP_L increases. This process of substitution continues until equilibrium is achieved. This combining may be limited by the ability of the farmer to vary all inputs. In the long run, all factors are variable, but in the short run one or more factors may be fixed. Important features of production, such as factory size are fixed over a short period. The scope to fund an expansion of the factors could be limited by the land available.

As $MC = P$, $MC = W \div MPP_L$ The (competitive) firm hires labour up to the point where $MC = MR$ and where $MRP = W$.

The MRP curve is the DEMAND CURVE FOR LABOUR. It describes quantity of labour to employ at every given return to the entrepreneur. It can shift when the price of the final product changes; the productivity of labour alters (i.e. the MPP shifts); or there is an increase in demand for the final product and so a need for a greater labour force.

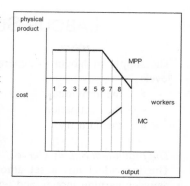

The industry demand for labour curve will be an amalgam of the firms' demand for labour curves but with a slight alteration. As the wage falls the employer will employ more workers and produce more output. Because the firm is small this increase in output will not affect the market price. On the other hand, if all firms increase output, the market price will fall, so shifting each firms MRP curve to the left (MRP_1 to MRP_2). Thus, the industry's demand curve will be steeper than the individual firms' curves. The industry demand curve is labelled D.

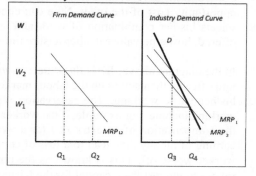

The elasticity of demand for labour will be high if:-

- The price elasticity of the final product is high. If the price falls, there will a shift in the labour demand curve to the left, leading to a lower wage and smaller working labour force. However a fall in the price of the good will lead to an increase in demand for it, and consequently, an increase in the demand for labour. If the latter effect outweighs the former, employment will rise. If the former outweighs the latter, employment will fall. The magnitude of the latter effect depends on the price elasticity of the product.

- The greater the proportion of total cost that is due to labour, the more sensitive total employment will be to a change in wages. This is key for food retail and care homes.

- The elasticity of demand for factors will depend on the elasticity of supply of complementary and substitute factors. If the wage falls, the increase in total employment will depend on the likely effect on the price of complements and substitutes given this will shift the demand curve for them, the former upwards and the latter downwards. With an increase in demand for complements, if their price rises significantly, this will severely constrain the increase in the size of the work force. With a decrease in demand for substitutes, if their price falls significantly, this will severely strain the increase in the size of the work force.

- The easier it is to substitute other factors for labour, and vice-versa, the greater the elasticity of demand for labour. If it is easy, any increase in wages will lead to the substitution of other factors for labour and a fall in the labour force. The scope for substitution will increase with TIME. The greater the time period you look at, the greater the elasticity of demand for labour.

LABOUR SUPPLY

The supply of labour is generally examined at three levels
- the individual,
- the occupation
- the industry

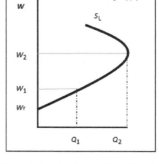

The Individual Supply Curve
The individual has a set amount of time to divide between earning money and leisure. There is a trade-off. To earn more money s/he must give up, or substitute leisure time. One is the opportunity cost of the other. S/he can choose the length of time s/he works and so selects his/her combination of work and leisure time on the basis of the wage rate offered, how s/he values his/her leisure time, and how arduous the work is.

In the diagram above, *Wr* is the *Reservation Wage*, he wage at which they are enticed into offering themselves on the labour market. Below this wage it is felt to be not worth his/her while working. The reservation wage will be related to the worker's non-working income. For example, if the worker receives £80 on the JSA and £90 working, the compensation of an extra £10 for a week's toil may not be enough. Indeed, the earning of money may lead to a loss of certain incomes from the state that makes the worker worse off. This is known as the poverty trap. The non-working income also relates to interest from capital for the leisured classes.

As the rate rises, the opportunity cost of not working rises. The worker will select a combination such that the opportunity cost of working is opportunity cost of not working. Thus, the worker will give up more leisure time the greater the wage rate, and consequently, s/he has an upward sloping supply curve. This is only true up to a certain point. There are two factors to the workers' earnings. Firstly there is the wage rate and secondly the number of hours worked. As the worker works more hours, the amount of time left to enjoy his/her earnings decreases. After a certain wage rate s/he will find that the cost of offering more work time given an increase above that rate will be greater than the benefit. Why is this? His/her income is such that s/he has an acceptable standard of living this will alter his/her perception of the benefit of working more hours. Also, s/he has a relatively small number of leisure hours and so his/her opportunity cost of leisure will be high. With an increase in the wage rate the perceived costs of working longer hours will exceed the benefits and the worker will substitute leisure for work time. We can say that an income effect, or the urge to offer more work time given a higher wage rate is greater than the substitution of leisure for income up to a certain wage rate then the substitution effect is greater than the income. Thus, the supply curve of the individual is backward bending after a certain point.

The *Industry Supply Curve* is the horizontal summation of the individual supply curves at every given wage.

The Supply Curve will shift with
*   A change in the size of the working population. This includes raising school leaving age, 16 to 18 years, retirement age for men and women to rise to 67 years; immigration.
*   Institutional factors - length of working week, holidays, participation rate (proportion of potential work force working or actively seeking work) which is affected by level of unemployment benefits relative to wage levels and social attitudes e.g. towards women.
*   Conditions of service affect the participation rate. Certain jobs may be less palatable than others. This will include working in arduous conditions, anti-social hours, more risky or dangerous, difficult or time consuming travelling to get to. These factors will lead to a smaller labour supply than otherwise, e.g. day vs. night, safe vs. hazardous, pleasant vs. unpleasant working environments.
*   Unearned income:- savings, benefits. If JSA is cut, the reservation wages of those not seeking work will be reduced. As a result, some will begin actively looking for work. This has the effect of shifting the industry supply curve to the right, leading to a lower market wage but more labourers in work.
*   Market access:- academic, occupational.

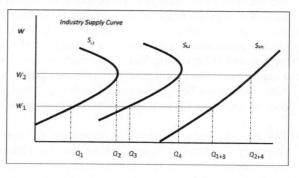

Elasticity of supply of labour
The elasticity of the supply of labour is a measure of increase in labour services offered due to a unit increase in the wage paid. It will depend on the factors discussed above. That is labour will be more elastic the cheaper it is to travel to work, relocate home, train for the job, and the better knowledge about the available jobs around. In common with other discussions of supply TIME will affect the elasticity. In the very short run labour is almost completely immobile. Over a slightly longer period it can move house and job. Over generations a mine worker's offspring can become a doctor.

Total supply of labour is not perfectly inelastic as higher wages will supply e.g. retired, students, married women. The supply of labour to a single industry will be elastic as an increase in an industry's wage rate will induce some workers to transfer from other industries. In the short run, barriers to entry will exist.

The occupational supply curve is based on the notion that there are barriers to entry or labour is immobile between occupations. Occupational immobility can be due to the talents necessary to do the job. These will include high levels of intelligence- to be a mathematics professor, strength- to work in the building trade, and skill- to be a surgeon. This will limit the number of possible workers. Many occupations require long training periods, during which time the trainee may have to be supported by their family. This will deter an individual wish to leave one occupation and training for another.

There are a number of occupations that require some financial outlay to enter, such as buying into a solicitors' partnership or funding a small business. Capital requirements will also limit the supply of workers to an industry.

The market supply curve is based on both the occupational supply with the added dimension of geographical mobility. Labour immobility can be analysed under monetary cost and psychic cost. The monetary cost refers to the expenses involved in moving belongings between abodes, and in the case of the home owner, the cost of selling one house and buying another. This in particular can prove to be a major barrier, especially when related to the co-ordination of selling the old one, buying the new one and the start of the new job. There has been a great deal of interest in the difficulty encountered by the low paid or unemployed worker, living in Council accommodation, who wishes to move areas to find acceptable work. The Council accommodation is generally allocated on the basis of a waiting list plus priority for needy cases. Because they moved to find work, finding themselves homeless, a person would not be seen as a needy case. The recent changes in welfare policy have altered this. Social Housing Associations are being encouraged to assist in the process to find work. A standard conclusion is that Council Accommodation severely constrains mobility.

The psychic costs of relocating relates to the need to acquire new friends, local shopping knowledge, a new school for the children, a new job for the spouse. Generally, the needs of the children at important times in their educational careers will leave many couples immobile between areas.

The location of the job may be some way from an appropriate workforce. This causes two problems: 1) the compensation needed to encourage workers to commute fair distances; 2) the compensation needed to encourage people to move house to that area. These compensations will be mirrored in their reservation wages.

Wage differentials between occupations and regions can be explained under market and non-market headings. The market explanation revolves around market supply and demand conditions with barriers to entry.

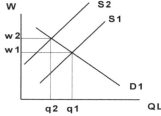

Given the same market demand curve, the wage will be higher the further to the left the supply curve is shifted. Let us begin from a state of no barriers. There is a single labour market and all jobs are equally arduous. The wage will be the same for all workers whose reservation wage is covered. If we introduce arduousness or danger, this will raise workers' reservation wage, shifting the supply curve to the left as workers will have to be compensated for the added risk.

If the skill factor required was relatively rare this would limit the numbers who could qualify for the job. The same would be true if the skill factor was attainable by many but the training period was long, hard and expensive.

The diagram right shows why there is a market premium for (n)ight work compared with (d)ay shift ($w_n - w_d$). The ONS estimate that 70,000 people now work mainly nights in the UK retail sector, which makes up 3% of the workforce. According to 5 Live Money the number has gone up 50% between 2007 and 2017, women by 77%. Shopping habit changed. Supermarkets, such as Tesco, open 24-seven in some stores, although this is declining. Online shopping

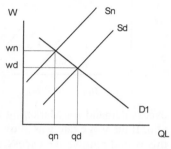

and delivery within 24 hours particularly online grocery shopping drives working shift patterns.

Not everyone will work unsocial hours. However, removing that night premium whilst boosting the basic rate will lead to excessive numbers wanting day shift work; more than there is work, perhaps, as illustrated in the diagram below, lower ($q_d - q_n$). Not enough will be happy with night shift, leading to some non-market rewards perhaps.

In Japan, the night shift is difficult to staff whilst not raising wages, so firms don't open at night or operate more family friendly policies. If there are 1.59 jobs for every applicant, but wages will not rise, then vacancies go unfilled. This record occurred in February 2018, the highest value since 1990. Unemployment stood at 2.8%. The value for part time work in April 2017 was 1.77. In contrast to the UK, Japan is keen to invite immigrants in. In 2012, there

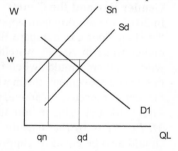

were 682,000 foreign workers. By 2017, 1,279,000 were in Japan, the increase representing about 20% of the total expansion of the workforce.

An interesting twist in this wage debate is the outcome for some lower paid workers is that the stagnant wages force them to take a second job. Take home pay may be the same as in 1997, but hours are up by 11%. In 2018, around 7.44m will work at least two jobs (11% of the workforce) up from 5.33m in 2015. Although this is behind the

US (around 20%) it is a notable shift in Japan, related to labour reforms. It could be a gig economy thing, yet nearly half of Japanese workers with two jobs are over 50.

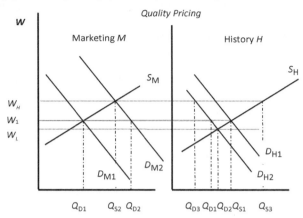

Left is analysis of the impact of common wages on different labour markets. Assume there is a market in Universities for lecturing staff. The current wage for Marketing and History lecturers is W_1. At this wage there are Q_{D1} Marketing staff (left-hand side) and Q_{S1} History staff. Students switch from History to Marketing leading to an excess demand for Marketing $Q_{D2} - Q_{D1}$ and an excess supply of History staff $Q_{S1} - Q_{D1}$. If the wage rate was allowed to fall to W_L in History and rise to W_H in Marketing, this would remove the excess. As work is of comparable worth, both groups could be paid W_H but excess supply of History staff of $Q_{D3} - Q_{S3}$. A solution could be to keep the wage the same but alter quality standards. Allow poorer quality Marketeers in but set greater expectations of Historians. This would undermine the work of equivalent merit argument – the staff are not. We conclude from this that the value of the work done cannot be viewed independently from the market conditions which produced that work. In the long run, lecturers retrain to become Marketing staff.

Gender Pay and the Courts

In 2017, the employment appeal tribunal upheld a ruling that workers in roles across the shop floor can compare their jobs with those done predominantly by men for a higher wage in Asda's warehouses. Typically, the gap was £1-3/hr. With unskilled work, workers should switch from tills to warehouse work, driving wages together. If there is no movement, the markets are separate and so there is a pay differential. From the lecturer discussion above, work is of comparable *worth*. The outcome is equal pay - not market clearing in both markets. For equal pay to correspond to market clearing, $MPP_T \div W_T = MPP_W \div W_W$: the productivity of till work (T) and warehouse work (W) should also be equal. If supply does not drive the wages together, a common cost of capital could. If it is easier to substitute in capital in till work than warehouse work, the wage rates could be different. Otherwise, the number of jobs lost due to automation would be greater for till work.

The Labour of Robots

In labour economics, what we teach is that if the labour market is becoming tight, such that there is pressure on wages, we move along the supply curve and wages are bid up. However, in the long run an alternative model is used, concerning price. If the price of labour rises relative to capital there is a substitution of capital for labour. In effect, labour is replaced by machines. Depending on the sector, the outcome is to accelerate the use of robots. Take farming. With global satellite positioning, robots can plant, fertilise and now harvest some produce. Importantly, for an aging farming population, it could drive tractors. Japanese farmers, average age 67, are looking to the driverless tractor to extend their working lives. Estimated to cost 50% more than conventional vehicles, like driverless heavy vehicles, the autonomous tractors could work alongside piloted ones. Uneven surfaces and steep fields make complete autonomy more challenging for tractors relative to trucks and cars.

Brexit forms an immediate concern. 29.7% of UK food manufacturing workers are EU nationals. Farming has been replacing labour since the industrial revolution. Can it fill the EU breach? In July 2017, the NFU reported that technology advances in the horticulture sector have made substantial improvements to the productivity of the sector – such as table top strawberry growing and poly-tunnels that facilitate work at a faster rate. But technology has not yet been developed to replace human pickers at an economically viable scale. Many crops such as berries, apples and pears require skilled hand-picking to avoid damaging the fruit. The scope for automation to replace labour is also limited in the livestock sectors where IT and technology will never be able to fully replace good stockmanship. Current expectations are that automation, where achievable, remains at least a decade away, and even then the cost of adopting new technologies may be prohibitive for many farm businesses. Thus, the technology is *enhancing productivity, shifting the demand curve for labour to the right*. However, where it can replace labour, *the lowering of the price of capital will facilitate more substitution, shifting the demand for labour to the left*, but for many farms that is some way off.

THE COORDINATION PROBLEM

The coordination problem entails the arrangement of groups of individuals with dissimilar goals in to a team with common goals. If uncontrolled, individuals will pursue personal objectives that may conflict with team goals. Thus, activity that requires collective behaviour requires the coordination of individuals. To subvert self-interest, co-operate or working interdependently requires an exchange of some sort: an individual must accept some satisfactory compensation. Moreover, a contract-specific task can be complex, mutually dependent and expensive to draw up. The individual contracting, coordinating and monitoring has *bounded rationality*. There is a limit to the entrepreneur's capability to envisage all possible problems associated with an array of contracts to perform a complex task. In general, it is possible that the risk of making an adverse selection will deter the information-poor party, whether they are a potential buyer, supplier or employer, from forging a contract with the information-rich party.

What are transactions cost problems?
An example of a contractual world in the news is insurance. Confused.com found that motor insurance premiums had risen from around £500 to £800 in the 4 years to June

2012. The industry provides its members with incentives to boost fees, which are ultimately paid by the culprit's insurer. Oddly, rather than acting collectively, the insurers bulk up the charges they levy on each other. A particular concern is the referral fee for injury claims.

Volkswagen withheld a payment of €385,474 over a dispute about €76.33. CarTrim and ES Automobilguss refused to deliver parts as a result. If production was brought to a holt it would cost €100m/week in profit. VW's relationship with the two soured after it commissioned CarTrim to develop new seat covers for high-end models and then cancelled the €500m deal in the aftermath of the diesel scandal, refusing to cover the €58m its suppliers had already invested. After 6 days, VW paid compensation of €13m. This shows *asset specificity* and weak negotiating position issues. These are strange ones to mention where JIT is prevalent.

A most awkward area with opportunism is the role of the financier when the business is close to failure. The business, by virtue of its dependence on the financier for forbearance, is an agent of the bank. Through access to the enfeebled business' books, the financier is in an unusual monopoly position, not subject to *asymmetric information*. The moral hazard is that it can force the business into receivership and acquire the business's assets on the cheap. RBS' Global Restructuring Group post 2008 was found by Promontory, a financial consultancy, to mistreat small businesses systemically. In other words, it was policy. Focusing on 207 of the 5,900 handled between 2008 and 2013, 86% were mistreated. Staff were coached in methods to extract fees and interest income from businesses that had already defaulted on loans.

Principal and Agent

Productivity is, in neo-classical terms, linked to [human] capital and incentives. Heterogeneity of the workforce and imperfect information are assumptions that lead to some practical realities:

- Workers differ in commitment and attitude, so their productivity is difficult to assess before appointment and often difficult to observe after;
- Productivity of a worker varies over time with a given level of human capital;
- Productivity per unit time is a function of innate ability, effort and the environment;
- Being highly productive can involve not following directives but acting on initiative.

The labour contract is split into two elements: Formal and Implicit. The former entails modes of direction and activity, and monitoring is often laid out: what is expected of the employee. These are challengeable in court. The textbook states that, as agents of the owners (shareholders), managers should seek to maximise shareholder value. The monitoring or oversight exercise by shareholders (principals) over their agents, the managers is often questioned. Specialisation is expected to improve productivity. Workers must be observed or monitored to prevent *shirking*. If this means that the worker moves beyond the monitoring capacity of their supervisor, the employer is forced to resort to other tactics to avoid opportunism. As monitoring and measurement can now be done by sophisticated machines or cameras, this observation may be virtual. GPS allows Deliveroo to monitor the performance of their couriers. Worksnaps will send regular screenshots from contractees' computers to contractors so they can check they are on track. Platforms, such as PeoplePerHour, allow entrepreneurs to address *monitoring* so that tasks can be auction to workers that may never meet their paymaster. The adverse selection is addressed by quality ratings from previous jobs.

Incentive schemes for workers can induce moral hazards: workers could behave badly where there is information asymmetry. In a drive to meet sales targets, between May 2011 and July 2015, 2m bank accounts or credit cards were opened or applied for by Wells Fargo employees without customers' knowledge or permission. Employees were trying to sell enough bank products just to keep their jobs. They were supposed to generate seven new chequing accounts and 42 other products every single day while making 100 phone calls each. Wells Fargo terminated 5,300 employees (about 1% of the workforce) in relation to the allegations. The bank was fined $185m; the CEO, John Stumpf, in September 2016, offered to forfeit $41m in bonuses; and in April 2017 $142m was offered to customers for fees and damage to their credit scores. In April 2018, it was further fined $1bn. The New City Agenda estimated that the 10 largest misconduct scandals cost UK banks and building societies £53bn in fines and other penalties, with PPI costing £37.3bn. Citibank was fined $425m as it employed Tom Hayes knowing he was a LIBOR manipulator and continued to do so whilst at Citi. The CFTC alleged that Citi was influenced by the possibility of $50-$150m profit from him.

Union Asset Management, based in Frankfurt, has found that litigation is a good tool to keep agents in line. It is suing Equifax over its cyber security breach in 2017 affecting 143m people in Georgia federal court. In May 2018, a class action lawsuit in the District Court in California alleged that the Wells Fargo made certain misstatements and omissions in disclosures related to its sales practices. The bank agreed to pay $480m to investors who bought stocks between February 2014 and September 2016.

Business Structures
Coase argued that one solution to transactions costs is the firm. The firm can be viewed as a nexus of labour contracts that are made loose and open-ended. Rather than specifying in a contract for each task or project for each artisan each day, the worker signs an incomplete contract. Workers are engaged on a 'permanent' basis and 'directed' by a supervisor to tasks that can vary from day-to-day. In other words, the contract is not task specific.

Coase addresses the bounded rationality problem, but what of opportunism, what stops the monitor behaving badly? From a Principal-Agent perspective, the owner is the ultimate monitor. For them the incentive to monitor is the profit. Everyone else receives a wage. Williamson, who took this further, suggested the monitoring problem where a team is involved will generate a **hierarchy** of bureaucracy. Assume that the owner or any other monitor can at best observe 4 people effectively. Once the business grows to 5 employees monitoring becomes less effective a deterring opportunism. By the time the business gets to 8 employees, the owner could employ another monitor. Indeed, there remains the opportunism of the employee-monitor. The owner could employ two monitors, and the owner monitors the monitors. The business could expand on this basis. With 64 workers there are an additional four tier one monitors and 16 tier two. From this one can see how a management hierarchy can evolve. Interestingly, in this version all monitors could be paid the same. They are only observing/ coordinating.

In the table right there are four resolutions to the coordination problem: the problem of organising people/workers to generate output. In Economics we envisage two routes

	Control	Flexibility
Internal Focus/ Integration	Hierarchy	Clan
External Focus/ Differentiation	Market	Adhocracy

to resolving the coordination problem: market and hierarchy. The market entails drawing up the design before construction begins.

To avoid opportunism, artisans are given formal, clear detailed, legally enforceable, written contracts. As mistakes happen, in this scenario all parties benefit from shifting risk; someone else carries the potential losses. One can see this issue with group of student renting a house from a landlord. Should the contract be signed by all and collectively they rent the house, or should there be individual lets? From the landlord's perspective, the former is better as the students must bear the risk of non-payment by one. Correspondingly, the latter would reduce the risk exposure of the student. There is no risk sharing. Here, the others could hold one party hostage on a job, but assuming repeat business, the 'cheat' will not be reemployed. But if there is low trust, the artisan may not see repeat business following and so behave **opportunistically**. This model works well where output is clearly associated with an individual entity. Measurement of output then is the mode of monitoring, reducing the scope for opportunism. However, this may only apply when the output is simple.

One dimension focuses on control. In the market, control comes through the contract. In hierarchies coordination and control comes from the supervision of the manager or principal. Output is a team effort, with no one entity being distinctive. Here a supervisor coordinates and monitors the team to address the problem of opportunism. Where the team member shirks, they run the risk of being fired. Monitoring can be becoming cheaper. Rewards are structured to encourage long-term relations, so that pay increments are based on years of service. The 'promise' of promotion will maintain the worker's motivation. So that there is long association, the wage is below what is merited in the early years and is over paid in the latter years. In effect, the MRP of an individual should reflect their wage in the long run.

A hierarchy fails when there is excessive ambiguity on performance evaluation. That is, a monitor cannot judge the quality of work. Under these circumstances an alternative mode of coordination is needed. Ouchi suggests the **clan** mode, which is based on self-control, is a solution. The opportunism that the expert can exploit is overcome through a *professional code of ethics*. The coordination problem, suppression of self-interest and the pursuit of congruent objectives, is achieved through socialisation. Here, the worker is pre-trained where traditions, customs, and a common way of thinking are inculcated into the worker. There is tight screening. Performance monitoring is not possible so, as in a high trust world colleagues are left to self-manage. Clearly, a rogue partner/ employee could take advantage of this light touch regime.

A further business form is the adhocracy. Minzberg and Quinn (1991) outline two forms of adhocracy: the administrative and the operating adhocracy. At their core is a structure to deal with a rapidly changing environment. The structure is highly flexible, loosely coupled, and amenable to frequent change, where problems exist in highly complex and turbulent environments. Adhocracy comprises highly trained technical experts in teams that are fairly fluid. Examples include high-technology firms where being leading-edge with technologies and strategies that must be developed to respond quickly and effectively.

The notion of insurance has its heart hold a moral hazard. By sharing the risk of what you do with others, so they bear some of the cost, you are more reckless. By taking out a loan where you can default, it encourages you to borrow too much. Indeed, the recklessness during an asset price bubble is based on this risk sharing with banks. However, banks and other businesses also share risk. The notion of too big to fail is much of a focus for the BoE. But then without this insurance some socially desireable activity will not take place. A classic example is the entrepreneur. Although that are risk neutral in theory. In practice, the punishment for failure should not out-way the benefits of the pursuit of profit. Here, through the drift from entrepreneur to the corporation and the institution of limited liability proffers variation of that social contract. If corporates only exist because they are useful social instruments, the way they are managed shows a break or the social contract. Profits and management salaries are disproportionally large and wages correspondingly small. The distribution of tax and dividends is equally problematic. One can see why the populist movements believe that their supporters feel short changed. What is ironic is that the nationalism associated with it is commonly about aliens when actually, it is their elite that has exploited them.

The Labour Arrangement – What is Self-Employment?
There are three types of employment status:
1. an employee, who enjoys the full range of employment rights;
2. a worker, who has less protection but is still entitled to the minimum wage and some other basic rights;
3. a self-employed person.
Platforms that represents a neo-classical labour exchange have been estimated by McKinsey Global Institute in the US, could add 72m full-time equivalent jobs or 2%

to global output by 2025. According to the Freelance Union in the US there are 53m freelance workers, including 21m independent contractors.

Relations can be seen in principal-agent or transactions costs terms. A firm is viewed as a collection of loose contracts where the employee, in return for accepting direction, is given incentives such as permanence and stable income. From a Williamson hierarchy perspective, this is likely because production involves a team that needs coordinating on an ad-hoc basis and no single contribution can be assessed. In Coase/Williamson's world there is a trade-off between control and security. In forgoing free will and accepting direction, the 'employee' (type 1) is given security. The employer accepts the responsibility of finding work to do and the risk of failing to do that. The obverse is the sub-contractor (3) who is contracted for specific tasks but the contract is the 'director' of effort, not an overseer. Are internet companies a market, where they act as an agent for both parties in bringing them together? Or are they employers where direction is given?

The UK Numbers
The TUC reported in January that, from 2008Q1 to 2017Q3 there were 895,000 new self-employment jobs and 1.65m employed (1.127+0.526m). In other words, 64.8% of job creation was in *employment* where 87% of jobs were located in 2008. Indeed, of the 2.52m new jobs 44.2% were permanent employee jobs.

	2008Q1	2017Q3	Δ	%Δ	% of totalΔ
EmpFT	19,122,857	20,250,428	1,127,571	5.9	44.2
EmpPT	6,459,020	6,985,036	526,016	8.1	20.6
SEmpFT	2,945,631	3,326,959	381,328	12.9	15.0
SEmpPT	931,944	1,445,860	513,916	55.1	20.2
Total	29,683,561	32,206,974	2,523,413	8.5	

The majority of self-employed was part time. The concentration of these new entrepreneurs is in the over 50-age bracket, making up half. They could be exploiting redundancy monies as well as their accumulated experience and contacts. The TUC pointed to a rise in non-regular employment and flexible labour markets.

In December 2016, the TUC estimated 3.2m workers (10%) were in some form of insecure work: 1.7m low-paid self-employment; 730,000 casual temporary or agency workers; and 810,000 on 'zero-hours' contracts. The ONS found that of the 848,000 jobs added to the total number of employees between 2012 and 2013, 34% were on zero-hours contracts and 36% were on flexitime. Only 16% were not classified as some flexible working. Sports Direct employs almost all of its 22,000 staff this way. But this is true of McDonalds and JD Wetherspoon as well. In the period April to June 2015, the LFS found that 744,000 were on a zero-hours contract, representing 2.4% of people in employment. This represented an increase is 120,000, or 19% up on 2014. The ONS survey in November 2017 of those on contracts that do not guarantee a minimum number of hours (NGHCs) indicates that around 1.8m are on NGHCs up from 1.4m in 2014. The Resolution Foundation reported that, workers on zero-hours contracts doing similar jobs as part-time workers earn 6.6% /year less (£1,000).

Is this Temporary work Temporary?
The OECD suggested that the temporary job is no longer the stepping stone to permanent employment. It found that 49% of temporary workers in 2008 went on to permanent jobs by 2011 in the UK. In Italy (26%), Spain (20.6) and France (20.5), the movement is less fluid.

The TUC analysing the Labour Force survey calculated that of the 740,000 agency workers 420,000 had been with the same employer for over a year. Of these, 11,000 have been there for 20 years and an additional 39,000 for at least half that. The average agency workers was paid £1.50/hr less than permanent staff. Many employers are using agency workers not as a temporary stop gap. JLR is such a company. In part, it a long-term strategy to keep costs down. Agency staff can be let go at less cost to the business. However, JLR treat agency stall like permanent, with the same pay progression.

This gives them the advantage of long term association before they are converted to permanent (which takes 3 yrs, on average). This is more like an efficiency contract than an efficiency wage.

Research conducted by the Association of Independent Professionals and the Self Employed, found that 37.3% of self-employed people did not earn a high enough income to be able to pay into a retirement fund. A further 9.1% were unsure of how to set one up. The RSA reported in February 2017 that 8% of the self-employed between the ages of 25-34 were enrolled in a pension, against 60% of employees. The typical earnings of the self-employed is £240/wk - 18.8% of them receive tax credits to make up their income; 10.6% of employees face this issue.

Unfair Wage or Competition?
JPMorgan's CEPS study of 260,000 respondents found a difference between physical and on-line work in the gig economy. As they are competing locally with people who face the same cost of living, physical taskers' wages, in countries such as the US tend to be much higher. By contrast, on-liners are subject to wage depression. Average earnings per hour on Mechanical Turk are below the US minimum wage, but 14 times the minimum wage in India.

Segmented Labour Markets
Segmentation occurs when the labour market is divided or structured in a way which is reflected in the forms taken by the employment relationship or contract. It is associated with the division between 'core' and 'atypical' employment in some contexts, and with that between 'formal' and 'informal' employment in others. In industrialised economies, a 'normal' or 'standard' employment relationship is full-time, indeterminate in duration, and based on a stable contract between the individual worker and a single, clearly defined employing entity. Atypical work takes the form of

part-time, fixed-term and temporary agency employment, and casualised forms of work, such as zero-hours contracts, spot contracts and Uber or Deliveroo self-employment.

In developing economies, segmentation is identified with a distinction between a 'formal' sector in which employment is stable and regulated, and an 'informal' sector of casualised work relations which are, in varying degrees, undocumented, untaxed, and beyond the scope of collective agreements and legislative protections.

One can see several versions of segmentation
- employers' organisational requirements (internal labour market theory)
- labour-use strategies (efficiency wage theory)
- the responses of unions (insider-outsider theory)
- the outsourcing of risk (the flexible firm)

The first 'dual labour market' theories of the 1970s identified a division of the market into a 'primary' segment consisting of stable employment in firm specific internal labour markets, and a 'secondary' segment. The markets had the following characteristics:
1. Upper primary: Pre-trained, lightly monitored, task flexible. In ILM – highly paid, promotion, good working conditions – white collar
2. Lower Primary: On-the-job training, heavily monitored (time and motion study), machine worker in limited ILM, union security – blue collar
3. Secondary: Virtually no training, few rewards and low level of job security, high turnover/low wage – McJobs

In an era of Monopoly Capitalism employment within the vertically-integrated firm was widespread. The primary employment was based on formal, bureaucratic rules and procedures. **Internal labour markets** (ILM) are markets internal to a company, so that candidates only compete with others from within the company for the internally advertised vacancies. We can see these themes in other areas. Williamson's hierarchies used transaction cost to explain identified stable employment with a series of loose contracts and monitors. Human capital theory predicted that long-term employment relationships and seniority-based wages would be found in contexts where firms and workers made mutual investments in firm-specific training.

By contrast, the ILM approach views the secondary market as governed by unfettered competition and transactions approach views this market as low-skill and low-discretion jobs and associated with 'spot contracting'. Workers' wages are influenced by external conditions

Efficiency wage theory from the early 1980s posits that the higher wage paid by employers in the primary sector incentivises its workforce to remain with the firm, lowering turnover costs. With asymmetric information, employers cannot fully assess the qualities of workers. So with workers' aptitude and motivation difficult to assess and having invested in their skills, employers increase wages and other elements of the work bargain above the market-clearing wage. It is thought that this leads to [equilibrium] unemployment possibly in a Harris and Todaro sense. The reliability also would encourage greater investment in the worker, increasing their productivity.

Insider-outsider theory focuses on the role of trade unions in segmenting the labour market. Segmentation, at least partly the result of union activity, is geared towards restricting the labour supply, and bid up wages in the primary sector. With the decline of factory work and trade unions, this model may reflect little in the economy today. However, today the law make act in the same way.

Atkinson – Flexible firm

The entrepreneur in transaction cost terms is viewed as a risk taker whereas employees are risk averse. It follows that the entrepreneur should bear risk but take the rewards (profit). The flexible firm shifts the risk of changes in market demand onto the worker and the wage.

There are two types of flexible labour. Numerical flexibility entails adjusting hours or number of employees to suit demand. Here,

Core worker:	FT, permanent, managerial, professional, Primary ILM Functionally Flexible
1st Peripheral group:	FT but semi-skilled Secondary Labour Market Numerical Flexibility
2nd Peripheral group:	PT Short term Contract Job sharing Public subsidy training
External	Agency workers Increased outsourcing Subcontracting Self-employment

we see the use of agency workers or causals. Functional flexibility involves labour that is task flexible (multi-skilled).

External workers are used for elementary work e.g. cleaning OR for highly specialised work. Outsourcing of government activities to the private sector places downward pressure on wages. To some extent, this is the dirty secret of the privatisation/ outsourcing agenda. If other costs are quasi fixed and economies are desired, privatising and lowering conditions of service fit the bill. The TUC and New Economics Foundation reported in March 2015 that outsourcing had a detrimental effect on pay and conditions. In the case of residential care, a worker before outsourcing could have been earning £9.45/hr and a nurse, £15.18. In the private sector this dropped to £7.23 and £13.74. A specific case is G4S in Lincolnshire taking over back office activities for the local police force in 2012. At transfer, the pay ranged from £8.84 to £10.40. Two years later the same job was being offered at £7.36. But then this backfires. Serco runs a private sector prison HMP Thameside. A prison officer earned £17,350 rising to £21,000. A nearby public sector one paid £24,500. The inevitable move of officers left Serco struggling. It now uses inmates as 'violence reduction representatives'; prisoners manage prisoners.

The cutting of pay shifts part of the wage bill to the tax-payer. Unison found that council workers were just as likely to be in receipt of tax credits as retail sector workers (11%), with only the hospitality worse (17%). Local government workers' real wage fell 15% over the period from 2006. The tax-payer contributes £6bn/yr supporting low wage earners, with tax credits for the lowest paid amounting to £21m.

Wage Support Diagrams

In the figure right, a wage subsidy over the free market wage is considered. W_1 is the free market wage. The wage is deemed too low by society and a credit is made available increasing the reward from forgoing hours of leisure, rotating the supply curve downwards. The new equilibrium would be at W_2 Q_2. Credit = W_2+credit − W_2. The cost of the credit provided raised = (Q_2) × $(W_2$+credit −

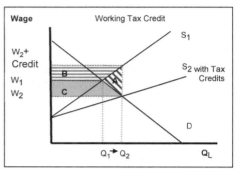

$W_{2t})$, which relates to areas A+C+B. Area B reflects the returns from working. Area C is the implicit employer subsidy and Area A reflects the deadweight loss.

In theory, more hours should be offered, but the subsidy may not encourage workers to work longer hours. Also, knowing the State will provide the subsidy, the system encourages firms to pay wages below a liveable level.

It was reported by the Joseph Rowntree Foundation that those living below a threshold of income that could provide adequate housing food and clothing in 2014/15 stood at 19m, up from 15m in 2008/9. This group will be affected by the post Brexit devaluation which pushed up food prices. In October, food inflation was 4%.

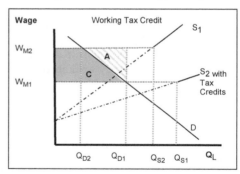

Assume the minimum wage W_{M1} is equivalent to £7.50/hr. At this level there will be Q_{D1} jobs and Q_{S1} looking for work. Unemployment will be $Q_{S1} - Q_{D1}$. Those in employment can claim a tax credit, which is a subsidy. The total subsidy would be areas C+A. Area A would be the welfare loss. If minimum wage was pushed up to W_{M2}, which is equivalent to £7/hr, this eradicates the subsidy, but at this level there will be Q_{D2} jobs and Q_{S2} looking for work. Unemployment will be $Q_{S2} - Q_{D2}$. The government has shifted the burden, but at the expense of fewer jobs.

Employment Subsidy

Rather than giving the subsidy to the worker, it could be offered to the employer in the form of an employer subsidy. In the diagram right, the demand for labour schedule shifts right as it is cheaper to employ the marginal worker. If the supply of labour schedule is upward sloping, there is a welfare loss of area A. The employer receives the subsidy directly. This time the policy drives up wages to W_2.

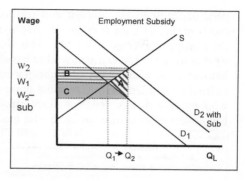

IN WHAT SENSE A GRADUATE JOB?

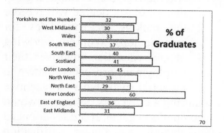

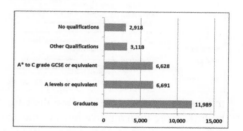

The Global Agenda Council on Employment (2014) report that in many Western European countries the proportion of the labour force with tertiary qualifications has grown at a faster rate than the jobs requiring a degree, which can lead to higher levels of graduate unemployment or over-qualification. In the UK, the proportion of graduates in the *working population* has double to 38% in the period 1992-2013. Indeed in 2013, there were 11,989,000 graduates of which 6,376,000 had an undergraduate degree (53%)[4]. The concentration of graduates reflects wage and unemployment. 60% of the Inner London working population are graduates.

Say's law states that supply creates its own demand. The skilled workforce available will spur entrepreneurs to utilise them. In the diagram below, there is an indication of the annual wage of a graduate and their employment rate. For example, the employment rate of someone in Business and Finance was 90% with an average salary of £30,000. There will be two competing forces. One would expect an area with excess supply would have a low wage and low employment rate. High demand would present the opposite picture. Marginal welfare analysis suggests the costs of the education should be outweighed by the social benefits. As a merit good, it should be subsidised. An over-skilled workforce is preferable to an under-skilled. Individual productivity, in

---

[4] A graduate is defined as a person who is aged over 20, not enrolled on any educational course and who has a level of higher education above 'A' level standard

part, depends on the amount and quality of the education and training they have received. In 2010, the average UK employee cost their business €266 in training costs; the European average was €511. This links to output. In the time it takes a British worker to earn £1, a German worker has earned £1.35. In a sense, the surfeit is like an innovation or a discovery of a cheaper resource. With job upgrading employers are using the qualification to screen out those not capable of undertaking current or future work perceived as skilled. Not all are capable of meeting the future needs of the sector. Employers want to hire someone who meets or exceeds a certain intrinsic quality that

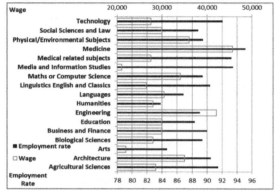

means they would be able to adequately perform the job they are being hired for. Graduates have signalled they have more potential than others.

Alternatively, one could suggest that getting a degree will reorder the ranking of candidates for existing jobs. Workers, knowing greater education improves their employment prospects relative to potential rivals have an incentive to acquire a degree. If this were the case, then acquiring a university education would be little more than a move in a simple positional competition game. If it does not need a degree to take it on so that the skills acquired from obtaining a particular qualification are superfluous, the graduate is over-skilled for the job. If someone has higher qualifications than needed to get the job, they are over-qualified. Employers, faced with better applicants, will select them over those with less education, even if both types of workers would be capable of doing that work.

Assume that there are two groups; a high and a low productivity group with a relatively high MRP for the former. Assume the employer cannot judge immediately who is more productive, but the employer is wanting to set up a separate, more productive group with a higher wage. The 'market wages' for the two jobs are W_H and W_L. From the diagram below, the transfer market would see Q_T transferring from the low to the high wage market if the costs of relocation were zero and the skill requirement was the same. The supply of movers would by S_T under those circumstances. The wages would be common but higher. Suppose employers in the higher wage sector maintain the higher wage but seek to separate out less productive workers, so access to the market is restricted. This restriction could be achieved by qualifications. Only pay the premium to the well-qualified workers. This would lead to a transfer market. If the cost of training to get this qualification is greater than $W_H - W_L$ amortised over a working life, no one would transfer. If the cost was $W_{H*} - W_{L*}$, Q_{T*} would undertake the training, narrow the differential to reflect the cost.

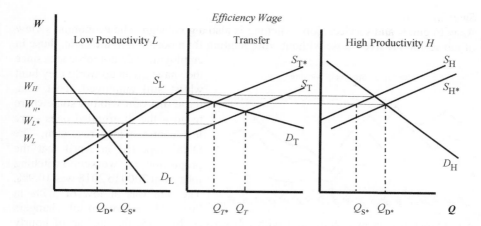

One could argue that enrolling on a degree programme is also a *signal* that the candidate has greater productivity. With an investment in human capital (the gap between S_T and S_{T*}), the student is taking a risk: a higher fee may be too risky for some. The Social Market Foundation (SMF) found that the number of students from disadvantaged backgrounds going to university was increasing fast, especially those entering with vocational qualifications, such as BTecs rather than 'A' levels. Between 2008 and 2015, students entering higher education from the most disadvantaged backgrounds with 'A' levels increased by 19%, but with BTecs increased by 116%. Graduates with a BTec *and* a degree earn 20% more/hr compared with a BTec as the highest qualification. The Augar report is concerned about the percentage of BTec diploma students achieving a distinction or distinction star, which rose by 40% between 2006 and 2016, possibly reflecting inflated points.

The same argument can be used for an efficiency wage premium. More productive workers would be paid a higher wage. If they were not, higher productive workers will not try so hard or they leave. So we end up with two markets. At any one time, a proportion of workers in the low wage market are highly productive. The supply of job shifter curve becomes S_T. But the gap between S_T and S_{T*} reflects the opportunism in moving. Q_{T*} represents the number who have good characteristics and can meet the higher productivity demands, justifying the efficiency wage premium $W_{H*} - W_{L*}$. Workers could then choose to move to higher wage firms or higher paid jobs within the firm. In return for the higher wage the employers would monitor workers and sack the lazy ones. Arthur Okun's toll, whereby the *MRP* > *W* in early years but otherwise later, is an incentive to stay with the company. It also gives the employer chance to judge the productivity of the worker – to shift them from lower to higher productive units of the company. Being a known quantity means you are taking less of a risk when you shift jobs, so one could suggest the larger premium for those changing company is based on the likelihood of fitting in.

Switching costs

As with goods and services, job switching is also a good sign. The economist's view of job search involves those without work hunting for a position. In the main, those in

employment do not job search once they have given up work; they hunt whilst still employed. That said, those that quit without somewhere to go – the disgruntled ones - are less common in a recession. The ONS[5] reported in April that the proportion of workers switching jobs from 2000 to 2018 was 10.9%. The rate was at low of 5.7% in 2010. The returns to job changers was higher pay growth compared with job stayers. In 2018, the median of hourly earnings growth for job changers was 7.3% compared with 3.0% for job stayers. Earnings growth for job changers is more cyclical and quicker to react to the economic downturn than for job stayers. Those that changed job within their firm saw a 6.9% pay increase, but between firms the increase was 7.6%. The premium for moving may in part be related to the risk entailed in shifting firms.

Potential growth is slowed when resources shift more slowly from poorly performing to better performing sectors. So, this should contribute to the productivity puzzle. What was noticeable was the number that switched within the same sector, which fell slightly. The big drop was the number that shifted between sectors. Since 2012, this figure has risen from 480,000/qtr to 650,000/qtr. This is related to the state of the

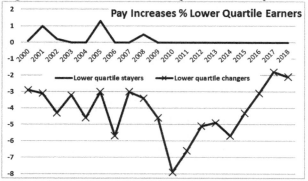

market. Those that move could be signalling their worth. However, those with poorer earning (Lower quartile) fared less well. The changers at the bottom end may have been forced into moves by job loss.

Does this signalling pay? In 2015, graduate (Non-graduate) unemployment stood at 3.1% (6.4%). Young graduates had a much greater likelihood of having a skilled job (56% vs. 31% in medium and low skill jobs) compared with young non-graduates (17% vs. 54%). Between 2008 and 2015, the

---

[5]https://www.ons.gov.uk/economy/nationalaccounts/uksectoraccounts/compendium/economicreview/april 2019/analysisofjobchangersandstayers#job-changers-and-stayers

median salary for young graduates of £24,000 (£31,500 for all ages) was £6,000 (£9,500 for all ages) better than non-graduates, but the pay had not grown since 2008. Since 2015, this gap has contracted to £4,500. The graduate premium over non-graduates in 2018 across all working age workers was £10,000, whilst the post-graduate premium above that was £6,000 suggesting the median annual earnings for a post graduate of £30,000 was £16,000 above a non-graduate. The latter premium from around 2011 was shifting from UG to PG, perhaps reflecting the increase in the number of graduates. The premium of £4,500 for having a post-graduate degree when young was growing.

In 2017, the proportion of overeducated workers in the UK was 16%. London had the highest. Results for London are out of line with the rest. This is

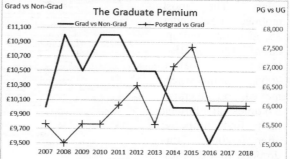

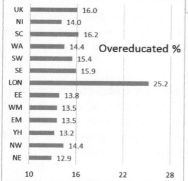

possibly a reflection of a relatively high proportion of immigrants but also graduates that flock there. Using a Harris-Todaro model, one might suggest rather than unemployed, one can be unemployed on the job waiting for a highly remunerated

opportunity to arise on one's doorstep.

In the diagram right, it is evident that the 'problem' of non-graduate jobs is

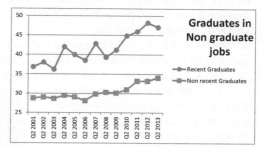

one affecting recent graduates, which has risen steadily since the financial crisis began. Recent is defined as aged 30 or under.

In the US, from 1975 until 2014, relative wages for those with a high school degree fell from over 80% to less than 60% of the amount earned by workers with at least a college degree.

From a survey of movers, the pay increases in London across 2017/18 were around 3.1% for those that did not change job, which is only slightly greater than elsewhere. However, for those that moved, the increase was 11.1%, an 8% premium. Note how the higher unemployment regions have the higher premiums otherwise.

The Resolution Foundation reported that in the last 17 years people are less likely to migrate between regions; the proportion dropping from 0.8 of the population to 0.6. This constitutes less than half the 1.5% rate in the US, but even then it has halved since the 1980s. The benefit of a move results in a £2,000/yr increase in salary. The most mobile, those under 35, also saw a drop, but of 20%. The BBC found that before 2008, homeowners moved, on average, 3.6 times, after buying their first property; after 2008 this dropped to 1.8 times.

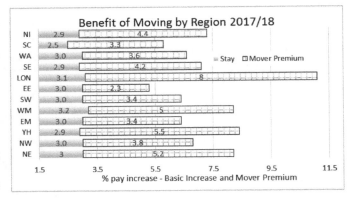

Benefit of Moving by Region 2017/18

The Resolution Foundation reported that in 2007/8 moving to London boosted salary by 15% in real terms; by 2015/16 this had risen to 18%. However, housing costs in London grew by 54% over the decade to 2015/16, deterring moves to London.

Turnover Costs
One strand of Efficiency Wage theory emphasises turnover costs. Staff turnover is inevitable but it can prove a significant cost to employee morale, productivity, and company revenue. Recruiting and training a new employee requires staff time and money. In 2014, Oxford Economics estimated the cost of replacing members of staff was £30,614/worker. There are two main factors that make up this cost:
1. Lost Output whilst the vacancy exists
2. Training and absorption costs of a new worker

Costs of recruiting are shown right. Once in, it takes on average, 28 weeks to reach Optimum Productivity, where one can do the job effectively. This cost is worth £25,181/worker. This time varies. For SMEs (with up to 250 workers) 24 weeks; over 250 workers, 28 weeks. Microbusinesses (1-9 workers) 12 weeks.

Hiring temporary workers before the replacement starts:	£3,618
Advertising the new role:	£398
Recruitment agency fees:	£454
Interviewing candidates:	£767
HR time spent processing replacement:	£196
Total	£5,433

Five sectors are considered - Retail, Legal, Accountancy, Media & Advertising and IT & Tech. Differences between the sectors are revealed in the table below.

The time varies with experience. Joining from the same sector, time-to-optimum is 15 weeks; from another sector 32 weeks; new graduates 40 weeks; unemployed or inactive 52 weeks.

In the US, the Centre for American Progress found average costs to replace an employee are:

- 16% of annual salary for high-turnover, low-paying jobs (< $30,000/yr)
- 20% for mid-range positions ($30,000 to $50,000/yr)
- Up to 213% for highly educated, executive positions.

	Optimum Productivity	Cost to replace worker
Accountancy	32 weeks	£39,230
IT & Tech	29	£31,808
Legal	32	£39,887
Media & Advertising	20	£25,787
Retail	23	£20,114

It was revealed by the National Foundation for Educational Research (NFER) in 2017 that teaching had a high turnover rate, particularly in their first five years. Between 2010 and 2015 about 10.4% of science teachers left the profession each year; 10.3% of maths; 10% of technology; 9.7% English; 8.4% art, drama and music; 8.5% humanities such as history and geography; and 5.9% of PE teachers. The government has claimed teacher retention figures in England remain steady. After 5 years about 70% remain. That would imply an attrition rate of 6.9%. A rate of 10% implies that 60% remain after five years and over half have gone after 6.6 years. Efficiency wage theory suggests a greater wage is needed.

Occupations and Job Influence

The CIPD, when analysing the role of graduates in the labour market proffered four perspectives. As with robots, more graduates could lead to a raising or declining fortunes. Greater productivity leads to a higher wage. But employers could just use graduates for non-graduate roles. The CIPD took the view, found in Braverman (1974), that high-skilled work is typically associated with elements of employee autonomy and decision-making. This corresponds with Core worker/ Clans and Upper-primary work. In a sense, this depends on the complexity of the work and the nature of the employer. In a declining industry, less discretion may be a function of pressure on profits. Nevertheless, change in the levels of influence and discretion are good markers. It proposed four areas of job type:

• Job upgrading – jobs with non-decreasing levels of graduate skill requirements and non-decreasing differences between the skill requirements of graduates and non-graduates.

• Job competition – jobs with initially positive but decreasing differences in skill requirement between graduates and non-graduates accompanying rising graduate shares.

• Job deskilling – jobs with falling levels of skill requirements.

• Graduate mismatch – jobs with zero or negative differences in skill requirements for graduates and non-graduates.

Occupations not seeing a decline in influence and discretion, but where graduates are performing increasingly less-skilled jobs are examples of **job competition**. Cases include managers in manufacturing, transport and communication and health associate professionals, including nurses.

Occupation	Increase in graduate share, 1994–2007 (%Δ)
Upgrading	
Managers in healthcare	8.2
Functional managers	11.5-15.3
Associate professionals in business services and finance	14.1
Public sectors associate professionals, vocational instructors, careers advisors	9.3-15.1
Associate professional in other community services, including: Media associate professional; Social welfare associate professionals (e.g. social workers); Protective service occupations (e.g. police officers)	8.1-37.4
Administrative occupations in other community services	9.5
Competition	
Managers in manufacturing	10.0
Managers in business services	11.6
Managers and proprietors in other services	15.2
Science and engineering technicians/technicians in manufacturing	11.2-14.1
Associate professionals in health (including nurses and therapists)	21.4
Sales associate professionals	15.0
Personal service occupations in education	9.6

Occupations where influence and discretion have been increasing over time, so **job upgrading** encompasses distinction between graduate and non-graduate work. Examples are graduate retail assistants; customer service occupations; media associate professionals; and public service associate professionals.

Deskilling accompanies tighter managerial control and a greater reliance on routine tasks. Less discretion is found in the NHS despite a clearly highly professionalised staff base. Indeed, the report highlights senior- and lower-level public administrators but this affects graduates as well as non-graduates. It is part of the new public management. Other examples were leisure and travel service occupations, such as travel agents, leisure assistants and air and rail travel assistants.

Mismatch	
Office managers	10.1
Managers in hospitality and leisure services	8.2
IT technicians	33.8
Administrative occupations in education	13.8
Administrative occupations: records	8.0
Personal services in business services	13.5
Childcare and related personal services	11.1
Deskilling	
Senior public administrators	12.0
Health associate professionals (e.g. nurses)	22.5

Sectors where graduate skills have not been key to performing adequately and so represent a **mismatch** include managers in construction, health and social care, and leisure and hospitality; administrators in finance, education and healthcare; record-keeping administrative occupations; and IT technicians. In some cases, the skills are comparable to what non-graduates have traditionally offered.

PARTICIPATION

Several factors have contributed to the rising demand for skills in the labour market: technological and organizational change, trade, deregulation of key industries, and the decline of unions. In contrast, reductions in the demand for labour appear to explain the participation decline especially for lower-skilled men. The graphic above shows the

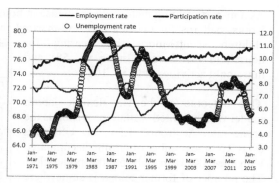

evolution of the unemployment, employment and participation rates. The unemployment and the employment rate (lower one left-hand scale) off set each other, suggesting that the participation rate is fairly stable. Indeed, it has a general upward slope.

Households and Participation

The number of working age HHs was 20.682m in 2015Q2. This will include at least one person of working age. There were 3.269m HH where no adult of working age was employed (15.5%); 5.9m where some but not all work; and 11.55m where all worked.

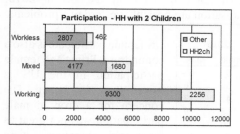

Of the workless households, 462,000 had two dependent children (10%), as opposed to 16% for all groups. The mixed category contains both working and workless members – probably a child carer. 1.68m or 29% of the total number of two dependent households fall into this category. Having 2 children may be a marker of a participant household.

The male participation rate in the US of those in the prime age groups of 25 to 54 is around 88%. This compares unfavourably with the 1964 rate of 97%. A simple linear trend suggests that by 2050 a ¼ of US men will be non-employed: Larry Summers expects ⅓. ½ will experience at least a year of non-work out of every five. He was too pessimistic. From 2016 to 2018 5m jobs were secured by new and returning workers of all ages.

A Time Use Breakdown in 2014 for prime age males overall compared with non-participating males is instructive. The big difference in non-work time is in Socialising, Relaxing, and Leisure, in particular watching TV. The working male would watch 154 minutes of TV/ day. The non-participant would watch double that (335m/day).

As non-participating men could specialise in household management whilst their wife works, patterns for married and non-married men should be different. Those with children spent more time caring for household members (73mins vs. 58) and household activities (112 vs. 108).

Prime age Men	Partic-ipants	Non Partic-ipants
Caring for Household Members	29	28
Caring for Non-Household Members	7	8
Education	8	25
Household Activities and Services	84	111
Socialising, Relaxing, Leisure	251	472
Watching Television	154	335
Work	316	7
Other (Including Sleep)	736	773

 One outcome of the US flexible labour model with a limited welfare provision is the crime rate. At around 1.5m, the US locks away 10× the number of criminals compared with the UK, with only 5× the population. The number of former felons is somewhere around 12-14m, which, given their record, makes them difficult to place in work. Another concern for the disadvantaged highlighted by Case and Deaton is that working-class white Americans have a high mortality rate. Uneducated white Americans now die at higher rates than other ethnic groups. In 1999, white male and females aged 50-54 with a high school education had a mortality rate 30% below black Americans, by 2015 it was 30% above. Much of this excess mortality is down to deep social dysfunctionality. Characteristics include suicide, alcohol and prescription drug abuse. Opioid abuse is estimated to cost 2.8% of GDP in the US in 2015. Uncontrollable immigration and deindustialisation are possibly yesterday's problems.

World Bank participation rates 15+	1990		2016	
Income group	Female	Male	Female	Male
High income	49	73	52	68
Upper middle income	61	82	56	76
Middle income	52	83	47	77
Lower middle income	42	83	38	79
Low & middle income	53	83	49	78
Low income	69	85	70	83
United Kingdom	53	75	57	69
United States	56	75	56	68
India	35	85	27	79

US female participate is also a conundrum. Prime age female participation in the US is lower than in Japan. The concern for a drop in male participation was not great as household incomes were rising: female participate made up for the decline. With both in decline there will be a household issue. The US stands out as being less supportive of the home maker-worker. Paid-parental leave in OECD countries increased from 17 weeks to over a year since 1970. In the US it remains at zero. Trump promised six weeks of paid maternity.

In the UK, the DoE found that 53% of stay-at-home mothers would rather work if there was suitable childcare. It was also found that 80% of working mothers relied on child care of which ⅔ use formal childcare. However, 36% of working mothers would rather not work if they could afford to. So around 6.3m children receive some form of child care.

Universal Income

McKinsey Global Institute reported in 2018 that global executives expect to replace over a quarter of their workforces by 2023, along side the possibility that 30-40% of jobs being replaced by technology. The latter has enormous political implication. One solution is to offer a Universal Income. In May 2018, Finland was half way through a 2 year programme when it was abandoned. Rather than €500 unemployment benefit, a candidate received €560 in a monthly basic income. This does not require someone to be a job seeker, which reduces stress. Interestingly, a recipient did not lose it if they worked.

Clearly, with 40% possibly persistently without work, a universal income is socially desirable. Five arguments have been mounted against UBI:
1. it is expensive if everyone gets it. Deficits and so interest rates will mushroom.
2. it will increase inequalities. Those getting targeted benefits will get less whilst the rich get more.
3. work offers a social capital, structure, meaning: it trains, challenges and rewards: along with pensions, it is the key means by which income currently disbursed. Delinking work from income, as we see from the US male, tends to be linked with dysfunctional societies.
4. it undermines the incentive to participate in work and possibly society. It encourages dependence
5. it deflects from looking for alternative solutions to the distribution of work issue. Rather than calling it part time, a full working week could redefine 16 hours/wk as full time. This is not so fanciful. IG Metall and Sudwestmetall agreed a 2-year deal covering 900,000 workers that entailed a 28-hr week in February 2018.

Linking it with pensions and participation, it was reported by Continuous Mortality Investigations in 2018 that the life expectancy for a female [male] at 65 was 24 years [22.1]. This was a fall of two months from 2017 and 12 months [10] from 2016. This boosted the share price of Insurance Companies.

THE POLITICS OF THE LOW WAGE

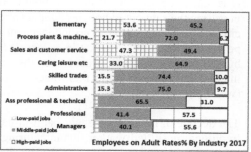

Employees on Adult Rates% By industry 2017

Although not mainstream theory, capital accumulation requires appropriate ratios of wage/profits and investment/consumption. The division between wages and profits determines the funds available for consumption and investment. Workers' income must grow at the same rate of the growth of output. Investor income and investment must grow as least as quickly as the output of capital goods. If workers' income is too modest, consumption will be inadequate to provide the rewards from production. If workers' income was too great, the funds available for investment will be insufficient to reproduce the necessary capital to generate the goods and employ the workforce. Real wage growth/year in the UK in the 1970s and 1980s was 2.9%; 1990s 1.5%; 2000s 1.2% but more recently the rate has been –2.2%.

In the US, the long-term average of wage/profit & interest is 63%. The labour share of the cake has been declining. Richard Lewis, on this theme, found that a decrease in the wage proportion in France, Germany, Italy, the UK, the US, Japan, Turkey and South Korea led to lower growth. But then Canada, Australia, Argentina, Mexico, India, China and South Africa saw higher growth. GDP fell 0.36% for every 1% fall in the labour share of the cake. Interestingly, the highest income earners are not rentiers; they are employees plus entrepreneurs. Moreover, lower wages had a negative effect on the proportion among trading partners: a low proportion infected other areas.

The division of the cake is central to the collapse of mainstream consensus politics, which can be characterised as the moderate left challenging the moderate right in liberal democracies – which constitutes part of the post war settlement and the triumph of the market economies over communism. Politicians were elected to moderate the excesses of the market and make is fairer for all. However, to a populist, this group was little more than a self-perpetuating elite that, as the agent of the people, was difficult to monitor and, in effect, ran the system at the expense of the people. A *populist* can be seen as someone that seeks to *challenge this 'status quo'*. Thus, in old language, a populist can come from the extreme left or the right.

A populist sees the ruling elite as not supporting the neglected majority; those that see themselves as poorly treated relative to less 'deserved' cases (those tolerated minority groups); those that are victims of globalisation (see Vernon Bogdanor[6]). Those that fit the bill can be identified by their links to the past and place. The alternative group are most likely to benefit from the system that filters out non-member through exams. Yascha Mounk, from Harvard, is scornful of the current US political system describing is as 'undemocratic liberalism'. Economic elites and narrow interest groups succeeded in getting their favoured policies adopted about half of the time. The views of ordinary citizens, they had virtually no independent effect at all. When elites have sufficient power they have little interest in reflecting the preferences of the public at large. The burden of structural adjustment from the 2008 crisis is seen as the key marker. The internal devaluation (falling real wages and cuts in benefits) affect the squeezed middle (well bottom) negatively.

The decline of trade unions goes hand-in-hand with the decline in the absorber of the traditional unskilled worker, manufacturing industry. Here, manual work could still bring home a solid wage that could be used to bring up a family and secure a roof over it. The decline of manufacturing from the 1980s left the less well educated exposed to a future of service sector work that was not well paid and not seen as clearly male-

---

[6] https://www.youtube.com/watch?v=_6Kc16BpbBs

oriented. The wave of globalisation that followed in the 1990s and 2000s intensified this whilst the elite post Mrs Thatcher went further in reducing the transfer of wealth from those that benefited from globalisation to those that did not. Furthermore, those jobs and homes that the losers in the great scheme could compete for were moved further out of reach with waves of immigrants with more human capital following trade arrangements such as the single market or NAFTA. In effect, there has been three decades of removing opportunity of work from the losers whist advocating the [profit] opportunities that free trade bring to the community [elite].

Minimum Wage

The minimum wage rate, initially set at £3.60 in 1999, rose faster than inflation and average earnings. The minimum wage is of no consequence if it is below the clearing wage. In 2010, the wage stood at £5.93, when the median wage was £11.08 and the mean wages £14.65. The

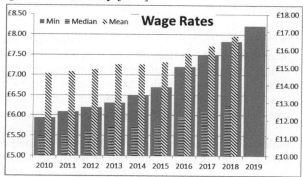

Low Pay Commission estimated the minimum wage's 12p/hr increase introduced in October 2013 would have raised tax revenues by £110m and reduced benefit expenditure by £73m; assuming linearities, 50p/hr could save the exchequer about £750m/yr. Card and Krueger, found that a higher rate did not destroy jobs. Their 1994 study of fast-food restaurants in two neighbouring US states showed a rise in jobs.

In 2013, 5% were on minimum wages and a further 10% were earning within 50p/hr of that. Of this 10%, ⅓ had been stuck there for 5 years and 20% for 10 years. The Resolution Foundation found that number of those earning less than the 'living' wage has increase from 3.4m in 2009 to 4.6m in 2013. In other words, the wage-wage spiral that the minimum wage could cause had not materialised. The Low Pay Commission reported that only the lowest 15% of earners (3.8m workers) saw a real wage increase over the 2007-2016. The pay dominated by the minimum wage of those working 26 hrs/wk rose by £180/yr in real (£400/yr nominal) terms. For the whole of the UK, the real wage fell by 1%.

Minimum Wage – at a Cost

In April 2016, mayors of California and New York signed in to law a minimum wage of $15/hr to be introduced in 2023 and 2018, respectively. The then Federal minimum of $7.25/hr is found in states such as Texas. Normally, a minimum increase is absorbed in price and profit. Alan Krueger sees $12 as beneficial but $15 as potentially introducing undesirable consequences to replace labour with capital. The Congressional Budget Office projected that a Federal minimum of $10.10 would cost 500,000 jobs, or 0.3% of the workforce, or 2 month's job generation. The consequence of pushing minimum wages too far are below.

In manufacturing, rising labour costs would provoke greater mechanisation. Labour intensive industries such as care homes cannot replace labour. In November, Allied Healthcare, which supports 13,000 people, admitted it was struggling with debts. The Care Quality Commission issued a notice saying it had serious doubts about Allied Healthcare's future. In April, Four Seasons Health Care went into administration. With about 322 homes, 17,000 residents and patients and employing some 20,000 staff, it was the biggest care home group to have gone into administration since Southern Cross in 2011.

In 2018, the Joseph Rowntree Foundation reported that since 2008 the minimum income standard had risen by 30% for a nuclear family but 50% for a pensioner couple. With 19m people in a household below this minimum, the increase of 3.4m over a decade is consistent with other measures of growing inequality. Concurrently, the Resolution Foundation found that between 2003 and 2016/17, the lower bicentile household real income adjusted for housing cost had dropped from £14,900 by £100.

Following the introduction of €8.50/hr wage, inequality in Germany fell more than anywhere else in the EU. Eurofound, an EU Agency, found no effect on employment. In the UK the minimum wage helped pay rise by 10% in real terms between 2015 and 2017 whilst employment rates were at record highs and falling unemployment rates. In June 2018, it was announced that German minimum wage would rise to €9.19/hr. But the push might be the route for better wages possibly destroying the High Street along the way.

GENDER BIAS

The pay gap between males and females is falling for the under 30s. This would be great news if it has real meaning. The driver is that men are earning less. The Resolution Foundation found they will earn at 30 £12,500 less than an equivalent cohort in 1993 compared with 2016. Men are increasingly doing low paid jobs. The proportion has increased by 45%. The number of men working in retail has gone from 85,000 to 165,000 and the number of bar staff from 45,000 to 130,000. By contrast female participation in business and finance has risen from 175,000 to 325,000 and teaching, a not well paid but solid and dependable work, has gone from 140,000 to 310,000.

That said, standard 'mid-skilled' jobs have declined. The number of secretarial posts has dropped by ⅔ whilst routine manufacturing jobs, the backbone of traditional Fordist work, has fallen by 40%. Only 7.7% of jobs are found in mining quarrying and factories.

The type of tenure selected by both males and females is questioned by the ONS. Are women content with part-time work? Do men dislike temporary work?

In 1992Q2 there were 825,000 temporary workers out of 25.64m in employment. By 2015Q2, there were 30.98m in employment and 941,000 temporary workers. The number of females dropped from 489,000 to 480,000. Of these, 46% were happy to be temporary employees, down from 52%. By contrast, male contentment increased from 31% in 1992 to 37% in 2015.

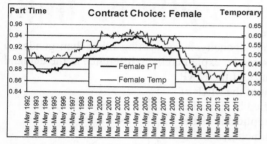

Of the 4.957m part-time employees in 1992 89% were women. The number of part-time males tripled to 1.5m as the number of total part-time employees rose to 6.866m. So, of the 5m more employees over the 24 years 1.8m were part-time. The proportion of part-timers that were women fell to 77%. Those that were content with the contract remained static: 86-89% for women and 65% for men. Part-time employment is a preferred tenure.

Examining the time profiles of both males and females we see a common pattern; a cycle of around 20 years. The peak is sometime in 2004/5 period, which corresponds strangely with house prices. Contentment may go with the business cycle. However, there is a clear difference. Males have a stronger preference for full-time work compared with females. With 85% content with a part-time contract, the concerns about tenure are women working are clear. 59% of employed women work full-time.

The spare capacity in this area – converting PT female employees is limited (only a further 4.2%).

Earnings by Degree
In the tax year 2016/17 the best degree that a woman could have as measured by median pay after 5 years is Medicine. Half of those with that degree earn over £45,800. This is followed by Economics at

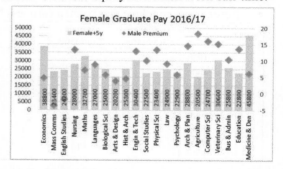

£38,800. The least remunerated were Agriculture (£20,500), Social Studies (£22,500) and Arts (£20,200). The premium earned by males over females was largest in percentage terms in Agriculture @22% (£4,600 premium). The smallest is Mass Communication @-3.8%.

A further 5 years adds an additional 14% to a female salary but 31% to a male's. The male premium really takes off in the second 5 years after graduation. Assuming graduating at 21 years of age, this puts this breakaway period in prime child birth age.

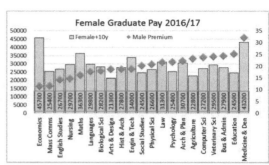

Female Graduate Pay 2016/17

Let's examine wages using simple labour market diagram. Assuming homogeneity in everything other than gender, a difference in wage for the same work can be explained by a difference in the demand for workers by group. In the diagram right the MRP of males would have to be to the right of the MRP of females for the difference to be justified by a market premium. Although not directly applicable Uber provides some interesting gender distinctions. Using data on 1m drivers in the US there was a 7%/hr gap in earnings. This was explained by

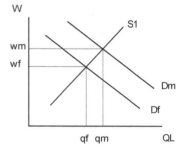

- Males drive 2.2% faster – so more trips per hour
- Males have more experience – they drive more hours per week and they have a longer association with Uber. Drivers with over 2500 trips earn almost 14% more/hr than their first 100 as they pick up tactics - learning by doing.
- Males tend to drive in more lucrative part of town.
- Researchers conclude that women earn less because of the choices they make.

Skill Level	Male Graduates	Female Graduates	Part Time
High	54%	50%	14
Upper Middle	31	21	12
Lower Middle	12	27	32
Low	3	3	40
Employment Rate	89%	86%	
Ave Gross Hourly Rate	£17	£14	

In the table left there is an analysis of graduate employment subdivided by gender and skill in 2013. A *high skill* level is defined as normally acquired through a degree or an equivalent. This would include 'professional' or managerial positions, such as senior government officials, financial managers, doctors, teachers and accountants. Half of graduates are in high skill jobs with very similar rates for males and females.

The hourly rate of pay difference could reflect the level of non-graduate work. The employment rate is relatively high at 86-89%, 8% of males are part time whereas 32% of female graduates are not in full time work. This is likely to do with time out of the labour market for child rearing, which is still viewed by society as primarily a female role. 1% of male graduates and 7% of females are out of the workforce for child raising purposes.

Options taken as school tell a story. 92,000 candidates took Maths in 2016.

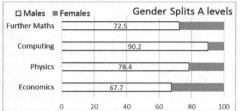

Gender Splits A levels

□ Males ■ Females	
Further Maths	72.5
Computing	90.2
Physics	78.4
Economics	67.7

0   20   40   60   80   100

As AS levels did not contribute to 'A' levels the 'AS' saw a 13.7% drop in entries. The STEM subjects show a worrying bias towards boys. Maths, Physics and Computing all have males making up over 70% of the candidates.

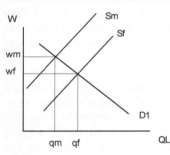

Alternatively, it could be there is a supply issue. The wage for females will be lower than that for males if there is greater supply. In the diagram right much like the explanation for night shift pay, women could earn less than men where they dominate. This explanation might work in sectors where average wages in general are low (e.g. mass communications). But interestingly, women earn more than men in these areas where they have a relatively larger supply.

A third possibility is union membership/industrial action. If females are less willing to

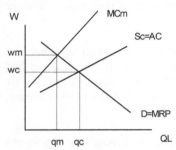

organise themselves, join trade unions or engage in industrial action, the wage might be lower. In the diagram right the competitive wage is w_c. This is determined where the demand for labour (MRP) equals the supply (AC). Restricting access to the sector or other forms of industrial action could be viewed as monopsonistic. The union could negotiate the MC of w_m, a higher wage. However, more women and a higher proportion of women join unions. Of the 6.22m TU members in the UK in 2016 3.398m were women. 25.9% of women workers were TU members as opposed to 21.1% of males.

Non-market explanations do become troublesome when articulated. Below are figures taken from the TUC based on gross median annual earnings for full-time employees from ASHE, 2017. The median wage was £28,758, with a gap of 18.6% between the genders. The IFS finds women's earnings gap is narrowing from 28% in 1993, 23% in 2003 and in 2016 18% per hr – about the same as above.

The wage differential widens steadily after birth of the first child, at a rate of 4% for each year out of paid work. One might question the experience issue if the tasks are easy to learn. However, one cannot escape the fact that women take longer breaks out of the labour market than men. Does this matter?

In April 2016, IPPR for the TUC found that full-time working fathers out-earn their childless counterparts by 21%. Fathers of two children earned 9% more than those with one. The report used data from the 1970 British Cohort

	All £	Male£	Female£	%
All	28758	31103	25308	18.6
18-	15396	16188	14363	11.3
22-	23294	24342	22037	9.5
30-	30097	31535	27865	11.6
40-	32433	35267	27867	21.0
50-	30967	34443	26022	24.4
60+	27073	29303	22662	22.7

Study, which follows the lives of more than 17,000 people born in England, Scotland and Wales from 1970. By contrast, full-time childless females out-did working mothers by 11%. The report pointed out that full-time working men with dependent children worked on average half an hour longer each week than men without children and full-time working women with children worked around an hour less a week than those without children. CVs from fathers were scored higher than identical ones from non-fathers whilst CVs from mothers were marked down against those from childless women.

The TUC claimed that mothers are still often treated as liabilities whiles fathers are seen as more committed by employers, perhaps reflective of a view that fathers were the main breadwinners while mothers were expected to fit in work around looking after their children. Indeed, in March 2018, the Parliamentary Women and Equalities Committee concluded that mothers who work flexibly often tend to be side-lined or downgraded at work. However, it found that fathers are even more likely than mothers to perceive that they would be viewed negatively by employers if they request to work flexibly.

Inconsistent with the above, in 2016 the TUC reported that women who become mothers before the age of 33 earn 15% less than similar women who had not had children. Older mums who worked full-time earned 12% more compared to full-time women without children. Less of a premium than with men but the same outcome, nonetheless.

Chartered Management Institute and XpertHR find that the gender pay gap is not primarily about men and women being paid differently for doing the same job. It is related to a weighted average: a higher proportion of men are found further up the organisation. Men are 40% more likely than women to be promoted into management roles. Working inflexibly might be a signal of commitment to the business affecting both genders.

Interestingly, Mercer, using Eurostat data, in June 2017, found that the gender pension gap in the UK and on average across Europe is 40%. This is, in part, related to the 40 year career-oriented pension schemes which do not correspond well with women. The Chartered Insurance Institute, in December 2017, gave this an added twist. Women live longer and spend longer in poor health. Women [Men] aged 65 won't be able to perform at least one task for at least 2.7 [1.5] years and will spend an additional 2.3 [1.5] years experiencing some difficulties with daily activities. The LSE estimate that care costs of £70,000 [£37,000] will be incurred before they die.

By April 2018, all UK companies with 250 or more employees must report the difference between the median and mean wages of men and women. This push to prevent sex discrimination in pay unfortunately will create more problems than it resolves. An example of a problem is TSB. 29% of its staff work part time. As an employer committed to providing choice in the workplace where work-life balance is accommodated, is likely to be found wanting. Of this 29%, 95% are women. Using schemes such as salary suffice to buy back holidays or child care vouchers whose uptake is greater among women, makes TSB look like a model of discrimination. A bonus scheme based on a % of salary would make this worse. A similar scheme at PwC has been scrapped because it makes the pay imbalance appear worse.

AN UNEMPLOYMENT PROBLEM?

In December 2006, John Hutton, the Work and Pensions Secretary, announced a review of the benefits system. He stated that: "the hardcore 'that can work but don't work' benefits claimants… [should] …compete for jobs along-side the growing number of migrants who arrive in Britain especially for work." Over 66% on job seekers allowance were prior-claimants and 12% (100,000) of them had claimed for 6 of the last 7 years. These are really on the margins of the labour market and may cause some interpretive problems for policy makers.

When presented with an unemployment rate of 7% one should be asking, what does this mean for policy purposes? It is likely this headline is a measure of **involuntary unemployment**. The number of [involuntary] unemployed is defined as *those of working age but without work and willing to work AT THE GIVEN MARKET WAGE.*

In April, China's unemployment stats shifted from claimant count of work-seekers to surveys. One can only be a claimant in one's home town, ignoring China's 280m migrant workers. The rates were 4% and 5.1%.

Those that are not willing are **voluntarily unemployed**. This group, which could include those that retire early, choose not to participate in the labour market. They were not of major concern. However, their capacity to switch when wages rise so adding to the capacity to produce is now making this group a focus of attention.

Those that participate form the labour force: they comprise the employed + self employed + unemployed.

Unemployment rate = Involuntarily unemployed ÷ Labour force

In an effort to reduce the use of illegal migrant labour, the Alabama State legislature in 2011 passed a law requiring proof of immigration status. It is one of 5 States that have acted to reduce the incentives to stay in the US. It was a great success. The number of illegal Hispanic immigrants was estimated at 120,000 in 2010; by 2013, ⅓ to ⅔ had left. The cost to the local economy was estimated to be $2.3-11bn, according to the University of Alabama. The illegal workers contributed both hands and mouths. The legislation should shift the supply curve of labour to the left, boosting the local wage. Unemployment fell from 9.3% to 7.1%. What also emerged was that some locals were not prepared to undertake the arduous work available for $9/hour, so Alabama producers faced a labour shortage. For example, for every 15 workers hired to undertake basic factory labouring, 11 would quit immediately. This looks like voluntary rather than involuntary unemployment and the claim about immigrants stealing jobs sounds hollow.

Full employment is where the number of people that want to work = the number of jobs available *at the given market wage*, so a marker of full employment relates to vacancies and unemployment. **Disequilibrium** unemployment occurs when there are more people looking for work than there are job opportunities for them.

U-V Analysis

A *U-V* curve traces an inverse relationship between vacancy and unemployment rates. In times of low demand, one would expect vacancies to be relatively scarce and unemployment correspondingly abundant. The figure right shows the ratio of the number of unemployed (by ILO) to the number of notified vacancies. You would have thought that, as there would be a job for each

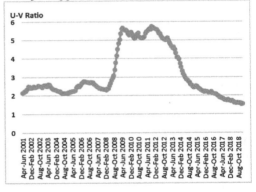

unemployed participant, a 1:1 ratio would imply full employment. However, it is estimated that only about ⅓ of vacancies are notified, so a ratio of 3:1 would be nearer the mark. The graphic then implies that disequilibrium unemployment emerged in the summer of 2008 and disappeared in summer 2014.

In the figure right, employment, unemployment and vacancies×3 are displayed. From 2013 the numbers of unemployed (left-hand scale) seem to fall in tandem of the number of vacancies and the number of employed (right-

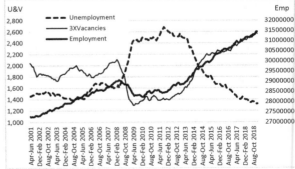

hand scale), but not before which is a puzzle in itself. Employment appears to follow real GDP. The U-V switch is evident in 2008, just before Lehman's collapsed. 'Normal levels' change. There is a mirror image suggesting that vacancies fall and unemployment levels rise. It is argued that the U-V locus shifted outwards in the 1970s and 1980s, indicating that there was an increase in the number of unemployed workers for every vacancy in this period. This would be consistent with a hysteresis, where new norms are established, very much like a structural change. Full employment can occur at a higher level of unemployment.

Equilibrium unemployment occurs when there are at least as many job opportunities are there are job seekers. Thus, at full employment rate there is equilibrium unemployment. This notion is captured by Friedman *et al.* and the natural rate of unemployment. The natural rate occurs because there are impediments to the labour market working perfectly. The natural rate encompasses Frictional + Structural + Geographic/regional unemployment.

Frictional unemployment describes the continuous flow of individuals from job to job in and out of work. As jobs are available, these potential workers are engaged in 'job search.' Frictional unemployment occurs because change happens: productivity improvements forever destroy jobs; innovation creates them. So, jobs are being lost here and generated there. If this creation/destruction rate increases, so does frictional unemployment. Also, life issues play a role. Some find that they change their job for family or career reasons. To reduce frictional unemployment, the State needs to speed up the rate of matching of vacancies with job seekers.
POLICY SOLUTION
Information:- The seeker may not be sufficiently well-informed about job opportunities, so more job information would speed up matching.
Incentives:- Job search can be expensive and disheartening. Indeed, the longer someone is unemployment, the more likely it is they become 'discouraged' and withdraw from the labour market. To support the job search, the State may provide some financial assistance or advice to improve the searching process.
Punishments:- it could be that the seeker has greater aspirations than the State views as appropriate - they could be too choosy. If so, the State may threaten to restrict their access to the benefits system.

The Dept. for Work and Pensions is keen to weed out false claimants. If someone is not looking for work, they are not really a job-seeker, so evidence of job seeking is an important indicator that they comply with the requirements. In December 2013, the Universal Jobsmatch website was launched. Employers could advertise vacancies, linking them with qualified seekers. This system could scan remotely job-seekers' efforts. Also, if they are throwing interviews, this could also suggest that they are not happy to take the job. If someone is willing to work at a higher wage, they may participate under more favourable circumstances, but currently, they are voluntarily unemployed.

Job Centre managers exhibited an unrealistic view of the sort of the matching function they play. A Job Centre in Hull was found to be advertising vacancies in Surrey, Watford, and North London as well as France and Turkey. These were viewed as 'local.' These far-a-field jobs were less skilled work, such as part-time cleaner or assistant aromatherapist. The reality, as ONS found from reviewing a 3-month period in 2009, is that commuting is really the domain of the well-paid executive. 9% of commuters outside and 36% within London spend longer than 45-minutes on their journey to work. The median pay of Londoners commuting for over 60 minutes was £18.80/hr and £14.30 outside. By contrast, commuting less than 15 minutes, the corresponding figures were £9.60/hr and £8.30. Moreover, in Britain, 36% of managers and professionals but only 12% of low skilled jobs engaged in long distance commuting. Thus, frictional could be redefined as geographical unemployment beyond a certain distance.

In a sense, at full employment all the involuntary unemployed are in-between jobs. However, 'time taken' to change jobs may entail geographical and occupational shifts. We describe these below:-

Structural unemployment is where there is a mismatch in the skills set between the jobs and the job seeker. As mentioned above, jobs are destroyed and created continuously. If the skill difference between jobs lost and created is significant, structural unemployment can become a major problem. Declining industries will be releasing workers with sets of skills that are not transferable to growing ones. Moreover, it is likely that while employed the worker skills capability is refreshed. Once unemployed, this is less likely: the longer someone is unemployed, the more likely it is they become structurally unemployed.

POLICY SOLUTION

Training:- A mismatch in skills suggests training is a solution. More drastic action, such as a change of career, will be costly. The State could provide subsidise training courses in preferred skills areas.

In the US, the probability of becoming discouraged and exiting the labour market is doubled if unemployed for 15 months. However, if these do secure employment, they tend to return to the industry for which they had previously worked, which, if it is a declining industry, points to a structural problem.

The ONS found that in 2013Q2 87% of those with a degree were in employment; 83% with 'A' levels; 76% with passes at GCSE level and 47% with no qualifications.

The CIPD reported in August 2017 that low-skilled vacancies had 24 applicants for each one; 19 for medium-skilled jobs; and 8 applicants for each high-skilled job.

Punishments:- It could be that the seeker is not that keen to retrain. If so, the State may threaten to restrict access to the benefits system.

Regional Unemployment is where there are job vacancies of the right task set but they are elsewhere, far from the job seeker's locale. There is a mismatch of location.

POLICY SOLUTION - relocate the work or the work seeker

Incentives for firms to set up/relocate to the area have been a standard approach for local and regional authorities. Providing soft loans, grants and tax holidays to multinational enterprises to locate direct foreign investment (branch plants) has led to competitive bidding. Ireland uses a low corporation tax rate of 12.5%.

Incentives for workers to move are less commonplace. There are pecuniary and non-pecuniary costs of moving. Housing is commonly a major pecuniary cost. If the cost to live in an area where the jobs are advertised or the costs to commute to that area outweigh the benefits, then job seekers will not resolve the regional unemployment problem. Key worker housing is often touted as a policy solution, but this needs to be subsidised by the State. A private buyer or builder will want a good price for the property, so building it at an affordable price and retaining it for key workers are problems that require State intervention. The right-to-buy policy of the 1980s has gone this way. In April 2013, the GMB reported that, of the 15,874 former council homes bought by their tenants in the London borough of Wandsworth, private landlords then owned 6,180. In other words, they went from State to private renting, and along the way someone extracted Ricardian rent. Their value had increased by a factor of 20.
Punishments:- it could be that the seeker is not that keen on commuting or relocating. If so, the State may threaten to restrict access to the benefits system.
Structural unemployment can be focused in an area leaving it persistently depressed. Labour immobility is often blamed, but for those with limited skills and unemployment being relatively high for all, the non-pecuniary costs plus being unemployed elsewhere are major disincentives to relocating to improve the likelihood of finding work.

Disequilibrium unemployment has two elements:
Cyclical (demand deficient) unemployment is related to the business cycle. Business conditions fluctuate - recessions, depression etc.. Reducing the intensity, duration and frequency of ups and downs of business activity can lessen cyclical unemployment.
Demand Deficient Unemployment as explained by Keynes fits here. Persistent or mass unemployment is caused by a lack of demand (particularly in the downswing of the business cycle). The *economy can be in equilibrium but the labour market does not clear* so the economy could occupy an underemployment equilibrium caused by insufficient aggregate demand.
POLICY SOLUTION - Government can smooth out fluctuation in economic activity by manipulating aggregate demand. Instruments include government spending and taxing (fiscal policy) or the monetary authority (central bank) can alter money supply or interest rates.
Real wage or neo-classical unemployment occurs when too many workers are enticed on to the labour market and others are priced out of work. The real wage is too high for the market to clear.
POLICY SOLUTION - Reduce the wage towards the clearing wage. This could involve reducing the power of Trade Unions and disbanding wages councils and minimum wages.

The topics above can be captured by the following figure. *WP* reflects the working population (q4), which is dictated by demographic, cultural and migration forces. Changing school leaving and retirement ages, extending the working week/ year and encouraging in migrants, can shift it. *N* represents the labour force at any given wage, and S_{eff} and D_{eff} are the effective supply and demand for labour. Here, effective supply means those that are employable now. Effective demand means there is a job that can/is filled. The number of people in work is the lesser of the two. In this case, demand is the constraint. The gap q2 – q1 is *real-wage* or *demand deficient unemployment* (disequilibrium forms of unemployment). These appear the same if the wage *w*1 is sticky downwards. Full employment occurs when the number of jobs

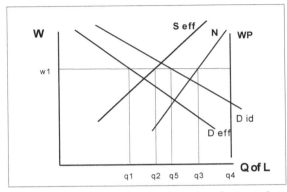

equals the number of (full-time equivalent) workers wanting work at the given market wage. The gap between D_{eff} and D_{id} (ideal demand) represents vacancies. As with the supply of labour, there will always be a number of vacancies reflecting the frictions in the labour market. At *w*1, the number is q5 – q1. The difference between S_{eff} and *N* captures *frictional, structural and regional unemployment*, which is q3 – q2 (equilibrium unemployment). At full employment the number of vacancies equals *frictional, structural and regional unemployment*. The *rate of unemployment* is (q3 – q1) ÷ q3.

In addition, there are some who do not want to participate in the labour market. As a result we can derive a *participation rate* q3÷q4 (the proportion of the population participating in the workforce). There are three more rates: the *natural rate of unemployment* is (q3 – q2) ÷ q2; (q4 – q1) ÷ q4 is the *rate of non-employment*, (those that could physically work but do not); and the *rate of employment* is q1 ÷ q4 (those that do physically work as a proportion that could do).

Male inactivity numbers are growing steadily, due to a rising number not interested in work. In the table right, in

March to May 2018 '000	Women	Men	Aged 16-64	Aged 65 and over
Full-time employment	8,968	14,888	31,190	1,208
Part-time employment	6,291	2251		
Unemployment	654	757	1,389	22
Economic inactivity (aged 16 to 64)	5,307	3,337		
Economic inactivity (aged 65 and over)	5,858	4,707		

2018, there were 3.34m males that were inactive, of whom 77.7% did not want to work. There is a decline in female inactivity due to fewer not wanting to work (5.3m 79.1%).

In December, it was reported that, since its 2013 employment trough the Eurozone has added about 9.6m jobs. Of these almost ¾ went to those between 55 and 74, when those between 25 and 54 accounted for only about a fifth. Indeed, over the last three years, around 3m Americans over 55 joined or rejoined the workforce. The ECB suggested that pension reform was forcing workers to stay in the labour market longer.

Inflexibility in Europe

In the 1980s, it was proposed that the natural rate of unemployment in Europe was subject to hysteresis. Authors have provided commentaries on the unemployment 'puzzle', where, unlike in the US, European unemployment continued to rise after the energy (supply side) shocks of the 1970s had past, where the natural rate follows the actual rate. Krugman argued that the welfare state was partly to blame for the rise in the natural rates of unemployment in Europe. It discourages those on low incomes from working by raising the reservation wage and, through the taxes imposed on those working, reduces the reward from pecuniary focused toil. Krugman's 'solution' to the puzzle is that poverty and low wages on one side of the Atlantic is mirrored by greater long term unemployment for the corresponding low skilled worker group on the other. What would unite the two is the low net rewards from labour market participation. What distinguishes them is greater wage flexibility in the US. Thus, the fall in demand for labour, a shift of the demand curve to the left. In the US, the wage falls; whereas in Europe, the quasi-fixed wage is sticky-downwards leading to an increase in unemployment.

Hysteresis can result from a major shock inducing the scrapping of geographically or industrially specific productive assets, reducing the economy's potential output, so shifting the production function downwards. We could label this phenomenon *production hysteresis*. The 1974-79 period had a lower rate of growth than from the mid-1980s. One could argue that the

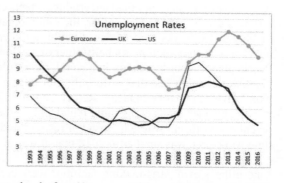

Lehman's collapse was the largest shock for 60 years. This analysis need not be confined to a large shock. Restrictive activities, possible enshrined in law, negotiated by Trade Unions, were blamed – inflexible labour market. Prolonged unfavourable conditions in the labour or goods markets may provoke or enlarge an output gap. Persistent and large gaps between actual and potential output may eventually prompt a re-evaluation of expectations and initiate the scrapping of capacity, or production hysteresis, and a change in the equilibrium rate of unemployment, or *unemployment hysteresis*. Consequently, there is a range of potential equilibria that the economy could move towards. Either a supply or demand shock may force manufacturers to change their expectations about the future, leading to the adjustment of capacity. Any subsequent stimulation of the economy could quickly lead to price and wage inflation as, once hysteresis has set-in, excess capacity in both the production and labour markets will be much reduced. Thus, the government may be left severely constrained by events. To reinvigorate the economy, the government ultimately needs to change both firms' and workers' expectations so that they respond to an increase demand by expanding output and employment.

Anderson in *Business Economics* Vol. 49 pp.2-30 proposed a new source of unemployment – *policy cost uncertainty hypothesis*. Here, political uncertainty provokes rational private sector managers to restrict the number of employees they hire because of the potential cost of employing them due to future changes in government policy. So the possibility of a new future payroll tax, greater paternity leave or a high minimum wage would deter employers from taking on the staff they need today. Moreover, the uncertainty affects employment through investment indirectly.

The firm is a value-maximiser. Managers maximise value over a longer run rather than maximise profit over a succession of periods. This implies that there is a multitude of economic conditions that could prevail at any time. The manager has some idea of likelihood of the current state changing and in what direction. These assumptions allow the manager to pre-empt a perceived change in the environment. Potential cost avoidance can lead to not recruiting someone when it is profitable so to do. This was evident in manufacturing output.

A case in point where political uncertainty affects expectations: a trade war for a global business can be seen in Caterpillar, the mining machines and construction bulldozers. In May 2018, it was evident that it could not keep up with a boom in demand. Like heavy trucks construction is a bellwether of economics conditions. Over a year its East Peoria plant saw orders jump, in general, three-fold. However, it did not respond. The plant was running just one shift, only four days a week, and its CEO, Jim Umpleby, won't invest in factory capacity. Rather, he will invest in new technologies, expanding its parts business and selling more rental and used equipment. This, in part, reflects the recent restructuring where it closed or restructured more than 25 factories and its full-time workforce was smaller in 2018 than it was at the end of 2012.

Caterpillar's own parts-making facilities were concurrently running three shifts, five days a week to provide it enough components to assemble. However, this was insufficient. Having switched to JIT, it was reliant on its suppliers increasing their output. Caterpillar blamed the backlogs on its suppliers' inability to keep up with the surge in orders. The Institute for Supply Management's index for order backlogs, one of the best U.S. metrics for 'elasticity of supply', stood at its highest level since 2004. The Commerce Department observed that in March 2018, orders for capital goods, a key measure of business investment, fell for the 3rd time in four months. Years of watching Caterpillar and other big manufacturers cut inventories, close plants and axe workers in the last downturn (2012 to 2016), has coloured expectations. Suppliers saw sales drop over 40%; worse than the Great Depression.

Even if they were so inclined to expand labour is a challenge. Kirsh, which melts iron and forms it into the rough shapes that will be refined for Caterpillar and others, could not source labour locally (Wisconsin) so it hired from outside, at possibly 3 × normal labour costs (inc. staffing company charges, hotels and expenses). Wolfe and Swickard Machine Company saw orders from Caterpillar surge 80% in 2018. It buys from Kirsh and others, shaping and polishing into final machine parts. With 85-worker shop it too could not locate the small number of skilled staff it needed. Some foundries decided not to expand. So, the industry response in the short term will be muted; employment will not rise much; labour skills and migration will be greater issues; vehicle margins will increase; lean production in a sector with large swings in demand will be rethought; and well expectations and history matters.

Kevin Murphy and Robert Topel[7] argue that these disturbingly high rates of unemployment are a result of inflexible labour markets. The labour market *insiders*, protected by union contracts, may gain from higher wages. *Outsiders*, those looking for work, are less fortunate. They pay with more than their jobs opportunities: they also lose the chance to accumulate skills and experience that would raise their future earning power. Flexible labour markets in the US and UK yield lower wages for some workers, but they are much better at putting people in to work. Without labour market flexibility, young workers are especially hard hit, and suffer permanent scars. Their employment prospects forever curtailed. The US youth unemployment rate was 12.3%, whereas Italy's (43.1%), Portugal's (33.8%), Spain's and Greece's (50.1%) were over twice that. Even if the economy and employment are growing, when growth in the demand for labour is outpaced by growth in the number of people looking for work, real wages will fall.

A reduction in benefits lowers the level of unearned income, possibly below the reservation wage of the non-job seeker. Also, it increases the opportunity cost of seeking rather than working. So, a cut in benefits should focus the mind of homo economicus. However, Jan Eichhorn of Edinburgh University argues that State benefit levels across the Europe 28 had 'no effect' on jobseekers' motivation to find work. There was a positive relationship between benefits and despondence. Luxembourg and Sweden were in the top quartile for both benefit levels and dissatisfaction amongst the jobless. The German unemployed were more dissatisfied than elsewhere in Europe, more than 50% higher than in Hungary. Romania and Poland, by contrast, were in the bottom quartile for benefit levels whilst the unemployed were the least and third-least affected by being out of work, respectively. In some countries, such as Spain, Poland and Romania, benefits had 'little effect' on perceived well-being.

---

[7] FT.com August 15, 2014 6:42 pm Raising the minimum wage is the wrong way to deal with low pay

INFLATION

Inflation is technically defined as a sustained rise in a weighted average of all prices, or a persistent increase in the general level of prices. Deflation is technically defined as a sustained fall in a weighted average of all prices, or a persistent general decline in prices. Disinflation is when the inflation rate is positive, but declining over time.

Traditionally, when discussing inflation, we consider the costs to society. Standard considerations are outlined below:

❑ There is a slot machine cost, where stated prices must be altered to reflect changing costs. As well as slot machines, it will also cover menus and brochures that must be altered or reprinted;

❑ The shoe leather cost concerns liquidity preference. Holding cash entails an opportunity cost. With higher inflation the holding of cash becomes more of a cost so one will visit the bank more frequently wearing out the shoes;

❑ As price rises are not uniform across products, inflation changes relative prices and, indeed, injects uncertainty into anticipated prices. This should deter entrepreneurs from investing, reducing potential growth. Also, one is spending more time gathering price information, wearing out shoes;

❑ Inflation pushes up interest rates, also reducing investment. The banks will be less clear about their returns from lending, so as to share some of the risk, the bank will offer the loan on a variable rate or on a fixed rate with a higher rate of interest;

❑ Inflation disfavours those on fixed incomes and favours borrowers. The purchasing power of those on fixed incomes will fall with inflation. In the developing world, food riots have occurred as the prices of essentials make them unaffordable. Also, the real value of debt will decline so that the real cost to the individual of repaying the loan declines;

❑ Inflation discourages saving and favours consumption. It shifts resources from the old (fixed income) to the young. Strangely, the government, usually the largest debtor in the system, benefits the most from inflation. So, there is a bias which credit rating agencies are keen to discourage.

Unanticipated inflation comes as a 'surprise', whereas anticipated inflation is the rate expected to occur. A means of reducing the risk of real values being undermined by inflation can be to index-link it or to share the risk. In a sense, the reward to the capitalist is based on risk taking, but some entrepreneurs may shift the rise in price on to the consumer. As inflation affects the purchasing power of money, the lender loses and the debtor gains. To compensate for the loss of the value of capital a greater interest rate is charged to the borrower by the lender, such as through a variable interest rate on a loan rather than shouldering all the risk with a fixed.

Measures of UK inflation are shown below. In 2017, CPIH was introduced. This adds owner-occupier housing costs and council tax to CPI. In April 2015, the CPI was negative, but CPIH was not. One way of boosting demand is to give the impression that prices will be higher.

Deflation
Deflation should have the reverse effects.
☐ The real value of debt rises, disadvantaging borrowers. The purchasing power of the fixed income rises and, by implication the stock or saving (wealth) is enhanced;
☐ Slot machine costs remain – so it is price *changes* that impose a cost;
☐ Nominal interest rates, instruments of monetary policy may become impotent. With inflation, nominal interest rates can move in line. Until 2015, one would claim nominal interest rates cannot be reduced below zero. But they can. It is not clear though what this means;
☐ Consumption is reduced. If prices are expected to be lower tomorrow than today, consumers will reduce their discretionary spending. Current consumption will fall, weakening enfeebled companies. (The standard view is that excess capacity puts a lid on price rises.)

Given the perverse world of Japan's deflationary pressures, a 40% phone charges drop was estimated to drive core consumer inflation down by 0.96 and education fees 0.9 percentage points in 2018/19. In October, Japan's inflation rate of 1% was boosted by the oil price. However, the price falls meant that this would taper off. BoJ believes Japan's inflation expectations are adaptive so 'negative price shocks' are remembered. This was compounded by the report that in 2018Q3 the output gap was −0.2%, falling from 0.7% above trend in Q2. In March, Coca-Cola Japan raised its prices for the first time in 27 years, by ¥20.

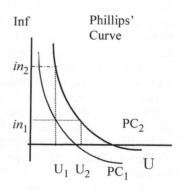

Shift or Shape - the Phillips' Curve Unpacked
The PC originally related money wage growth to unemployment. When unemployment was high, trade unions would be in an enfeebled bargaining position or employers could easily find staff without the need to offer a greater wage incentive. Tighter labour markets would see higher wage increases. As an X-efficiency wage perspective, once staff began to leave in large numbers, the employer would raise wages for all to retain some. Alternatively, when unemployment is high, there was the threat that those outside the firm could replace the insider, making the insider more compliant. Let us go through possible breaks in the argument.
1) The outsiders are not a threat

Krueger, Cramer and Cho argued that the long-term unemployed do not affect wages and inflation so they should be stripped from the unemployment figures. In effect, this implies the Phillips' curve *shifts* outwards. Unemployment needs to be higher to place downward pressure on prices. It also means there are more in the labour market that are structurally unemployed. The workforce schedule shifts to the right relative to the supply of labour. It also can be interpreted as hysteresis. There is a higher level of unemployment for a given rate of inflation, or higher inflation for a given level of unemployment. If these are removed from the equation, full employment will be met at a higher rate of non-employment.

  2)   It is machines, not people, that threaten

The Phillips curve in this sense could be flat for much of it away from full employment – and as Keynes envisaged, money wages are sticky downwards. TODAY from a Marxist perspective capital is not constrained by labour. Hines modelled wage increase based on trade union power. The number of workers involved in labour disputes in the UK in 2017, at 33,000, was the lowest ever recorded. This reflects a decline in TU membership to 6.23m or 23.2%. Alternatively, the threat of money wage increases results in substituting in capital. Wage-wage and wage-price spirals might have been a function of the era of the manual worker. A Spar manager, facing an increase in the living (minimum) wage to £7.20, would let some staff go, others working harder to make up the gap. At £7.50, they installed a self-service checkout machine. Sainsbury's announced in March 2018 that it would raise the base wage to £9.20 from £8/hr. The cost is that the workers lose bonuses and paid breaks. With that threat to benefits and jobs, market power has shifted to the capitalist. Thus, there is also the possibility that it has *flattened* so that the rise in wages/prices is not as pronounced as unemployment declines. Yellen was seeking to explain how the fall in unemployment was not putting the usual pressures on wages and inflation, signifying less of a need to raise interest rates.

  3)   Non-Participation is rising

The problem with skills and the labour market arise in the US. Long-term unemployment is defined as that over 26 weeks. Between August 2008, before Lehman's and February 2014, the count doubled to 3.8m. The proportion of long-term unemployed in the unemployment figures rose from 19.8% to 37%. The long-term unemployed are very much at the margins of employment. Their likely spell of non-participation could be prolonged but temporary, implying that the output gap becomes smaller and the Phillips' curve *shifts* inwards. The US unemployment rate dropped to 3.6% in April, the lowest since December 1969. Whilst average hourly earnings rose 6¢ (0.2% or 3.2% annually), 490,000 people left the labour force in April, the most in 18 months. It was the fourth straight month of workers dropping out of the labour force. The participation rate dropped to 62.8% from 63.0%, shifting the divide between unemployment and non-participation – non-employment remains the same.

  4)   Wage Increase are suppress by Monopsony Employers

Another reason to suggest the Phillips' curve has *shifted* in the US is based on profit margins pushing prices up at every level of unemployment. Corporate profit margins before depreciation are inflated when price is high relative to labour cost. As corporate output makes up 52% of US GDP, producer prices are estimated to be 350bps (3.5%)

higher than they would be if the profit margin was at its long-term average of 31.3%. Goldman Sachs estimated that US wage growth since the early 2000s were 0.25%/year slower because of corporate and union concentration. The Resolution Foundation reported that in 2003/4 the top five companies in 600 sub-sectors in Britain had a market share 39%. By 2015/16, this had risen to 43%.

5)   Wages are not a good indicator of compensation

Japan faced an unemployment rate of 2.3% in February. This low level is lower than in 2018 but wages still remain stubborn. In March 2016, Japanese wages were rising at half the rate they were in 2015: in 2017 they were lower again. Without wage inflation, price inflation >2% was not possible. Toyota paid a ¥4,000/month basic wage increase in 2015. In 2016, it awarded ¥1,500, ¥1,300 in 2017 and ¥10,700 in 2019. By contrast, Honda agreed a ¥1,400 deal, up from ¥1,700 in 2018. The wage system is highly structured so that a basic wage increase affects all layers of a company. This wage growth may reflect a desire not to increase costs. The BoJ believed that compensation in terms of holidays and family friendly polices (see day-night shift) is off-setting the wage rise. Cutting out wasteful unproductive hours of work will increase productivity per hour. In December 2017, hoping for a wage-wage spiral Abe called for a wage rise of 3%. A bid of 4% was expected to provoke a 1.98% outcome. In 2018, according to Rengo, the trade union federation, wages rose by 2.07%.

6)   Unemployment is Not a Good indicator

Blanchflower proposed that the pay puzzle what not a sign of the Phillips curve not working, but that the spare capacity indicator was poor. The underemployment in the economy is increasingly related to constrained hours rather than job access.

In the quarter to May 2015, the ONS reported that both wages and unemployment in the UK rose. The unemployment rate rose from 5.5% to 5.6% when there was a notable 3.2% increase in average weekly pay. In effect, this conflicts with a Phillips' curve analysis or the PC shifts outwards. It could be that some shifted from non-participation to offer themselves on the labour market. However, employment fell 67,000 as well. There could be

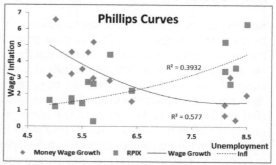

a restructuring. The number of people working as full-time employees increased 45,000 but there was a much bigger drop in the number of self-employed, part-time and temporary workers.

7)   Firms only need to Attract

Haldane argued that wage increases went to job shifters. With fewer shifters, the fear that others would move jobs is not the same threat to employers to retain staff that it once was.

AGGREGATE SUPPLY AND DEMAND

The Aggregate Demand Schedule plots the quantity of real GDP demanded at any given price. It slopes downwards because of:

- the real balance effect:- As prices rise, a consumer's money wealth and income will buy fewer goods. Therefore, less will be demanded as prices rise. Correspondingly, as prices fall, a consumer's real wealth and income will increase. As people become richer, they purchase more goods/services;
- interest effect:- as prices rise, consumers demand larger money balances. This will lead to an increase in the rate of interest. As the interest rate rises, investment expenditures fall. This will lead to less aggregate demand in the economy;
- international effect:- as UK prices rise, British goods become relatively expensive compared with foreign imports resulting a fall in the purchase of goods/services by both British and foreign citizens.

A change in the average price level will lead to a move ALONG the AD curve. The AD curve will shift when there is a change in demand conditions at any given average price level. The AD schedule will shift outwards to the right when:

- the nominal money supply increases - this would lead to a fall in the rate of interest in the money market and so an increase in investment expenditures;
- there is an increase in government spending or cut in taxes;
- there is an increase in the income of foreigners. This would increase the demand for normal and luxury UK exports.

The Aggregate Supply Schedule plots the quantity of real GDP supplied at any given price. It has three phases.

Keynes assumed that, under the conditions of huge under-employment, with an increase in aggregate demand, average price does not rise – it is fixed. This is important. This means that we assume that the government can spend money without increasing prices, i.e. no inflation. In this phase, the AS is horizontal. By contrast, neo-classical economists believe that the economy has flexible wages and prices in the short run. This implies that the economy automatically operates around the natural rate (full employment) in the long run. Any pump-priming can increase output but only in the short run: in the long run it will lead to an increase in prices only. This occurs at the natural rate of unemployment. (Q_n full employment output.) In this phase, the AS is vertical and occurs in the long run - hence LRAS. In the third phase, the AS slopes upwards because of:

- prices of factors:- if firms wish to increase output, they will demand more factors of production. This increases wages and prices of raw materials. Thus, the increased output will be accompanied by an increase in the costs of factors of production;
- general prices:- change in the average price level will lead to a move ALONG the AS curve. A price rise will present more opportunities to make profit. Firms expand output but costs rise limiting this expansion.

This third phase is associated with the Phillips' curve. This phase can shift more easily relative to the other two. It is the short run trade-off and is labelled SRAS.

When there is a change in supply conditions at any given average price the AS curve will shift. That is, prices are fixed but firms change output. This includes:

- a wages fall reduces overall costs and, therefore, increases profit. We would expect businesses to expand output: SRAS shifts to the right;
- a fall of the costs of raw materials or the non-wage costs of employing labour falls. These will reduce overall costs and, therefore, increase profit of firms. We would expect businesses to expand output: SRAS shifts to the right;
- an increase of the output per man will increase GDP output for given input. In other words, the AS has shifted to the right. The same applies to the application of new technology. These are incremental changes;
- a supply shock, such as a natural or institutional change in supply conditions, which usually shifts the LRAS to the left. Examples of this are the OPEC oil price shocks of 1973/4 and 1979. One could include the banking collapse of 2008/9. Hysteresis is associated with this shock. Labour market participants may change their attitude to work fundamentally, perhaps withdrawing permanently; moving from employed/unemployed to non-participant.

An AS/AD diagram is shown right. The AD intersects with the SRAS at Q_1, which is to the left of Q_n. A fiscal stimulus should shift the AD curve to the right, reducing the unemployment rate but at the cost of higher prices. This is the trade-off portion of the SRAS schedule.

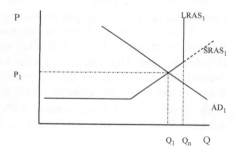

Demand pull inflation

Keynes made particular assumptions about an economy when in a deep recession. He suggested that the economy would be in equilibrium significantly below full employment. The theoretical forces moving the economy back to full employment (later interpreted as the natural rate), flexible wages and prices, do not exist. He suggested that wages were *sticky downwards* and as the under-utilisation of capacity would prevent factor prices from rising. So, an increase in aggregate demand would not lead to an increase in prices. In the diagram below, the starting position is P_1Q_1. A collapse in demand shifts the AD curve to AD_2 at output level Q_2. The price level and output have fallen. However, the depth of the recession means that a stimulus package could shift the AD curve to the right to AD_3 and output to Q_3 without prices changing.

Demand pull inflation is a necessary evil to be accommodated if the policy is to move the economy to Q_1. Keynes presumed no inflation until full employment, so this is related to a different theory.

Keynes advocated a counter-cyclical policy based on running a budget deficit in a recession [G > T]. Thus, one measure of a government stimulus package is the extent of the borrowing requirement to cover the deficit. Government borrowing could have a counteractive impact. Fully funding the deficit requires increase borrowing. This could raise interest rates or at least crowded-out private sector borrowing. Alternatively, it could support the fiscal stimulus, by increasing the money supply (print money). Note that Keynes did not project the upwards sloping AS curve and he was not focused on a structural deficit.

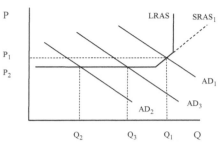

Demand pull inflation entails too much money (demand) chasing too few goods. In the diagram right, the initial position at P_1/ equilibrium real natural output Q_n.

An increase in aggregate demand to AD_2 leads to an increase in output above real natural output. Here, there is excess demand. This could be viewed like an inflationary gap (but isn't). Keynes would suggest a reduction of government expenditure would resolve this problem. The AD would move back to the left. An EAPC model would see movement back to Q_n as those workers fooled on to the market in the hope of a real wage increase withdraw. The fall in the numbers in the labour market will shift the SRAS to the left, to $SRAS_2$.

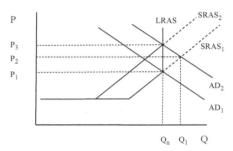

Cost Push Inflation
Cost push inflation entails an increase in prices when the economy is not close to full employment. It involves an increase in the costs of production, leading to the shift in the AS to the left. In the diagram right, the initial position is P_1Q_1. Under these circumstances, prices rise and output falls (implying unemployment rises).

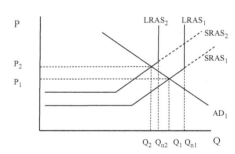

A **supply side shock** shifts both the long run and short run AS schedules to the left or right. Importantly, the full employment level of output, Q_n, also moves. In other words, the capacity to produce goods and services is persistently reduced and the natural rate of unemployment increases. The output gap decreases from $Q_{n1} - Q_1$ to $Q_{n2} - Q_2$. Why? LRAS can shift to the left as a result of:

- prolonged unemployment;
- a collapse in demand for certain skills;
- an increase in the rate of technological change;
- a rapid and significant change in costs.

With deep recessions firms and workers become more cautious/ pessimistic, which lowers the investment rate and willingness to look for work. Firms scrap productive capacity. The collapse of manufacturing industry in the north and west of the UK in the 1980s left many structurally/ regionally unemployed. Moreover, the longer someone is frictionally unemployed, the more likely it is that they become structurally unemployed.

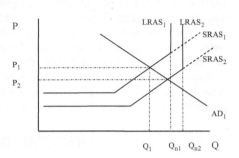

Not discussed often, but must be the case, is the supply side change that increases the capacity to produce goods and services. In other words, the LRAS shifts right. The initial position is at P_1/Q_{n1} with an output gap of $Q_{n1} - Q_1$. With a shift in productive capacity and prices do not fall, the output gap will increase to $Q_{n2} - Q_1$. However, lower prices with a fixed wage increase the real wage, participation and output.

Oxford Economics estimated that for every \$20 fall in the price of oil, after a 2 to 3 year lag, leads to an increase in growth of 0.4%. One could suggest the shock is not symmetrical. There is not a restructuring, so the change costs are not there. A fall in costs does not have to lead to a fall in prices. A fall in the oil price in 1986 led to a rise in growth to 4.6% in 1988, a figure not again seen until 2000.

As discussed under unemployment, there is such a concept as the non-employment rate. This will vary with:-
- Benefits:- higher benefits will deter some from seeking work;
- The recent rewards from job search:- lack of reward from job search will discourage workers from seeking work;
- The rate of job generation: a more dynamic economy will generate more jobs but increase the dislocation between the unemployed and skills. More will be in training, shifting the supply of labour curve to the left;
- The greater the number of women of child bearing age;
- The greater the number approaching retirement:- some will retire early;
- The greater the rate of female participation:- this point can be cultural see participation;
- The reward from working:- if the after tax, real wage is falling, this will lead to workers withdrawing from the labour market. This would be consistent with the EAPC and participating only if the reward is sufficient.

Policy RIP
By the end of the 1970s, the problem of stagflation, where the recession is accompanied by rising unemployment and inflation, left demand management advocates in a policy paradox; whatever target the government pursued, another would worsen. This led to a rejection of Keynesian policies and a switch to Monetarism. Stagflation, associated with a supply-side shock, would affect the natural rate of unemployment and the long-run growth trend. A short-run deviation from trend becomes ossified with the scrapping of capacity to produce and, hence, induces a long-run effect. Oddly, it could be that the quantity theory of money, the cornerstone of Monetarist theory, was abandoned in July 2009, as the MPC found the relationship not reflected in the results of Quantitative Easing. One could say Keynesian demand management died in 1975/76 following the oil crisis of 1974.

INCOME MULTIPLIER

The Keynesian model uses terminology and symbols as follows:

Y (national income) = E (expenditure) = Q or O (output)
J (injections to the economy) = I (investment) + G (government expenditure) + X (exports)
W (leakages from the economy) = S (savings) + T (taxes) + M (imports)

Y_d = disposable income = $Y - T$ $\qquad$ Marginal propensity to consume $c = \dfrac{\Delta C}{\Delta Y}$

Marginal propensity to pay tax $t = \dfrac{\Delta T}{\Delta Y}$ $\qquad$ Marginal propensity to import $m = \dfrac{\Delta M}{\Delta Y}$

Average propensity to consume $= \dfrac{C}{Y}$. The income multiplier shows that an increase in an injection will feed through to create a much greater increase in income than the stimulus that induced it. This will not happen instantly, but will build up over a period of time.

The derivation of a multiplier in an open economy
The model is in equilibrium when $E = Y$ or $J = W$. The general expression for expenditure in an economy open is $E = C + I + G + (X–M)$. The consumption function can be written as $C = cY_d$ i.e. consumption varies with disposable income. The level of import varies with disposable income $M = mY_d$. Disposable income will be income retained after taxes $T = tY$. Substituting in produces the expression:

$$Y = \left(\frac{1}{1-(c-m)(1-t)} \right)[\, I + G + X \,]$$

$$\Delta Y = \left(\frac{1}{1-(c-m)(1-t)} \right)\Delta A \qquad \text{where} \quad A = I + G + X$$

$\Delta Y = k\,\Delta A$ where k is the multiplier.

The simple multiplier discussed in text books would have it that the stimulus, represented by ΔG, would be spent on employing workers to dig holes, build hospitals and roads etc., which should put money into workers' hands. This is spent on domestically produced goods. Domestic firms, seeing a fall in inventories, will employ more domestic workers, reducing unemployment and increasing output.

In an open economy $(c - m)$, the addition to the model of the consumption of non-imported goods, strongly influences the magnitude of the impact of a stimulus package. With an MPC of 0.8, a simple multiplier, where savings are the only leakage, is equal to 5, but this is reduced to 2.78 if the average income tax rate is 20p in the pound, and is reduced further to 1.47 once imports are taken into account. A larger the gap between MPC and MPM induces a larger multiplier. Giving money to those with a high MPC should boost the multiplier. But if that group's preference for overseas' goods counters this, the strategy would be undermined.

Cambridge Econometrics estimated that for every £1 invested in super-

MPC = 0.6	K	MPC = 0.7	K	MPC = 0.8	k
MPT = 0 MPM = 0	2.5	MPT = 0 MPM = 0	3.33	MPT = 0 MPM = 0	5
MPT = 0.2 MPM = 0	1.92	MPT = 0.2 MPM = 0	2.27	MPT = 0.2 MPM = 0	2.78
MPT = 0.2 MPM = 0.2	1.47	MPT = 0.2 MPM = 0.3	1.47	MPT = 0.2 MPM = 0.4	1.47

fast broadband by the government the UK economy benefited by £20. A short-term gain of £1.5bn and 11,000 jobs in network and construction would grow by 2024 to £6.3bn/yr, associated with 20,000 jobs and because some could work from home, an additional £45m/ year in savings. The government would provide an initial subsidy of £530m to the private sector to induce this.

HOUSING

Rent

With a perfect capital market, people should consume property services up to the point where their utility is equal to the rent paid, subject to a budget constraint. As a capital good, property ownership, though, whilst it is being utilised, possibility bestows a capital gain. As a result, renting and buying a home are not perfect substitutes; there is no Modigliani-Miller notion of indifference. However, as the price of a property falls, one would expect the rent to decrease correspondingly. Following from the basic idea that the value of agricultural land (agricultural value) is based on the present value of discounted agricultural rent $r^a/_i$ where i is the discount factor, the same relationship holds for housing rents. House prices and rents should move together in the long run. Of course, this is predicated on perfect capital markets. If the buying and renting markets are segregated in some way and the arbitrage / adjustment is very slow, it could leave the two market prices moving in opposite directions for some periods.

Market Rent

Using supply and demand analysis, we consider the market effect of rent controls and vouchers. First, rent controls. The diagram right is for an idealised market for rented accommodation, where the dwellings are homogenous and have common locational characteristics. The short run supply schedule for dwellings (SRS) is vertical. As we know from a discussion of elasticity of supply over time, landlords are able to switch accommodation from alternative uses into renting over the long run (LR). The demand for housing services will be downward sloping. If the market is allowed to allocate rented dwellings, the

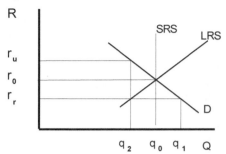

market rent would be r_0 and the quantity supplied would be q_0. It is decided that the market rent is too high for some poorer members of the community and a 'fair' rent is imposed. This controlled rent r_r is below market rent. As this alters the price and not supply or demand conditions otherwise, there are movements along each schedule. Now, the demand for accommodation increases to q_1. Under these circumstances, landlords would filter out the less desirable tenant; the more-likely non-payer.

Over the longer term, landlords will switch some accommodation from the rented to the home owning market or some other land use. Thus, switching to the long run supply curve (LRS), the number of units that landlords make available drops to q_2. The result in the long-term of rent controls is that there is excess demand of $q_1 - q_2$. Those that find rented accommodation are great gainers from the system and so are less likely to move for a job opportunity elsewhere. With a smaller reward, landlords have less of an incentive to maintain their properties, which means a worsening of the housing stock will follow. Also, the owning market will see a fall in price either because the discounted rents income stream is lower or because the number of properties in that market increases.

A shadow market may arise where some renters, so desperate for accommodation, pay r_u. Landlords could charge for elements not normally associated with the renting of property, such as key money or a non-returnable deposit, etc..

An alternative to rent controls is the rent subsidy or voucher. Again, the short run supply schedule for dwellings (SRS) is vertical and the starting point is r_0 q_0. It is decided that the market rent is too high for some poorer members of the community and they should be in receipt of a rent voucher, or housing benefit. Assume it is a lump sum

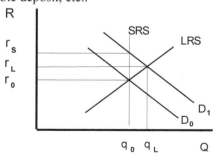

subsidy, so shifts the demand curve to the right to D_1. In the short run, this drives market rents upwards from is r_0 to r_S.

Over the longer term, landlords will switch some accommodation to the rented sector from the home owning market or some other land use. With the voucher system, the long run rents fall back to r_L, which is above r_0. Also, the dwellings in the rented sector increases to q_L. Those that had a contract at r_0 may find landlords seek to renegotiate the rent or they attempt to evict those on 'low' rent and re-lease the accommodation to higher payers. A variant of this was reported in February when Greek hoteliers complained a boom in home-sharing properties via Airbnb for tourists in the capital Athens was hurting hotels, pushing up residential rents and forcing locals from their homes. Growing at a rate of 25% it generates €10bn or 10% total tourist spending in the Greece, which makes up 25% of GDP. Situated near the Acropolis, in Athens, the suburb of Koukaki 83% of available rental properties were registered for short-term lets. Rents in Athens rose over 9% in 2018. It was reported that some owners in some neighbourhoods were evicting local families in order to rent their properties via Airbnb.

According to Dept. for Communities and Local Government, the end of a tenancy has been a common cause of homelessness. In 2009Q4, 1,060 households in England became homeless after their private tenancies were ended. In 2014Q1 it was 3,330 and two years later it was 4,650. With a greater reward, landlords have more of an incentive to maintain their properties, which means an improvement of the housing stock will follow.

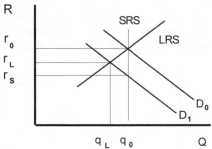

A third possibility is for the State to build 'affordable' housing or more rented accommodation. Again, the short run supply schedule for private rented dwellings (SRS) is vertical and the starting point is r_0, q_0. The new property takes out some of the demand for private rented accommodation so shifts the demand curve to the left to D_1. In the short run, this drives market rents downwards from r_0 to r_S. Over the longer term, landlords will switch some accommodation from the rented to the home owning market or some other land use. Thus, switching to the long run supply curve (LRS), the number of units that landlords make available drops to q_L.

A Child of Forward Thinking
Hungerman and Buckles found that, rather than coinciding with the business cycle, pregnancies appear to be a forward indicator, with a lead of 6 months. The explanation is that pregnancy is an indicator of consumer confidence. In effect, planning to expand the household is similar to consumer durables; you engage when you feel you can

afford to. The Royal Economic Society reported in 2017 that fertility was associated with home ownership. A 10% rise in house prices was linked to a 2.8% increase in child birth. But this was offset by the 4.9% drop in fertility among renters. Overall, from 1995 the birth rate has dropped 1.3% - or 9,000 births/yr.

House Price Accelerator
It is argued that the prices of homes bought by those already owning a house would be more volatile than those in a starter home market. Assuming a loan-to-value (LTV) of 80% and a steady growth of loan funding, a €20,000 deposit would merit a maximum loan of €80,000 for a property worth €100,000. Also assume the annual average house price growth is 9%. If a capital-constrained buyer purchased a house on that basis and during the subsequent year it rose in value by €9,000, the price increase would be 9% but the home-owner's equity in the house would rise by 45%. The leveraged property has an implied equity multiplier [of 5]. The now repeat-buyer has a €29,000 deposit, which puts a €145,000 within grasp. Increasing house prices boosts equity and fortifies purchasing power. By frequently revisiting the market, the borrower, operating at the limit, accelerates house price rises. This price acceleration is a function of the LTV.

The house price-earnings ratio (loan-to-income ratio) will mollify the acceleration of price. With a ratio of 4 and an income of €20,000 the maximum mortgage that could be offered is €80,000. The buyer initially jumps both ratio hurdles. If income grows by 5%/year, the maximum they could borrow after year 1 is €84,000. Combined with the €29,000 equity, the house price they could qualify for is €113,000. This is a 13% increase in the value of a house within the grasp of a second time buyer. Hanging on for a second year generates a far greater capacity to buy. The house is now worth €119,000; and the income of the buyer is €27,560, with a maximum loan of €110,000. The second house that is affordable within two years is worth €149,000. A loan to income ratio of 3.5 is below that of 2.7m existing mortgagees.'

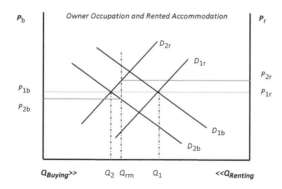

Kennedy and Stuart of the Central Bank of Ireland proffered an analysis of the complementary goods of house renting and owning. In the short run, the supply of accommodation is fixed, shared between the renting market and owner occupation. The cost of buying = mortgage costs + taxes + depreciation + maintenance costs − expected capital gains = user cost of capital. The cost of renting = rent.

Assume no transactions cost. In the diagram left rent = P_{1r} on the right-hand scale. The demand curve = D_{1r} slopes upwards. This intersects with the demand for buying schedule = D_{1b} which slopes downwards.

The quality rented is Q_1 running from right to left. The quantity owned is Q_1 running from left to right. Suddenly, buying is made more challenging (e.g. LTV, and/or the LTI ratios are lowered). This shifts the demand for buying to the left to D_{2b} and the renting demand curve D_{2r} also to the left so that Q_2 is the intersecting quantity. Assuming a one-for-one transfer, neither price changes. However, not all switch so that the demand curve does not move as far as D_{2r}; dropping out of the hunt for a house purchase so both price of renting and buying, falls. An alternative question is that some owned properties cannot be rented so that the max quantity that can be rented is Q_{rm}. Now, the renting price rises and buying price falls. This is a short run problem. The return for renting is relatively high.

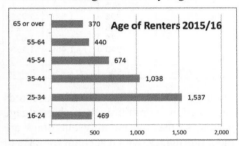

Rent-not-Buy

There were 4.528m in the private renting sector identified in the table below. 1.537m or 34% of those in the private sector were aged 25-34. One can glean movement from rent to renting and from renting to buying from the table below. Of the 1.828m moves, half were within the renting sector. Indeed, 13% of renting households moved in that sector in 2015/16, against 3% in the owning sector.

Of the stock of 14.33m home owners, there were 60,000 joiners and 400,000 OO move home but remained owners. Of these, 58,000 moved to own outright. A further 156,000 (38+9+97+12) shifted to the

TO	Own		Renting		Join
From	Outright	Mortgage	Private	Social	
Out	128	14	38	9	5
Mort	58	197	97	12	57
Private	21	151	787	84	196
Social	1	18	52	158	60
Variance	232	-325	123	-87	-55
Total	7,732	6,598	4,528	3,918	262

renting sector. Going the other way, 191,000 changed from renter to owners. Variance compares tenure changes over 2014 and 2015 with moves. 262,000 households not accounted for. These include deaths and migration.

The proportion owned outright passed 50% in 2012/13. 78.1% of those owned outright are either occupied by an individual or a couple without dependent children. In other words, the OO market is made up of retired people, without children, living in large houses. Then again the lone person need not be retired. The number has risen in 10 years from 7.23m to 7.74m out of 26m. One would expect this to be an aging population problem. However, it is more a 45-64 problem, where there is a 470,000 growth. This could reflect the rise in divorces.

'Generation Rent' characterised 48% of households of those aged 25-34 in 2013 up from 21% in 2003. Private rental accommodation rose from 11.9% of tenure choice to 18%, whilst social renters fell from 31.4% to 16.8% between 1980 and 2013. The former year is when the right-to-buy legislation came in. Private renters comprised 4m HHs, of which 987,600 were on housing benefit. The housing benefit bill of £21.1bn was 117% higher than in 2001 and the number on benefits was up by ⅔.

Surveying 15,000 Europeans, ING reported in September 2015 that 80% believed that it was becoming increasingly difficult to buy a first home, with 89% baffled as to how a first time buyer would ever buy a property in the UK. 72% of respondents, particularly renters, believed that society would benefit if house prices fell. The

Resolution Foundation estimated that ⅓ of Millennials (born 1981+) owned their own home in their late 20s compared with 52% for Generation X (1966-1980) and 60% of Baby Boomers (1946-1965). GenX had real incomes 54% higher than the Boomers in the early 30s, but Millennials are only 6% better off than GenX. The CML found that 65% of households born in 1970 were

Household Income Quintiles	Own '000		Rent '000
	with mortgage	Outright	
1	296	1,535	2,725
2	628	1,806	2,122
3	1,224	1,638	1,692
4	1,940	1,459	1,158
5	2,511	1,295	749
Tot 22.8m	6,598	7,732	8,446

homeowners when they were 35. Due to the rising unaffordability, 44% of households born in 1980 were homeowners at age 35. One reaction to prohibitively high mortgage costs is to spread the load over a longer period, so that the monthly outgoings are affordable. The Halifax revealed that repayment mortgages, which account for 88% of new lending, was being repaid over a longer period. In 2015, 26% of FTB took out a 35-year mortgage when only 15% were taken out in 2007. By contrast, 30% had a mortgage term of 20-25 years, when in 2007, 48% of loans were of this duration.

Civitas reported that there has been a decline in the proportion of single-person households among younger adults, most notably because of a marked increase in the

proportion of young adults living with their parents. In the table right comparing 1996/98 data for households with non-dependent (i.e., adult) children, there was an increase in the number of 20-34-year-olds living with their parents across the UK of 791,600. This represented in England an increase of 24.05% but in London (41.25%), and the South East (37.06%). Oddly in the North East, it was only 17.4% and Yorkshire Humberside 13.65%.

	1996/98		2014/15		%Δ
	With parents	% of all 20-34s	With parents	% of all 20-34s	over 96/98 14/15
NE	117.1	21.96	139.8	25.78	17.40
NW	323.4	22.76	399.5	27.62	21.36
YH	207.6	19.16	240.4	21.78	13.65
EM	164.6	18.69	198.3	22.68	21.33
EM	237.5	21.33	306.4	28.11	31.82
EE	211.5	19.71	3.8	26.99	36.90
LON	309.4	16.77	530.6	23.69	41.25
SE	299	18.63	402.9	25.54	37.06
SW	173.9	18.19	217.1	22.29	22.56
ENG	2,044	21.20	2,735.8	26.29	24.05

Housing Ladder

A simple housing ladder entails a small number of distinct dwellings placed in a hierarchy of quality. The discussion above implies there is a flat, a [terraced] house and a [family] house. A first time buyer (FTB) household is one just joining the property-owning sector for the first time. Given wealth, income and credit constraints, the FTB is limited to the lower end of the housing hierarchy. Through a series of acquisitions and disposals, the serial buyer household, injecting fresh capital, exchanges a smaller for a larger dwelling, rising up the ladder, likely to be affected by mismatches between family housing requirements to dwelling characteristics. Once the children have left the family home, to

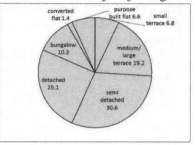

complete a life-cycle, the household could trade down back into a flat or into a bungalow. The buyer's age is an important indicator of their income, family unit and the relative value of their property.

The size of dwelling is a feature. 25.1% of OOccupied dwellings are detached and a further 30.6% are semi-detached. Despite terraced housing and flats making up a relatively small proportion of the housing stock in 2011, they accounted for 47.5% of sales.

In the figure right, the pattern of sales by type of dwelling shows the Terraced to be the most traded. This is consistent with the housing ladder discussion. As a relatively affordable type, households will acquired this and then trade up. As price increases the owner's equity in their (Terraced) property (the

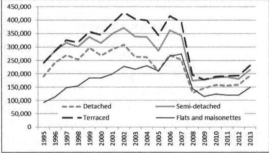

value above the outstanding mortgage) increases. Thus, the credit-constrained household has their budget limitation relaxed. As with other asset markets, the amount that can be borrowed increases, leading to pro-cyclical lending. If the home owner is already participating in the housing market, their borrowing and so purchasing power is enhanced, leading to an acceleration of house price inflation. In an accelerating era the repeat buyer (RB) is priced *in* to the market. More sellers join with little time or cost constraints, adding turnover volatility to the markets when prices are already accelerating. The seller may have no urgency to move, so need not price-to-sell. In a low demand era the seller may engage in 'fishing', where they continue to participate in a thin market with a high asking price hoping for a match with a buyer. Moreover, loss aversion may prevent the vendor from reducing price in the face of falling demand.

Affordability and Moves

Compiled by the Centre for Economics and Business Research, the Post Office Money's Cost of Moving study, reported in November, found that both renters and buyers were using the majority of their cashable savings to cover the cost of moving. Renters need £944 for the next security deposit and spend £525 on moving costs such as rental van fees, childcare and agency fees. Homebuyers require £10,132. The breakdown is seen below.

Stamp Duty	£2,019
Estate Agent	£4,815
Surveyors	£600
Conveyancing	£1,619
Removals	£1,079

The same research unit found that the average property across 20 of Britain's largest cities in 2018 took 102 days to sell, 6 days longer than in 2017. London slowed, taking 126 days, when it took 111 in 2017. Properties in Edinburgh and Glasgow spend the shortest time on the market, with homes typically selling in 39 and 48 days respectively, quicker by 2 days. Other cities away from London, although taking over 100 days, also speeded up: Liverpool 106 (112) and Belfast 111 (119) days.

Lloyds-TSB found that the average age of a second time buyer (trading up to their second home) had risen from 37 in 2002 to 40 in 2012. The type of house buyer changed between 2007 and 2013. The number of cash buyers fell from 417,000 by 18%; first time buyers from 360,000 by 31%; home movers from 654,000 by 50%; and the buy-to-let buyer from 183,000 by 57%.

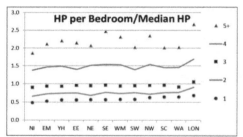

The price of an additional bedroom varies from region to region. In the Figure left, the median house prices for each size of dwelling is benchmarked against the median dwelling price of the region. The median price is just above that for three bedrooms for all but London and the four bedroomed dwelling is around 50% more than the median. As a guide, any dwelling with more than 4 bedrooms is around double the median. However, this factor is more unstable than others mentioned.

The dwelling of preference of the well-educated retired owner is the four bedroomed detached, which presents a blockage issue. The International Longevity Centre argue that there is not a suitable supply of dwellings for the retired to move to; stamp duty makes it costly; but in the main, people could not see the benefits of moving. Older folk do not move out of larger houses, in part because they own the property, are rich, and want somewhere for the family to stay when they visit. Savills estimated that 2.9m homes are occupied by over-65 year olds with two or more extra bedrooms. The exit rate of 90,000/yr is just too low and needs boosting.

The average new home was described as a rabbit hutch. A typical semi-detached in 2013 had 3 bedrooms and covered 925sqft. In 1920, there would be an additional bedroom and a further 622sqft. The equivalent numbers for a new terraced of 645 sqft are again a loss of a bedroom and 375sqft. At least there is still approximately the same space for 3 bedrooms. Affordability is the key. If land is expensive, then to utilise it more intensively, what is built is smaller.

Help to Buy

From a life-cycle/housing career perspective, a child's father buying a dwelling at the age of 25, having that child at 30, passing on at 80, leaves that child with the possibly of inheriting the parental dwelling at 55, just about the same time that their mortgage is paid-off. Fifty-five would be the life-cycle peak earnings period, so an intergeneration transfer of wealth to a FTB is far from improbable.

Intergenerational equity transfers through bequests, gifts, or housing equity release transfers, support or accelerate the rate of appreciation of first time buyer prices. Importantly, a geographical shift from the London area could release equity whilst preserving a four bedroomed family home, spreading wealth to low priced regions.

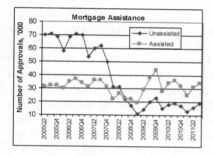

With the assistance of parents, FTB can continue to join the housing ladder when normally out-priced, so that equity growth can be self-refreshing. It is conceivable that a housing ladder can be maintained without many FTBs. Clarke of the Council of Mortgage Lenders (CML) suggested that intergenerational transfers make up a significant but stable volume of mortgages. There were an estimated 31,000 UK FTBs that were 'assisted' in the second quarters of both 2005 and 2011, and yet the number of unassisted FTBs dropped by 78% to 16,000 over the same six years. So, whilst the number of 'assisted' FTBs remained stable, the 'assisted' proportion rose from 31% to 66%. More recently, Clarke estimated the proportion of unassisted FTBs stood at 38% in 2014, which is around the rate post-2008 in Clarke. The added complication was two Help-to-Buy programmes providing additional support. Notably, the assisted FTB in 2014 bought a more expensive abode (£175,000) with a smaller loan (£120,000) than the unassisted (£147,000; £129,000). Weale takes a rather sanguine view of intergenerational transfers. Rising prices represent a transfer of wealth from future generations. If parents feel this is wrong, they can adjust their planned bequests. Savills estimated that in the year to September 2016, £2.8bn of family financial support was injected. 34% of FTBs relied on it in 2013/14 and a further 9.6% used inherited monies. This allows purchase to occur 2.6 years earlier (London 4.6) compared with the unsupported. In June 2019, the National Audit Office reported that 63% of recipients could have bought a home without Help-to-Buy funds. Between 2013 and 2018 over ½ of the sales in England made by Redrow, Bellway, Taylor Wimpey, Barratt and Persimmon involved Help-to-Buy. Persimmon the biggest beneficiary increased their profit on each house from roughly £20,000 to £60,000. Fran Boait of Positive Money argued that Help-to-Buy has mainly been a subsidy for a housing bubble, benefiting property developers and existing home owners.

Pryce and Sprigings find that, as buy-to-let (BTL) purchasers occupy the same portion of the housing market as FTBs, purchasing a dwelling for rent sucks cheap housing out of the owner-occupation market, possibly being rented to those that would have bought. BTL might be the significant blockage to the FTB. The Resolution Foundation estimated that over the 2014-16 period there were 1.9m BTL landlords. Additionally, 1.4m own second homes. Between them, they absorbed at least 0.9m (=0.5+0.4m) dwellings, over 8 years. 1.1m were newly built in that period in England.

Moving, what Moving?
Jamei & O'Brien (2017) reviewing the FTB in both Ireland and the UK, find that they have accounted for a very stable share of housing transactions since the early 2000s, with a rising proportion of cash buyers. The decline in the RB market is notable. Between 2004 and 2012 across the British Isles, movers accounted for more than half of property purchase mortgages. By 2016, movers' share of new purchase mortgages had fallen for six successive years in the UK and two in Ireland. Hudson & Green (2017) suggest that there has been a dearth of around 400,000 transactions each year since the bubble burst in the UK compared with before. Of these 80% are mortgaged movers. There is a shift to cash and there is an older population, who are less likely to move, which explains much. However, they highlight 140,000 missing moves that can be attributed to a decline in the rates of moving among mortgaged home-owners. Positing three factors: their desire to move; sufficient funds; and the availability of a home they want to buy, they find insufficient equity is the dominant factor holding back the mortgaged mover rate. Interestingly there find the period between 1990 and 2008 is the unusual one, not the current phase. In an era of financial deregulation, falling inflation and interest rates, although there was modest income growth, home-owners could borrow and service more debt to buy or move up the housing ladder. Real house price increases bestowed equity windfalls onto those in home-ownership. Those who bought in the 1960s through to late bubble in 1989 saw high nominal interest rates and high inflation. In the post 2008 period, there has been little house-price growth and little wage growth.

Unfortunately, the relative decline of movers may suggest reduced market liquidity. This limits the supply of second-hand properties for sale, possibly because movers have low or negative equity, they have an attractive mortgage rate that they do not want to lose or because of relatively high transaction costs. This has a knock-on effect on sales where those willing or able to sell may struggle to find a suitable property to buy. Between 2014 and 2017 the number of transactions in London dropped by 20%, while sales across the UK had fallen by 1% in 2018. A casualty of this is the estate agent. Accountants Moore Stephens, reported in July that more than 7,000 (27%) of UK High Street estate agents were struggling to survive. In August, Countrywide Estate Agents announced an emergency equity raising of £111m. This effectively wiped out the value of existing shareholders. Struggling with net debt of £212m, income was down 8.7% to £306.6m. Losses were £218m in 2018, compared with a £207m in 2017. Online agents Purple-Bricks and Emoov had been an additional factor.

As house prices escalate and with the rise of the buy-to-let buyer, FTBs are priced out of the market and renting has boomed. Savills estimated that renters paid around £54bn to buy-to-let landlords in the 12 months to June 2017. Of this, £20bn was paid in London or £24bn by younger people. Interest paid on mortgages by OO was £26.5bn, down from £32.9bn in 2012. Over the same 5 years the amount paid to landlords rose by £14bn.

The diagram left also shows interest payments as a proportion of gross disposable income. The peak in terms of interest payments occurs in 2008Q4, which corresponds with not numbers of buyers but mortgage rates. After this there is a decline in the cost but not in numbers, which remains flat for all three types of buyer.

In 2016, FTBs account for just under half of all mortgage lending for house purchases and had an average LTV of 83% on an average £190,180 purchase price. The average London deposit for FTB was £91,409, 2.78× the UK average. The Association of Letting Agents and the Centre for Economics and Business Research estimated that they spent an average of £68,300 on rent before they could afford to buy a home. In England, the amount was over £50,000. London's population continues to grow. Migration and births see to that.

For banks and regulators though, this presents a problem. The prospect of a ¼% increase in mortgage rate is estimated to increase the servicing by £15/month. However, the current market dependence on variable rate is around 40%. Those most likely to be exposed to changing interest rates are those in their 40s and 50s. A rise in business rates again is less profound than is was a decade ago. Then the share of profit to meet debt servicing was 25% now it is around 10%. Worse, in 2016, Halifax raised the mortgage age limit to 80 and Nationwide to 85. Because lenders cannot easily further extend the term of a mortgage if a borrower gets into temporary trouble with repayments, the result is more likely to be more home repossessions.

The ONS estimate that 18% of 35-39 year olds left London between 2014 and 2016. In 2009, 51,000 of 30-somethings left London; in 2015, 66,000. Overall, 283,000 migrated from London to the rest of the UK. By contrast, 4% of the borough of Epsom and Ewell were interlopers from London.

In June 2018 it was reported that almost a decade from the start of the financial crisis and 12 years after the peak, Irish banks have an averaged non-performing loan ratio of 14%. Of the €100bn of outstanding mortgage debt, €10bn was non-performing, or in arrears of more than 90 days. About €6.5bn were more than two years past due, of which €3bn were more than five years in arrears. The average new house cost 10× average earnings, with secondhand houses in Dublin @ 17×.

Regional Comparisons

In the table below there are data on house prices, house prices per metre sq and per room. The next column concerns rent as a proportion of disposable income. To give some context, GVA and GVA per head is reported. Data for the lowest and highest

2014	HP £'000	HP/ m²	HP/ room	Rent %Y	GVA/ head	High NUTS3	Low NUTS 3	Total GVA £'000	% UK GVA
England	220	2248	50318						
EE	233.5	2410	54205	23.1	23,970	29,097	17,524	145,651	8.7
EM	163.5	1541	35677	21.7	20,929	27,645	16,978	97,887	5.9
Lon	365	5627	112279	31.6	43,629	292,855	17,053	378,424	22.7
NEast	142	1236	28795	25.1	18,927	24,585	15,475	49,677	3.0
NI	125			20.2	18,584	35,023	13,919	34,410	2.1
NWest	156	1435	33129	24.7	21,867	32,314	14,523	156,872	9.4
SC	165			22.3	23,685	36,963	15,128	127,260	7.6
SEast	263	2893	64637	25.2	27,847	41,581	17,273	249,174	14.9
SWest	210	2209	50869	27.5	23,031	30,850	15,600	126,007	7.6
Wales	155	1328	31279	23.9	18,002	22,783	13,411	55,788	3.3
WM	170	1669	37684	21.7	20,826	31,705	15,762	119,769	7.2
YH	155	1460	33688	22.1	20,351	27,466	16,170	109,704	6.6
E&WA		2194	49219						
UK	212.5				25,351			1,666,342	100.0

NUTS3 area are displayed.

In 2014, the median house price in the UK was £212,500. The average house price per habitable room in England and Wales was £49,219 and this corresponded with a price per meter squared of £2,194. Habitable rooms exclude bathrooms conservatories, kitchens and utility rooms.

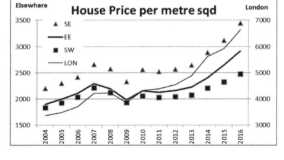

Renting over the period 2012-2014 cost the average renter in Wales 23.9% of their disposable income.

The latter is measured after benefits and direct taxes are paid. Using Wales as a benchmark, London is much more expensive. A more realistic comparison is with the East Midlands. Median house price was 5.48% higher, but the price per room was 14.1% greater. By contrast rents were 9.8% lower per £1 of disposable income.

Renting has become more expensive, rising from 14.2% across 2002/4 to 25.1% in 2012/14 in the North East. Despite its relative poverty and the low cost of renting it is still high relative to income.

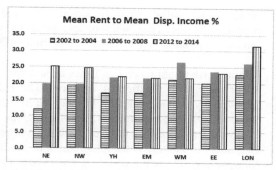

In the figure right, there is a plot of the median price of a house based on its footprint. The cheapest of the four is the South West. The right-hand scale is twice that of the left. As the patterns are very similar it implies that London house prices per unit area grew at about the same rate. The price in 2016 was greater than at the peak of 2007. Compare these with the rest of the country. Here, the values in 2016 appear not dissimilar to those in the south in 2004.

In general prices are lower the greater the distance from London. Indeed, Wales, North East, North West and Yorkshire Humberside were, in 2016, still below the 2007 peak.

Productivity	Lincolnshire	UK
Wheat	1	2
Cloth	3	4
Output 1		
Wheat	50	25
Cloth	16.67	12.5
Output 2		
Wheat	87.5	0
Cloth	4.17	25
Output 3		
Wheat	75	0
Cloth	8.33	25

INTERNATIONAL TRADE

Returning to the Primitive Society in Lincolnshire, assume Lincolnshire and the rest of the UK have the same levels of productivity. As the opportunity costs would be identical there would be no benefit from trade.

In the table left one can see that it takes Lincolnshire one unit of labour to produce one unit of wheat but the UK requires two units of workers. To produce one unit of cloth takes four hours of labour in the UK but only three in Lincs. If there is demand for an additional unit of cloth, two units of wheat must be foregone in the UK. This is the opportunity cost. In Lincs, it is worse. Three units of wheat must be foregone. Surely it is better for the UK to forgo the wheat? Assuming a 50:50 split in both regions and 100 units of labour, Lincs initial output of wheat is 50 and cloth is 16.67. The rest of the UK produce half that. Thus, without specialisation, wheat output is $50 + 25 = 75$ bushels and cloth output is $16.67 + 12.5 = 29.17$ units (Output 1).

Although we might teach that Lincs should specialise in one and the Rest the other, it is not clear with the figures we have. The maximum output of cloth that can be achieved by the Rest is 25. To stay within the tradable zone there are then two extremes. One can maximise wheat output given the total cloth output should be 29.17. This would require 4.17 units of cloth to be produced by Lincs. This needs $4.17 \times 3 = 12.5$ hours of labour. Thus, 87.5 remain to produce 87.5 bushels of wheat (Output 2). Alternatively, the maximum output of wheat should be 75, harvested by 75 workers. The remaining 25 workers in Lincolnshire should produce some cloth as well ($25 \times 0.33 = 8.33$) (Output 3).

We have not mentioned prices. In the event of an improvement in productivity, the price of wheat and/ or cloth should fall, even if there is no trade. It is not clear that all benefit. Prices come down in both regions but incomes may fall as well.

A sign of changing times is evident in trade figures. For the first time since the 1930s, global GDP growth was outstripping trade growth. With expanding trade, there has been a 2 to 1 ratio of trade to GDP growth. Between 1980 and 2011 the figures were 7% and 3.4% annually. The IMF and WTO estimated growth in 2013 should be 2.9% when trade should expand by 2.5%. The trade consultancy, Delta Economics, estimates that 40% of global trade is now south-south trade. This is associated with capital movements. By the end of 2013, McKinsey estimated that capital flows across G20 borders had fallen 68.5% from the 2007 peak. However, China-African trade in 2013 ($200bn) outstripped US-African ($110bn). India now supersedes the EU as the largest exporter of agricultural products to the very poorest countries. The price of its exports undermines producers in the poorest countries.

From Ricardo's theory of international trade, countries benefit from specialisation and trade. The Marshall Islands in the South Pacific is not the best example of trade. After WWII when they became a US trust territory, the inhabitants changed their diets. Out went domestically produced coconut and fish. In came flour, white rice, fatty meat and sugar. This is financially and physically crippling. Not only was it expensive to import but the Islands had the 3rd highest prevalence of diabetes in the world. The preference for a western diet over what a coral atoll could muster could be viewed as a choice failure.

India halted progress on the Doha round of WTO negotiations in July 2014, defending its farmers. It was protecting its agricultural support programme; a programme of food security. India's right to food law allows for the subsidy of grain. Each of the 70% of the poor covered by the law is entitled to 5kg. To stimulate production, a price minimum is set for wheat and rice with any surplus purchased by the state. However, over the last 10 years prices have doubled, leading to large harvests and stockpiles.

The WTO conference in Nairobi, Kenya from 15 to 18 December 2015 is notable. At the end the Doha round of negotiations seemed to be concluded. During the conference the biggest tariff-reduction deal since 1996 eliminated restrictions on the $1.3tn trade of 201 IT products. It was estimated to increase GDP by $190bn/yr. Trade in IT goods accounts for 7% of total international trade, greater that in automotive goods, and textiles, clothing, iron and steel combined. There was also agreement on abolishing subsidies on farming exports. For developed countries this should be by the end of 2018.

In the diagram below, the free movement of goods and the welfare changes that follow can be analysed. The initial position entails no trade so country M operates at a higher price than country X. With free trade, there is an equalisation of price at P_e. The export schedule XS is derived from the differences between the supply and demand curves in Country X (excess supply). The import schedule MD is derived in a corresponding manner using differences between the supply and demand curves in Country M (excess demand). Trade drives down price in country M as consumers purchase the cheaper version from country X.

There are welfare changes. Consumers are worse off in X (area A) but better off in M (E+G). Producers are worse off in M (E) but better off in X (A+C). The free movement in goods has resulted in a net welfare gain of G+C.

Free(r) trade in wheat may benefit UK farmers. As the 14th largest exporter at 2m tonnes, it is well set. However, currently Spain and Portugal are key markets. A low

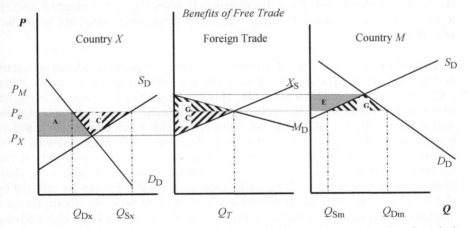

pound may help but with without some support, farming will be exposed to the winds of commerce. The US in 2016 had a fourth bumper harvest of grains in a row. Yields are at record levels.

It is customary to analyse the movement of goods only. Trade theory and Customs Union theory presumes labour does not move so as to preserve relative productivity or relative labour costs. The free movement of labour can be analysed in the diagram below. The initial position entails no movement of factors so Country *B* operates at a

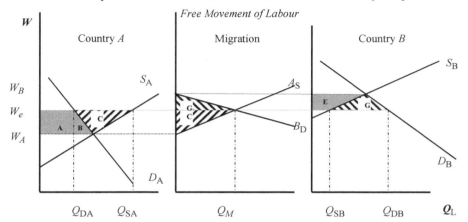

higher wage than Country *A*. With free movement of labour, there is an equalisation of price at W_e. As the wage rate is higher Q_M (= $Q_{SA} - Q_{DA}$) workers relocate from Country *A* to Country *B*. This drives wages down in *B* and up in *A*. Correspondingly, there is a shift of production from country *A* to country *B*. Employers in Country *B* gain E and G because labour is cheaper and there is more of it. Employers in Country *A* lose area A in higher wage costs and B in lost output. Workers that migrate gain B+C in rent (higher wage). Those that remain in Country *A* gain A. Country *B* workers lose E as the wage has fallen. The free movement in labour has resulted in a net welfare gain of G+C.

As implied above, free movement of goods means the production is reduced in country *M* (the US?) and an equalisation of prices. The movement of labour to country *B* (the US?) leads to an equalisation of wages. This can be seen to be operating in the US labour at the bottom end of the skills and wage hierarchy. Forbes estimated that the median wage in Beijing of $329.53/wk is just below what a fork lift operator at $12.75 is making ($382) in a warehouse in the US. Asian economy wages grew by 5.7% annually from 2006 to 2011. In the developed world the rate was only 0.4%. Euromonitor estimate that Chinese wages had tripled between 2005 and 2016. Thus, those at the bottom of the skills hierarchy more than any other group are affected by globalisation. Their work has gravitated to China (demand curve for labour, left) and migrants from Mexico have moved to the US (supply curve for labour, right) driving wages down.

The car industry has moved east in Europe, but migrants have moved west, to where wages are higher. This has led to growing labour shortages in the east and a huge interdependence with Germany's car industry. In January, employees at Audi's plant in Gyor, which employs 13,000 people, were awarded an 18% pay increase. Industrial action led to a suspension of engines produced in Gyor, causing Audi's plant in Ingolstadt had to halt production for two days. This victory is within a country where its parliament passed a labour law in December allowing employers to seek up to 400 hours of overtime/yr.

Hungarian union focused on wage relatives with comparable production units. Audi and VW workers in Poland (39%), the Czech Republic (25) and Slovakia (28) earned at least a quarter more.

Larry Summers argued that it is hard to see today how some in the West benefit from free trade:
1. The benefits of reduced tariffs and quotas are now very small. Protectionism in the textbook sense remains in areas steeped in cultural symbolism, such as agriculture. Trade agreements now are more about regulatory harmonization and the protection of investment, such as in intellectual property.
2. The benefits of freer trade have assisted the developing countries spectacularly. In the West, freer movement of factors has benefited the owners of capital and a cosmopolitan elite. The losers have been the poor, where wages, harmonizing with those in factories in the developing East, have fallen in real terms, so much so that reshoring is viable. Worse for politicians, the middle class are feeling the costs rather than the benefits, with the US median real wage unmoved for four decades. Inequality is shifting from a developing to a developed nation issue. The benefits of free trade by-pass the less-skilled [American] worker. Between 1979 and 2013, the top 1% saw their income rise 188%. The middle and lower income brackets grew by 18%. The protection of intellectual property benefits the skilled elite. An innovation may boost employment in both developed and developing nations – such as the iPad. The influx of migrants into the rich West from the poor East is of benefit to capital but a threat to less skilled labour. The Euro elections in 2014 and in the US and UK in 2016, 2017 and 2019 revealed discontent.
3. REAs that make sense geographically or have a clearer strategic purpose are more likely to succeed. Trump cancelling REAs as soon as he took office and GSP two years later is making a statement about his view on trade. Interestingly, China takes a different, more inclusive approach.

TRADE PROTECTIONISM

A standard theme in International Trade Programmes is the issue of trade protectionism and the question, why protect an industry? In previous *Updates* there has been a wealth of diagrams showing trade protectionism outcomes with the conclusion that interference leads to a net welfare loss for a small country. As we know from the discussion of international trade theory, in a Ricardian world, free trade leads to country specialisation and an improvement in the allocation of resources. However, the outcome will not favour all sectors in all countries; some must lose resources for them to be reallocated. This means that various sectors in every country will experience restructuring costs, some difficult to bear. It is common for countries to advocate free trade when it is to their advantage, but squeal about unfair competition when it is not (America first?).

Protectionism leads to a greater misallocation of resources:
❑   The large lobbying supplier extracts economic rent, so it redistributes wealth from the consumer to the producer in the small importing country.
❑   A key outcome is that it raises domestic price
    o   production expands in protected markets – Producer Surplus increases PS↑
    o   consumption decreases in protected markets – Consumer Surplus decreases CS↓.
❑   Less competition may foster inefficiency – this point is relevant where the market is dominated by oligopolies – but then Ricardo is based on perfect competition.
❑   It increases (less efficient) employment in protected markets.
❑   It reduces the volume of imports (but not necessarily the value).
❑   A tariff raises revenue for the State.
❑   It may encourage firms to relocate to the protected market.

Explanations for Protectionism
Standard explanations for trade protection revolve around the avoidance of the disadvantage of international trade. These include the defence of infant or senile industries; maintaining a diverse industrial structure, which can include possibly being self-sufficient in a sector where security of supply is vitally important; or there is a wish to retain a way of life worth protecting. The loss of jobs in certain sectors can be highly emotive in many countries and governments might step in to protect those jobs by restricting access to the domestic market, such as agriculture. Moreover, an importing country will face external balance issues. As any trade disadvantage grows, either a balance of payments deficit or an exchange rate deterioration develops. Where an exporting country subsidises its exports (dumping) both jobs and trade balances are put under pressure in the importing country leading to domestic producers losing market share in the home market. To counter act this, under WTO international trade rules, the importing country is permitted to use countervailing measures, including an antidumping duty.

Another reason why protectionism might emerge is that the advantages of international trade fall thinly on the many (consumers) but the disadvantages fall heavily on the few (producers). Producers, having more power in the market place, are better placed to lobby the government for special treatment, either individually or collectively through associations. Market power is related to the last set of points. Countries with market power could exploit it by engaging in trade protection domestically in such a way as to alter world price, imposing the costs of trade protection on others.

Trade Diagrams and Maths

We could apply supply and demand analysis to trade diagrams. Assume the following:

$Q_S = P - 15, Q_D = 60 - .5P$. This results in a domestic price = £50 and quantity = 35 units, in the diagram right. Assuming the world price = £20, at this price imports = 45, domestic production = 5 and domestic demand = 50.

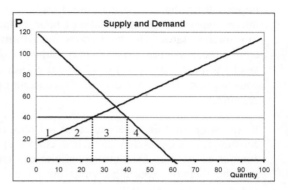

Assume that the small importing country imposes a lump sum tax of £20. This would move the domestic price with tariff to be £40. At this price imports = 15, domestic production = 25 and domestic demand = 40. As a result of the lump sum duty, domestic price is increased by £20, imports are reduced by 30 units and domestic production is increased by 20 units: 10 units less are consumed. The balance of payments is improved and so is domestic employment but what about overall well-being? CS↓ by areas 1+2+3+4 = £900 PS↑ by area 1=£300 Gov't Rev↑ by area 3= £300. Combined, well-being↓ by areas 2+4 = £300.

A similar outcome is achievable using a quota. The quota should be equal to 15 units. This can be achieved by using the supply function $Q_S = P$.

The balance of payments is improved and so is domestic employment but what about overall well-being? CS↓ £900 PS↑ £300 Gov't Rev↑ = 0. Combined, well-being↓ £600. As there are no tax revenues the welfare change is worse for the same price change. The producer takes what would have gone to the State.

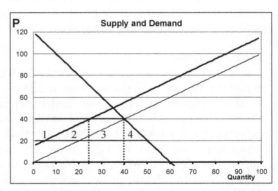

Rich economies seeking to reduce trade barriers in services have shifted to plurilateral agreements. These are not made available to all WTO members, so contravene the most favoured nation clause.

New Ideas

The case for protectionism moved forward. Lawrence Summers, Gauti Eggertsson and Neil Mehrotra tied together a secular recession, a liquidity trap and the paradox of thrift. By increasing savings, China reduces consumption (thrift) and the demand for imports from the U.S, generating a trade surplus. The surplus savings depress US interest rates, with an appreciating Dollar. In the US, a trade deficit is combined with low interest rates. The latter does not offset the former so domestic output and employment is depressed as, in part, Chinese excess have driven them to liquidity trap levels. With $(X-M) + (G-T) + (I-S) = 0$ it was thought that a trade surplus would boost consumption. Here, a reduction in consumption in China depresses US domestic demand.

It was suggested that the source of a China trade surplus (currency manipulation, consumption suppression, or a low currency) is immaterial. US policy should be countervailing. Neo-mercantilist policies alleviate the secular stagnation of the country pursuing them by exporting savings, but at the expense of the trading partner. Krugman is a supporter of this view.

In March 2018, Donald Trump imposed steel (25%) and aluminium (10%) import tariffs. Canada and Mexico were exempt from May 2019. 7% of UK Steel exports go to the US, worth £360m. EU members were made exempt until June. South Korea, also exempt from the tariff, was subject to a quota of 2.68m tonnes (70% of annual steel export). In exchange, it doubled the import quota of US cars to 50,000.

Structural Issues in Trade Wars
Diversion
Chinese producers began diverting their steel shipments to Vietnam "immediately" after the duties were imposed. In retaliation in May 2018 anti-dumping duties of 199.76% and countervailing duties of 256.44% on imports of cold-rolled steel produced in Vietnam were imposed. The assertion was that as much as 90% of the product's value originated from China.

Third Party beneficiaries
Trump was undermining the very point of a REA, deepening integration. US wheat exports to Mexico fell 38% by value, to $285m, in the first five months of 2018, and to all countries by 21% ($2.2bn). Mexico, dependent of US wheat, was investigating alternative supplies in July. Russia/ Ukrainian, was one source. During 2018Q1, wheat exports to Mexico totalled 243,000tns, nine times that in 2017Q1. At $202-$208/tn the wheat is cheaper than the $240 in the US. However, if the Mexican government imposed tariffs on US wheat large Mexican millers were considering near neighbours of Argentina and Brazil. At the back-end of 2017, Mexico imported a test cargo of 33,000tns from Argentina, with the plan to buy 100,000tns ($20m) in 2018. 8 milling operations in Mexico booked the Argentine wheat purchase, even though it cost $1 or $2 more/tn than US. Corn imports from Brazil rose by a factor of 10 in 2017 over 2016. Logistics are difficult to adjust quickly. The Russian wheat has a cost advantage. However, unexpected increases in US rail costs make Argentinean wheat more cost competitive.

By the end of September, a 10% tariff (rising to 25% on Jan 1st 2019) on $3bn worth of Chinese seafood imported into the United States forcing US importers to stockpile frozen Chinese squid and tilapia. In July, China imposed a 25% tariff on US seafood leading to exporters from Canada expanding to China. At Halifax Stanfield International Airport, total cargo rose 42% in July, and 55% in August. Canadian shipments of live or fresh lobster to China nearly doubled to 1.25mkg in July.

Targets that Hurt
The Mercantilist seeks to maximise the benefits of trade whilst minimising the costs. In trade wars, the instigator would seek to maximise the pain on the economy or the elite of the rivals. American agriculture is a political vote that US President Trump relies on. On 6th July, both China and the US had imposed tariffs of $34bn on each other. Some 91% of the 545 products China was placing a tariff on are from the agriculture sector. In response to the steel tariff on 4th August India imposed tariffs on 29 goods, including almonds, walnuts and chick peas. India is a large buyer of US almond exports and so the move was expected to hurt farmers in America.

Trump scheduled for that India and Turkey to be excluded from the US's Generalised System of Preferences (GSP) in May. India is the world's biggest beneficiary of that trade concession, and its withdrawal would be the strongest punitive action against the country since Trump took office in 2017. The US imported $1.66bn in 2017 from Turkey under GSP.

The European Union introduced retaliatory tariffs on US goods worth €2.8bn (£2.4bn) on products such as bourbon whiskey, orange juice, Harley Davidson motorcycles, cranberries and peanut butter. The majority carried a tariff of 25%. 50% duty fell on footwear, some types of clothing and washing machines. In January, Harley Davidson reported that the 25% tariff in the EU and China and the 10-25% tariff on imported components would cost it $13m worldwide in 2018Q4. Along with restructuring costs of $23m it reported a net income of just under $0.5m – no profit.

The FT estimated that subsidies to 3,545 Chinese listed firms rose 14% to $22.3bn in 2018, or to 4% of total net profit.

Storing Up Problems
By November, unable to sell to Chinese buyers, US farmers had a problem with their harvests. Normally, any surplus they could store or sell to a local elevator - giant silos usually run by international grains merchants that store grain. As their elevators were already full these were not buying as much grain. Across the United States, grain farmers were ploughing under crops, leaving them to rot or piling them on the ground, in hopes of better prices in 2019. For example, up to 15% of the Louisianan oilseed crop was too damaged to market or ploughed under. Expecting to meet China's expected demand for 60% of their soybeans, US farmers planted 89.1m acres in 2018, the second most ever. The 25% tariff effectively closed the $12bn market. Compensation of $837.8m had been paid out by mid-November.

Grain storage bag retailer, Neeralta, saw sales of their product were up 30% from 2017. At some Midwest river terminals, farmers were paying 60¢/ bushel to store soybeans until the end of 2018 - more than twice as much as in 2017. Dockage rates of between 60¢ at $1.20/ bushels at Bunge Elevators in Tennessee - more than three times as high as in 2017. This was made more acute because before the autumn harvest, around 20% of total grain storage available in the US was full with corn, soybeans and wheat from previous harvests,

As the trade war hotted up, in July Alliance of Automobile Manufacturers (inc. GM, VW and Toyota), told the US. Commerce Department that the 25% tariff on imported cars and parts would raise the price of an imported car by nearly $6,000 and the price of a US-built car by $2,000, displacing 2m vehicle sales/yr and cost more than 117,000 auto dealer jobs (10% of the workforce).

A Swine of a Problem
Just before trade barriers went up, the Dept. of Agriculture (USDA) predicted that global supply growth of pork would outpace demand in 2018, sparking 'fierce competition and lower prices.' Retaliatory pork duties of 62% in China and up to 20% in Mexico reduced exports and so drove US bacon and ribs prices down. Tariff battles raised feed prices. Because their prices are tied, the world's third largest exporter, Canada, saw producer fortunes declined with the US's. In August, pigs worth C$115/head were below the C$150 it costs to raise them.

The fall in US hogs and cattle prices is contributing to the change in American diets by boosting supplies of pork and beef. Restaurants were seizing on the increases to promote hamburgers instead of chicken, while grocery stores featured pork. What resulted was Americans lost their taste for chicken.

In late 2018, an outbreak of African Swine fever in China raised alarms. The ASF virus, endemic to Africa, is fatal to pigs and has no cure. The current wave of cases began in Georgia in 2007 and spread to parts of Eastern Europe and Russia before, in August, reaching China. It had half the world's pigs @ 430m losing 130m animals when China's 1.4bn people consume 55m tonnes of pork, presents a significant food issue.

In March, China purchased 24,000 tonnes of US pork, the highest amount in almost two years. By April, the running total was 127,000 tonnes. Hog contracts for June settlement were 96¢/lb on the Chicago Mercantile Exchange in April, up more than a quarter on March 1st. Morgan Stanley also pointed to Brazil as being well positioned to benefit from exporting pork, beef and chicken to China. More so when China cancelled contracts covering 3,247 tonnes in retaliation to Trumps new tariffs in May.

In July 2018, China imposed a 25% tariff on US cotton, putting the high-quality fibre at a disadvantage to supplies from Australia and Brazil. But after the government ran down large state reserves, they purchased net 178,000 bales of US-grown upland cotton in early April, the second-highest weekly volume in two years. Indeed, China's import commitments for US upland cotton total 2.86m bales, only about 100,000 below the level of 2018.

Missed Targets
By February, the tariffs on aluminium and steel were almost a year old. There was a notable increase in US aluminium but China was a major beneficiary of the exclusions process with approved import tonnages, leaving it not far off actual volumes in 2017. Petersen Institute estimated that over 90% of the Chinese products targeted were intermediate inputs or capital equipment. Aluminium, in semi-manufactured product form, surged 21% (5.8m tonnes) in 2018. The Commerce Department's January 2018 report targeted raising capacity utilisation from 39% (2017) to 80%. By December 2018, it was at 63% (1.15m tonnes). Alcoa reported a 2018Q4 operating loss in its aluminium segment.

For the non-switchers, the Peterson Institute estimated that the steel and aluminium tariffs increased the price of steel products by nearly 9%, pushing up costs for steel users by $5.6bn. This shifts the supply curve for those goods to the left. Caterpillar's production costs rose by more than $100m in 2018. It increased prices. Facing a similar increase in 2019, Deere cut costs and increased prices to protect its profits.

In May, Trump was threatening to raise further tariffs but this raised the awkward question, who loses? From February 2018 to March 2019 new tariff revenue was $15.6bn. Customs duties for the half year from October 2018 rose 89% to $34.7bn. However, most importers of Chinese-made goods are US companies, or US subsidiaries of foreign companies that import goods from China. The Economist estimated that 30% of the value of the goods China exports to America originated from third-party countries. The expected increase in US tariff revenue from 25% on $50bn and 10% on $200bn worth of goods should be around $32.5bn/yr. In 2018, tariff revenue of the $49.7 was up by $14.5bn on 2017. The expected increase in Chinese revenue of $15.5-18.5bn in tariffs was met with a tax revenue *fall* of $2.2bn ($42.1bn - $44.3bn). The consumer loses: - A US Congressional Research Service report in February found that the tariffs had led to an increase of as much as 12% in the price of a domestic washing machine. Federal Reserve Bank of NY, Princeton, and Columbia Universities found the metals tariffs cost companies and consumers $3bn/ month in additional taxes. Producers lose further: - companies lost further $1.4bn in inefficiency costs in 2018.

China was not using its full arsenal of weapons, including its quasi monopoly of rare earth or its holding of US sovereign debt. Why? China might have suspected it was not the real target and so sought to block rather than strike back. It could be that it was about deterring US firms from producing overseas. Consider the US attacked its two key allies, Mexico and Canada. Ford scrapped plans to produce in Mexico. However, after the raising of tensions, President Xi Jinping visited a rare earth plant. Between that day (May 20th) and early June dysprosium metal rose 14%; neodymium rose by 30%; gadolinium oxide 12.6% in price. These are critical to the production of some magnets, high-powered lamps, nuclear control rods and medical imaging. Some thought China would weaponise rare earths.

Who Bears the Cost of Free Trade in General?
If Trump was appealing to an electorate that feared migration and globalisation; where working-class Americans were looking for someone to blame, it has a strong upside. Trump makes pronouncements and then the Democrats protest free trade issues, alienating the Blue-Collar vote.

The complaint that freer trade costs jobs is not unreasonable. An MIT study estimated that rising Chinese imports of all good from 1999 to 2011 cost up to 2.4m American jobs. The Economic Policy Institute in Washington estimated that the granting of market economy status to China would endanger between 1.7m and 3.5m jobs in the EU. Competitive disadvantages are found in aluminium, bicycles, ceramic, glass, car parts, paper and steel; with 639,000 jobs vulnerable in Germany; 416,000 in Italy and 387,000 in the UK. Aegis Europe (30 industry bodies in numerous sectors including the vulnerable sectors) was campaigning against China's WTO market economy status.

Growth in the US between 2009 and 2013 may be seen as jobless. The export - jobs multiplier can be assessed in the following way. In 2009, exports created 9.7m. Each additional billion dollars of exports created 6,763. Although exports generated more jobs in 2013 (11.3m), the jobs/$ exported fell to 5,590. This could mean that the US is shifting towards capital-intensive exports - perhaps overturning the Leontieff paradox. This may be due to the cost of production in the US. Thus, Trump is hoping to reshoring US jobs through trade restrictions – overturning Vernon's product life cycle thesis and the NIDL. Automakers are unlikely to uproot billions of dollars of investments in plants and supply chains. Rather those that cannot comply with standards for passenger cars could simply pay tariffs of 2.5% (around $800 to $900 per vehicle) and buy low-cost parts from Asia to offset the cost. Trucks are different. More than 40% of GM's 2017 U.S. pickup truck sales were built in Silao, Mexico (400,000). Under proposed new rules 75% of the vehicle's content should be made within North America, with 45% at $16/hr wage, to qualify for tariff-free import from Mexico or face a 25% tariff. That said Ball, State University estimated of the 5.6m US manufacturing jobs lost 2000-2010 85% due to automation and only 13% due to trade. The use of automation is related to capital intensity, facilitation the reshoring of output. Klaus Kleinfeld, CEO of Alcoa, argued that [Lean] production requires production to be close to the R&D unit and customers. However, the labour needed is likely to be highly skilled, so not addressing the concerns of those blue-collar workers left behind.

ECONOMIC ASSOCIATIONS: WHICH ONE?

REAs encourage trade among a subset of the world. As such, the benefits of free trade should be bestowed on member countries and this should off-set any distortions. The benefits from specialisation and an improved allocation of resources should produce a welfare benefit. This should be gauged against the pre-trading arrangements. In Custom Union theory, if the group of countries constitutes a high cost group, trading among themselves rather than using the lower, world price, could result in trade diversion and so possibly a welfare loss. By contrast, if the group operate at the lowest cost of production as the rest of the world, it should lead to a welfare (static) gain. This corresponds to trade creation.

Additional benefits of a REA include scope to exploit further economies of scale. Assume that 10 countries of similar size and stages of development form an REA, so that, from expanding output, each firm can lower unit cost whilst serving a market of 10 countries. Clearly, not all can grow; some can expand whilst other, high cost producers, become uneconomic. Economies of scale are not part of the H/O and Ricardian worlds. Krugman's geography and trade thesis predicts a core-periphery outcome where economies of scale ideas produce much the same outcome as perfect competition and free trade: there will be a spatial division of labour, specialisation and more trade.

Another argument concerns the nature of manufacturing. It is common for oligopolies to emerge in an industry, leading to exploitation of the consumer, X-inefficiency, etc.. Moving from one country with 3 producers in the industry to 10 countries with 30 producers collectively should increase the degree of rivalry among oligopoly suppliers, driving firms to be more cost sensitive and innovative. However, the above point about economies of scale applies. The tendency to exploit economies of scale should lead to a shakeout, mergers and a smaller number of larger producers again. If one aim of forming a greater governing unit is to exercise greater power over large firms, this strategy of enlarging the political grouping, such as the EU, should succeed, but only in the short run, as the firms grow larger also.

Particularly when reducing unnecessary duplication, developing countries should be well placed to exploit economies of scale. Resources necessary for growth could be pooled, such as a jointly funded power plant by Brazil and Argentina. Here, the group of countries might be interested in import substitution or export promotion. These could apply to both primary and secondary goods. Import substitution could be seen as part of a self-sufficiency strategy. The infant industry argument for developing nations is a strong one. Additionally, outward looking policies, such as export promotion, would appeal to an export base model as the explanation for growth. Here, from a Thirlwallian perspective and an export base model, income elasticity matters. Agricultural staples, which have income elasticities around zero, are likely to leave the country or group as part of the periphery. Furthermore, from a balance of payments constraint perspective, the developing country cannot grow beyond certain limits.

Also, such a policy may hit a trade barrier from developed countries. The multi-fibre agreement and agricultural barriers have prevented free access to developed economies' markets. So an export-led growth strategy is not an automatic choice for a developing country in a non-neo-classical world.

Importantly, for the welfare gains to be made, countries should be at the same stage of production and produce the same goods. For many REAs involving developing countries, they operate at different stages of the development process and produce different goods. The benefits of specialisation must come after, not before, joining. If they already have specialised, trade diversion is likely to emerge. Worse, commodity-exporting countries are less likely to find the intra-union trade will grow much. If they already have a focus on more lucrative international markets, boosting demand in a low growth area may not be worthwhile.

CU theory does not address factor movements. Free movement of labour is predicated to produce good outcomes, but cumulative causation may suggest otherwise. A core may grow at the expense of the periphery. In a Krugman sense, countries could concentrate on (be a core country in) a narrow range of goods, so that all could specialise and trade. However, cumulative causation is a non-product model that implies resources in general could be surrendered by the periphery to the core, so that national/ regional unemployment may get worse. Labour, capital and goods may flow in the same direction.

Increasing integration comes at the cost of a loss of sovereignty. In the case of monetary or tax harmonisation, the country loses control of the levers that can be pulled to steer it along an independent road. In effect, the country ceases to be a separate entity and becomes part of a super-state. However, it must be stressed that up to 1973, one could put a case for the EC membership of a CU. With the inclusion of poorer states, the case for EC/EU membership really became one of political influence and control of borders, rather than an economic one. Moreover, allowing free movement of labour with very large disparities in national wages without a robust regional policy would lead to mass exoduses from poorer, smaller countries. The core would become over-crowded, leading to congestion problems, and the accusation of stealing a generation of skilled workers; the periphery would become an economic backwater or home for the elderly. As this appears to have happened between Spain and Germany, one must conclude the politicians were not concentrating on the ball.

Trade Creation
Upon joining a REA, a small importing country removes a lump sum duty. The REA operates as a low cost producer (= world price = £20). This lowers domestic price by £20. Imports are increased by 30 units and domestic production is reduced by 20 units: 10 units more are consumed. The balance of payments is harmed and so is domestic employment. But what about overall well-being? CS↑ £900 (1+2+3+4) PS↓ (1) £300

Gov't Rev↓ £300 (3). Combined, well-being ↑£300 (2+4). Centre for Economic Policy Research (CEPR) estimated the welfare gains from the TTIP for the EU as up to €119bn/yr, or €545/yr for a family of four. For the US, the values were €95bn/yr and €655/yr.

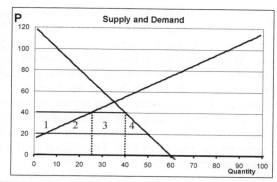

Trade Diversion

Below the REA is a high cost producer (EU price = £30). Domestic price drops from £40 to £30. At this price domestic production = 15, domestic demand = 45, so imports = 30. Imports increase by 15 units and domestic production decrease by 10 units, but 5 more units are consumed. Breakeven occurs when well-being from joining a CU does not change (2 + 4 = 5). This occurs at EU price =

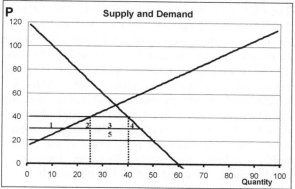

£27.64. If EU price > £27.64, there is a net welfare loss. If EU price < £27.64, there is a net welfare gain. Leaving a high cost arrangement should lead to trade creation. If Europe is a low cost car producer, it could make cars more expensive, but this form of trade diversion could boost demand for UK-made components for UK cars. The percentage of British parts in a British-built car has risen from 36% to 41% since 2013.

The UK-European trading options are as follows:
1. Norway: Staying in the EU Single Market and leaving the Customs Union would mean full access to the Single Market for both goods and services, but the UK would have to continue to abide by the EU's four freedoms, including freedom of movement.
2. Turkey: Creating a new customs union with the EU – so must abide by the CET.
3. Leaving the Single Market and Customs Union, but negotiating a new bespoke bilateral free trade and customs agreement.
   a. Swiss: Multiple bilateral deals: Switzerland has a bespoke arrangement with the EU, based on more than 120 bilateral agreements developed over the last two decades.
   b. Ukraine: Deep and Comprehensive Trade Area. Ukraine's association agreement with the EU provides for nearly-full access to the Single

Market through a special arrangement designed as a potential first step towards full EU membership.

   c.   Canada: A FTA

4.   World Trade Organization (WTO) option.

In effect, 1 is a contradiction – the single market is a Common Market = CU+ movement of capital and labour. So, 1 suggests the single market is not a common market, allowing for the UK to pursue its own independent trade policy, though in practice Norway, along with other countries in the EFTA, often negotiate as a bloc. This is because of the interwoven bonds. The European trading environment; respectively, European Free Trade Area or the European Economic Area have the following groupings:

The EFTA = Iceland + Liechtenstein + Norway + Switzerland.

The EEA = EU countries + Iceland + Liechtenstein + Norway, OR

The EEA = EU countries + EFTA – Switzerland.

Estimated by the government, a FTA with the US would boost GDP by just 0.2% and China and India between 0.1% and 0.4% vs. the loss of 5% with a FTA with the EU. The WTO anticipates shifting from EU to WTO rules for UK exports to the EU would reduce goods by half and services by 60%. Oddly, a Liechtenstein model might also suit. Liechtenstein has a customs with Switzerland but only one of them is in the EEA. Standards must match the destination market and importers are reimbursed if the EEA tariffs are lower than Swiss. However, there are border checks at the Austrian border, which is a problem for Ireland.

Most Traded Goods % of Exports

Good	%
Pharmaceuticals	2.1
Gold	2.2
Telecoms equipment	3.9
Integrated circuits	4
Vehicle parts	2.4
Passenger cars	4.4
Crude petroleum	3.2
Refined petroleum	4.2

In May 2017, post-Brexit customs system was 'costed'. The separate customs areas would use technology to reduce friction and costs at the border. This "max fac" could cost businesses £17-£20bn/yr. The Liechtenstein model would involve each collecting tariffs on its behalf the other, so declarations are not required for goods crossing the border. The cost could be £3.4bn/yr.

The UK car industry employs 169,000 directly with 78,000 in the supply chain. 52.6% of the 1.24m industry's exports go to Europe (see right). Cars are the most valuable exports globally, worth $697bn (4.4% of all exports). For the UK car industry, the prospect of Brexit and tariffs looms large. As can be seen above, vehicle parts are the 6th most valuable good. It is not final products that are the most concerning for the UK car industry.

Country	%
Japan	3.3
China	6.2
Other	9.2
US	17.9
Turkey	2.3
EU	52.6
Australia	2.1
South Korea	2.1
Canada	2.1
Russia	1.4
Switzerland	0.8

Britain's total goods or services exports to the EU fell from 54% in 2000 to 43% in 2016. But goods or services used in supply chains rose from 61% to 69% (in 2014). A Bentley SUV, built in Crewe, uses components that have travelled 2,200miles crossing the EU border 3 times. Bumpers are painted in Germany, made in the EU but in between are shipped to Crewe for inspection. The Delphi fuel injector, fabricated in Stonehouse using steel from Europe is shipped to Germany for heat treatment before returning for final assembly. It then is sold to truck-makers in Europe who install the injector exporting the finished vehicles back to Britain. 18 of the 20 largest vehicle components manufacturers have operations in the UK. Vendigital estimate that of the £15bn of material used in UK cars, £12bn come from overseas. ¼ of UK £150bn exports to Europe by value go via Calais, a port ill-suited for non-EU border checks. The number of UK customs officials in 2016 was around 5,000. An extra 5000 would cost £250m/yr. 4.5m heavy goods vehicles traversed Britain's border in 2015. Of these Dover saw 2.56m and the Channel Tunnel 1.64m. There were 30 staff at Dover in October 2017, dealing with 500 vehicles to and from non-EU countries. That will rise to 10,000/day. A lorry takes less than 2 minutes to board a ferry. Any slight delay e.g. adding 2 minutes to the process, would generate a 17 mile queue. Adding 6 mins would result in a M25-Dover queue. Manufacturing uses JIT/JIS which cannot cope with major delays at Dover or Calais.

It has been the case that DFI is invited in by the host to improve/ develop the industrial structure. The clustering of companies around an assembler's factory using JIT/ JIS techniques can alter the industrial and skills structure of the country/ region. The Nissan plant in Washington has left a major footprint on the local/regional economy of the North East of England. There are 5,000 directly employed by the plant. Through its first tier suppliers, a further 13,500 are dependent on it. Overall, one fifth of all

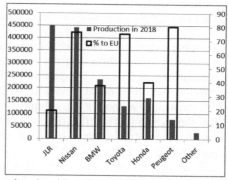

North Eastern manufacturing jobs are associated with Nissan. Nissan produced 507,430 vehicles in 2017 but 442,254 in 2018.

A letter sent to Nissan in October 2016 offered to ensure that its exports will be exempt from tariffs. This led to an investment promise. This was extended to other car markets. Indeed future investment plans were put on hold or are subject to guarantees form the UK government desperate to cover-up the true cost. Japanese car companies came to the UK as a base for European exports. 75% of Toyota's 180,000 cars are exported to the EU. Nissan has the same emphasis whereas Honda is less so. In January both Ford and JLR announced large redundancies: the latter 4,500 white on top of the 1500 blue collar jobs lost in 2018. On February 1st the EU-Japan FTA came into force. The world's biggest such deal covers nearly a third of global GDP and 635m people. The deal's headline is about eradicating duties on 97% and 99% of Japanese and European imports respectively. Almost immediately, Nissan switched the plan to produce the Q30 car and QX30 sports-utility vehicles from Washington to its Kyushu plant in Japan. Two weeks later Honda announced that it will close its only British car plant in

2021 with the loss of up to 3,500 jobs. The SMMT points to the sale of diesel cars in the UK tumbling by 30% in 2018.

WHAT IS MONEY?

Money is an indirect claim on assets. Money can be exchanged for a wide variety of other assets. It can itself be based on an underlying asset that has intrinsic value, such as a cow or a camel. Alternatively, it has little intrinsic value but users have faith in its value in exchange, such as a rock or a piece of paper. Mostly, it is guaranteed by the State (fiat currency) and has a single source of supply: the central banks, such as the Reserve Bank of India, hold the monopoly on producing this paper money within the borders of a Sovereign State. India scrapped the R500 ($7.60) and R1,000 notes in November 2016. The reason given was to reduce the size of the black economy (23.2% of GDP in 2007). As these represented 86% of India's cash supplies, this led to a cash shortage, reducing GDP growth by possibly 1.2%. The ratio of currency to GDP in India of 12.2% is higher than countries such as Russia (11.9%), Brazil (4.1%), and Mexico (5.7%), indicating the dependence on cash.

To some extent, money is what money does. Importantly, money can be seen as any asset that is *generally acceptable as a means of payment*. In effect, a trade or exchange process entails a swap. The parties sacrifice one set of things for another that should provide them with equal or greater utility. Money acts as a temporal intermediary in this exchange. Without it the volume of exchanges will be lower. As such, we presume that the most important function of money is that of being a *medium of exchange*. For money to act as an intermediate asset, there is an incompatibility between what the two parties to an exchange 'want.' One is willing to accept money on a temporary basis. This money is then exchanged with a third party for what is desired. There is a time delay between the exchanges. For money to facilitate the exchange process it must hold its value. If it did not, why accept money in exchange for goods when that money would be worth notably less in a short space of time. Thus, money must act *as a store of value* to make future purchases. Interestingly, cash withdrawals on Fridays are typically 5 to 6 times greater than other weekday nights.

A variant on this is the *standard of deferred payment*. Investments, where there are returns but over an extended period, are central to the growth process. The investments are funded by the sacrifice of current consumption, in favour of greater future consumption. If you purchase a bond, you want some notion of the benefits of such a sacrifice.

We presume that people make the best use of their endowed assets. To achieve that, they exchange one set of goods for another. Those choices are made on the basis of relative prices. That is, they need to know how many of good A is acquired compared with good B for a given endowment. Money provides that rank ordered set of prices. In other words, it provides a *unit of account.*

Cash is not disappearing but there are reasons to expect it to. Cash represents only 3.7% of GDP in the UK. Mobile phone apps and debit cards for the youngster are the norm. The older consumer may not trust banks and prefer cash. Millions of US residents do not have accounts. Criminals and the informal economy rely on cash. The total value of goods and services purchased in 2013 in the UK, according the BRC, was £191bn, up from £151bn in 2009. Cash made up 53% of the number of transactions but only 27% of the value of purchases. The average value of a cash transaction was £9.47. This is less than the £40.81 for credit cards. In May 2015, card overtook notes and coins for the first time: cash transactions by consumers and businesses stood at 48%. Transport for London stopped accepting cash payments on the London bus network in 2014, claiming this would save £24m/yr in handling costs.

Crises stimulate the holding of notes. In Greece in May 2015, cash in circulation was at €45.2bn, a level last seen in June 2012. The holding of larger denominations reflects the urge to hoard cash in the face of bail-ins and bank failures. Not wanting deposits, banks will penalise the retail consumer, encouraging them to hoard cash.

Barter is one of those standard market failures corrected by the facility of money. The double coincidence of wants makes barter inefficient. However, this double coincidence is an information thing. An increasing number online could being together those who could, through exchange, improve their well-being without the need for cash. In the poor areas there is a serious liquidity problem: barter is a poor substitute. Across 78 municipalities, the Asturian network of barter communities has 1,500 users. It creates digital money, equating a 'copin' with one Euro. The community network's platform enables users to barter directly, or to accumulate copins to spend on goods and services from others in the community.

When consumers lose faith in money they seek other means of exchange. The 57% inflation in Argentina has driven many to revert to barter clubs. These existed in previous crises of 2001-2002 and 2009. However, the double coincidence of wants problem is eased by Facebook. Trades before exchanging goods in person take places in places like the railway station. A chart posted on the San Miguel group's Facebook page outlines a points system for certain goods. A 1 kg (2 lb) pack of flour serves as the central currency or reference = 1 point or hypothetical value of 30 pesos. One bottle of sunflower oil = 2 pts. One cake = 4pts, and adult jeans = 3pts. Barter can lead to consumer surplus extraction so the Facebook recommended 'prices' seek to ensure fairness in trades.

Recently, the BoE reviewed the monetary system. It makes seven points:
1. Banks are more than financial intermediaries. Their liabilities are generally accepted means of payment (money). Bank deposits make up 97% of broad money.

2. The money multiplier is a myth; there is no strict relationship between money stock and bank deposits. Central banks can create reserves at will (e.g. QE). It supplies these reserves to banks if demanded and at a price.
3. Credit creation is based on risks and rewards. Banks will only lend if they see a profit in it and only take deposits accordingly. Borrowers cannot be made to borrow. If borrowers or lenders are more risk averse, lending drops.
4. The central bank can alter the returns that banks hold with it. As the bankers' bank, the central bank intermediates between the banks to facilitate settlements so all have accounts with the central bank. Each regulated bank is obliged to hold deposits with the central bank. It could, lending elsewhere, receive a higher return. Thus, market interest rates should be at a premium over bank deposit rates.
5. Lending can be influenced by other regulatory requirements, such as reserves and liquidity requirements. If, as is common, lending by banks is secured against an asset, this boosts its demand, and price, increasing the scope for more lending. This risk needs to be moderated with lending restrictions.
6. QE entails swapping bonds with bank reserves at the central bank. The money multiplier has been possibly zero, so QE has boosted bank reserves and also lowered yields across a range of assets.
7. Banks do not need to lend out their reserves, they can create loans without that need, by the stroke of a pen. Money is created at that point. It is destroyed when a debt is repaid. Credit easing, where corporate bonds are purchased, will cut out banks as intermediaries in the first instance, but the corporates will increase their deposits at the bank.

The Duel Currency
As a generally accepted medium of exchange, a dual currency has to provide the holder with additional returns compared with the primary coin. Examples include Lewes, Ambridge, Brixton, Totnes, Stroud, the Lake District and Lambeth. The multiplier effect is much reduced by leakages; monies leaving the locale. A local currency boosts the local multiplier. Ultimately, people need to be paid in the currency, particularly their salaries. Shops not only need to accept but be able to buy their produce from local suppliers using that currency. They should have work done on their business units by local artisans so, the currency allows for some indirect monitoring of the supply chain. A bank, acting as a key intermediary, needs to take deposits and issue loans. Local authorities have been key in the buy-in or the accepted aspect of the currency. If you can pay your local taxes in the local coin, you are more likely to accept the currency rather than pounds.

A credit card is not money. A credit card has no intrinsic value. What it offers the user is credit. Cash or even electronic money does not require the owner to forgo any future consumption to clear any debt, whereas credit must be repaid. But money is credit of a sort. Alfred Mitchell-Innes argued that money is a promissory note or IOU that circulates or is exchanged in a trade. A sale is an exchange of a commodity for a credit. Bills of exchange were the effective currency of Victorian Britain. When bank loans replaced bills, the notion of a credit note was lost. However, when banks create money they are creating a credit. March 4th 2018 election in Italy brought anti-establishment parties together who wanted to have tax cuts and aggressive spending. To pay for this the proposed issuing non-interest-bearing Treasury bills in branded as MiniBOTs. These would be printed, rather than electronic, using the State lottery's ticket presses – but it claim they are not money. This parallel currency may be accepted by customers as they can pay back the government, for example through taxes or fines. Shops may not be so willing. It was anticipated that there would be a market for them operating at a discount, whereby pensioners and state creditors lose say 10% of the value in exchange for €s. This would redistribute wealth from those on benefits to financiers. As a means of circumventing Article 106 (only the ECB can issue the €), if MiniBoTs are introduced on a large scale, political strains could eventually force either Italy or Germany out of the €.

MONETARY POLICY INSTRUMENTS

One of the Bank of England's two core purposes is monetary stability. Monetary stability means stable prices and confidence in the currency. Stable prices are defined by the Government's inflation target (of 2%), which the Bank seeks to meet through the decisions taken by the Monetary Policy Committee (MPC). Monetary policy in the UK usually operates through the price at which money is lent – the interest rate. In March 2009, the MPC announced that in addition to setting Bank Rate, it would start to inject money directly into the economy by purchasing financial assets – often known as quantitative easing (QE).

The Reserve Bank of India's roles are to operate the currency and credit system of the country to its advantage; to regulate the issue of Bank notes and keeping of reserves with a view to securing monetary stability in India and generally to operate the currency and credit system of the country to its advantage; to have a modern monetary policy framework to meet the challenge of an increasingly complex economy, to maintain price stability while keeping in mind the objective of growth. Norges Bank, the Norwegian central bank:-

* promotes price stability by means of monetary policy
* promotes financial stability and contribute to robust and efficient financial infrastructures and payment systems
* manages the portfolios of the GPFG and the bank's own foreign exchange reserves in an efficient and confidence-inspiring manner.

The South African the constitution, requires the Reserve Bank to protect the value of the currency in the interest of balanced and sustainable economic growth.

Monetary Policy as an Exchange Rate Policy.
The Central Bank of China's monetary policy objective is to maintain the stability of the value of the currency and thereby promote economic growth. Nationalbank, the central bank of Denmark, operate a peg of 746.038 DKr per €100 ± 2.25%. Denmark is the sole member of the ERM II.

A central bank may have a number of interest rates that it can manipulate. The deposit rate is what banks receive from deposits at the central bank. Some monetary authorities compel domestic banks to deposit a minimum amount, possibly under the heading of a *cash ratio*, related to the extent of the banks' deposits.

Bank Rate
Bank rate, or discount rate, is the rate of interest that a central bank charges on the loans and advances that it extends to commercial banks and other financial intermediaries. Changes in the bank rate are often used by central banks to control the money supply. Bank Rate is a long-term measure and is governed by the long-term monetary policies of the Central Bank concerned. NB. the **repo rate** is a short-term measure, i.e. applicable to short-term loans and used for controlling the amount of money in the money markets. In June 2018, India raised its Policy Repo Rate from 6 to 6.25% in response an April inflation rate of 4.58% and a projection 4.7% by 2019 which pushed the target 4 ±2%.

Reserve Ratio Requirement (RRR)
The reserve requirement is the minimum reserve each commercial bank must hold (rather than lend out) as a proportion of total customer deposits and notes. The reserve ratio (RR) can be used as an instrument, influencing the country's borrowing and interest rates, by changing the amount of loans available. The FED has not altered the RR for 20 years. The use of ratio requirements is more the domain of the developing nation with less sophisticated capital markets. The Philippine Central bank cut RRR by 2% from May to July 2019 releasing $3.62bn in liquidity.

Statutory Liquidity Ratio
Statutory Liquidity Ratio is the amount of approved liquid assets that a financial institution must maintain as reserves with the central bank. SLR Rate = the liabilities of the bank which are payable on demand, divided by those liabilities which are accruing in one month's time due to maturity. In May 2019, India's was 19%. The Swiss National Bank can require banks to hold up to 2.5% of their risk-weighted assets, in a buffer. This is preferable to raising interest rates, which would affect the value of the Franc.

Open Market Operations
Controlling the money supply in the West is more likely to rely on OMO as commercial banks work on low excess reserves. In the US, the FOMC manages the money supply, through OMO.

The Transmission between the Money and Real Economies
The rate of interest is seen as the price that has to be paid to persuade people to forego the advantage of holding money. It is the price that must be paid in order to overcome people's liquidity preference. As interest rates rise, as there is an opportunity cost from holding cash, people will hold less cash and visit the bank more often. Keynes was

interested in using the inverse relationship between bonds and interest rates. If a bond (e.g. Government Stock or Gilts) offered the owner a fixed sum of money per year regardless of what s/he paid for it, then the cheaper it is, the better the yield (or rate of return on the investment) for the owner. The price of the bond follows the laws of supply and demand. If consumers wish to buy more bonds, demand shifts to the right, the price rise and the yield falls. Keynes' model implied that there were two types of assets; money and bonds. The speculative demand will vary with expectations about future changes in interest rates. For example, if interest rates are high and bond prices are low, speculators, who expect interest rates to fall, will buy bonds. Speculators will hold cash if they anticipate a rise in interest rates i.e. an expected fall in bond prices should result in holding cash. Thus, the Money Demand schedule MD is downward sloping.

Indirect Transmission Mechanism
Keynes' indirect transmission mechanism entails increasing the Money Supply MS from MS_1 to MS_2 in the diagram below. With this additional cash in idle balances, speculators buy bonds. As the price of bonds rises, yields fall. As a yield is a rate of return, interest rates in the economy falls from i_1 to i_2. This *may* have an impact on the real economy.

For investment to be worthwhile, its rate of return must exceed the opportunity cost of investment (the rate of interest). Thus, as the interest rate falls, the level of planned investment will rise. There will be an increasing number of projects that yield a rate of return sufficient to cover the cost of capital. The relationship between the level of investment and the rate of return on investments is called the marginal efficiency of investment (MEI). This schedule is downward sloping. The fall in interest from i_1 to i_2, lowers the costs of borrowing leading to greater investment from I_1 to I_2. Investment is an injection into the circular flow of income. The aggregate demand schedule shifts to the right. Assuming some unemployment, greater output, employment and growth follow.

Liquidity Trap
A liquidity trap occurs when interest rates have reached, what is perceived as, their lowest level, i.e. where bond prices have attained their maximum level. Any purchase of bonds will result in a capital loss on irredeemable bonds, so speculators will hold cash. If the Money Supply schedule is to the right of

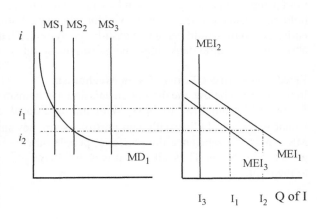

MS_3, an increase in the idle balances of speculators will NOT lead to an increase in demand for bonds and so no fall in interest rates. Money cannot influence the real economy in this liquidity trap.

Alternatively, when interest rate elasticity is zero so investment is insensitive to interest rates, as with MEI_2, a decrease in interest rates will not increase investment. Money cannot influence investment. Keynesians would not advocate the use of monetary policy in these cases. A third case entails the MEI shifting to the left to MEI_3 as quickly as interest rates fall. Consistent with a deep recession, economic conditions worsen as quickly as the cost of capital falls. Thus, investment does not increase despite falling interest rates.

Krugman, Gavyn Davies and Tim Congdon extended the notion of a liquidity trap. Krugman's trap is focused on changes in the price level of goods and services. Krugman posited that at zero short rates, unless monetary policy raises the expected rate of inflation, the real rate of interest precludes the full utilisation of resources. With low or negative inflationary expectations, consumers will withhold expenditure.

Davies tied the two together. He suggests a full liquidity trap has three crucial characteristics.
1. short rates should be (effectively) at zero;
2. bond yields should be at their lower limit in the risk/return sense;
3. the real economy should be operating below capacity because real interest rates, though very low, are stuck at levels that are too high to induce sufficient aggregate demand. Underlying inflation rates should therefore be declining.

Note:- the demand for money curve is predicated on a liquidity trap. As bond prices do not automatically have an upper bound, the trap cannot exist with negative nominal rates of interest rates. Does this mean that the money demand curve retains its negative slope at interest rates below zero? Keynes and Fisher assumed yes. But what sort of money? Gavyn Davies argues that if central banks pushed the yields on bank deposits too far into the negative zone, banks and eventually their customers would choose to hold cash instead of the negative yielding deposits. Ultimately, if pushed too far, the entire economy would become a cash-based system. That is, the real constraint on the ability of the central banks to set negative interest rates.

Friedman's Direct Transmission Mechanism
In the diagram below, the direct transmission mechanism entails increasing the Money Supply MS from MS_1 to MS_2. With this additional cash, people find their cash balances are out of kilter with their portfolio so money supply exceeds money demand MS > MD. To rebalance the portfolio, people purchase a range of assets, including goods and services. Thus, all asset prices rise. In the real economy, the AD curve shifts to the right.

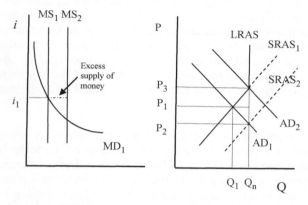

A deflationary gap can be analysed from the perspective of active or passive monetary policy. The economy is operating at Q_1, to the left of Q_n and below trend. In a neo-classical world, with flexible wages and prices the market wage must fall, which reduces the cost of labour and thus the SRAS shifts to the right to $SRAS_2$. Prices fall and, as a consequence, the level of aggregate demand increases. The money supply has not changed but there is movement to Q_n and the price level falls from P_1 to P_2.

With inflexible wages, as in Keynes' world, increasing the money supply could be a solution. The AD curve shifts to the right from AD_1 to AD_2. Price rises from P_1 to P_3 whilst output moves towards Q_n.

The Term Structure of Interest Rates

The yield curve plots the yields of similar-quality bonds against their time maturity periods. In a world of certainty the curve will reflect only liquidity preferences. As there is a greater likelihood that unforeseen events will undermine the investment, with uncertainty, a risk-averse investor needs to be offered a risk

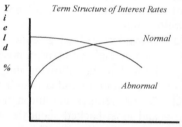

premium for holding a long-term investment, rather than a short.

The figure above shows a *normal* term structure with a higher rate offered to those more willing to lock their capital away in a bond with a longer period to maturity. In other words, in equilibrium, holders of long and short dated bonds have equal compensation, accounting for risk.

In the event that interest rates were expected to fall, where short term rates are higher than long, yield curve becomes inverted or 'abnormal.' Longer dated stocks are more exposed to uncertainty. Borrowing on a short term basis when interest rates are about to fall may be cheaper than if you borrow long. Inflation can play a significant role. Market sentiment suggests is a pending economic recession. It implies the yields offered by long-term fixed income bonds will fall in the future.

If inflation is expected in the future, holders of long dated stock must be compensated with higher returns. A steepening curve is associated with rising inflation expectations.

Commonly, this comes about due to a tightening labour market and stronger economic activity. Higher policy rates are anticipated. When the yield curve is steep, banks are able to borrow money at lower interest rates and lend at higher interest rates. Deflation implies the opposite. From December the, 2-year, 10-year Treasuries differential floated around 20bps, the lowest since just before the onset of recession in 2007. 10-year US Treasury [German Bund] yields in June 2019 were 2.1% [-0.2%] down from 3.3% [0.47%] in November 2018, indicative of a global slowdown and less expected inflation.

Work by Engstrom and Sharpe suggested that the traditional warning signs of recession (2-year to 10-year gap) may not be as powerful as analysis that focuses on shorter term rates. Rather, the yield curve around 3-month and 18-months served as a stronger predictor of recession in the coming year by capturing the market's conviction that the FED would need to cut rates soon in response to a slowdown. 18th March, the 3m-2y yield differential flipped.[8] At the beginning of May the 2y stood at 2.39% below the 10y @ 2.51% but also below the 3m @ 2.43%.

Over the recent past, economic policy instruments have appeared unfit for purpose. Some governments have resorted to developing unconventional methods for managing the economy. If one goes to the Reserve Bank of India's website, one can find a review of **Central Banks' Unconventional Policy Measures**. It suggests some of the following:-

❑ Quantitative Easing entails central banks buying all sorts of assets from commercial banks (as opposed to only gilts and highly rated paper). This should boost liquidity allowing the commercial banks more scope to lend. If the banks hoard liquidity rather than lending it, then this option will not work.

❑ Direct credit easing: through the purchase of commercial papers, corporate bonds and asset-backed securities the central bank could extend liquidity support to corporates directly. This is a means of avoiding using banks as an intermediary of monetary policy.

❑ Indirect (endogenous) easing entails expanding the size of the central bank's balance sheet by lending to banks at longer maturities, against collateral that includes assets whose markets are temporarily impaired. This option could widen the pool of collaterals that may be accepted by the central bank for refinancing operations.

❑ Forward guidance: in the zero lower bound interest rate era, the signal of a cut of rates was no longer possible. Guidance does not require a target, but that might help manage expectations. Credibility is everything here. Offering guidance which turns out not to be followed or fails to achieve any stated ends would devalue the usefulness of future statements. Guidance may matter less now zero is no longer the lower bound. Indeed, Swiss, Canadian, Singaporean, Swedish and Australian central banks all engaged in unpredictable interest rate policies in the

---

[8]https://www.treasury.gov/resource-center/data-chart-center/interest-rates/Pages/TextView.aspx?data=yieldYear&year=2019

first 4 months of 2015. In March 2018, the BoE was signalling an increase in interest rates. Economists and the market lined up behind that. Then, in the following April and May it changed tone, wrong footing the market, the way forward guidance should not.

❑ Twisting the yield curve entails targeting a certain period to maturity e.g. one associated with mortgages, to alter a key rate in the real economy. The degree of monetary stimulus is marked by the shape of the yield curve. The flatter yield curve, the greater the stimulus. This raises the price of long term bonds strengthening the bank balance sheet that owns them. The BoJ uses yield curve control, setting a target of 0% on 10-year government bond yields. Unfortunately, failing to achieve its 2% inflation target, after heavy printing, is leaving it with few options. Rather than raise inflation expectations, by capping long-term rates, Central Banks could lower them deterring current expenditure.

❑ Negative interest rates on offer at the central bank. This should act as a disincentive for high street lenders to leave their surplus with the central bank. This tack, introduced by the ECB in June 2014, entailed a cut its deposit rate from 0 to –0.10%.

❑ Helicopter money is a gift to all citizens from the central bank. This boosts the money supply. As QE persistently increases the money supply in the way OMO does not, one can see why it's viewed as the peoples' QE. It avoids banks and rich folk. However, to ensure the money is spent, it should be offered in the form of vouchers, with a limited life, so that it cannot be horded.

QE ARGUMENTS

As QE was tried, tested and amended, a number of explanations of the transmission mechanism emerged.

1. As a variant of OMO, QE improves bank liquidity. This should boost bank lending, putting money in to people's hands, so increase in nominal spending. Charlie Bean stated in 2010 that there was a need to get consumers to save less and spend more, (shifting the AD curve, right). This was achieved in 2017Q1 when the savings ratio at 3.7% was at its lowest annual level since 1963.

2. QE lowers interest rates. By purchasing bond prices across all maturities bond prices rise and yields fall, pushing down interest rates, which, through the indirect transmission mechanism should boost investment. A variant on this is Yield curve control and Operation Twist, where a particular interest rate is targeted, which affects the well-being of mortgagers. By reducing the likelihood of default, this helps the solvency of banks: by reducing the servicing of mortgages, this could boost spending.

3. QE boosts asset prices.

   a. From the direct transmission mechanism, the excess of cash holdings will cause an imbalance in a portfolio. Asset prices will rise as agents to rebalance their portfolio, shifting their asset holding away from and cash to shares, gold, commodities and goods and services. Thus, the AD shifts. The

BoE found that the rise in asset prices favoured the top 5% that hold 40% of the UK's personal assets. The richest 20% save ⅓ of their income and contribute 40% of all consumer expenditure. QE is the basis for huge inequalities.

b.   From a permanent income perspective, permanent consumption is based on wealth. An increase in wealth due to a rise in asset prices will lead to an increase in consumption. So asset price increases should raise demand in the economy for goods and services.

c.   As the asset rises in value, the family home provides a greater unit of collateral against which more borrowing can be made.

4.   QE lowers returns on investment grade assets. Investors turn to higher yield corporate bonds and equities. So companies can raise record levels of capital at a low cost. Henkel ($500m-2yr) and Sanofi (€1bn-3yr) issued debt at negative yields (-0.05%) in September 2016, the first corporates to do so in Euros. Even if the companies do not invest, this cheap debt improves their chances of survival. Banks also benefit. With fewer failures banks are less exposed to corporate debt defaults. Share buy-backs are driving up stock exchange and CEO remuneration. More worryingly, from a competition perspective QQE was funding Japanese banks taking over regional competitors. This trend is not so welcome.

5.   QE is a means of helping banks switch bad assets with good and build up reserves to improve their solvency. QE entails buying up corporate debt, some of which may have a lowish credit rating. This socialises the risk of failure, lowering the cost of borrowing. The IMF estimated that systemically important banks, too important to fail, received an implicit subsidy of $150-590bn. The subsidy is imputed from the cost of borrowing that the largest banks enjoy that would be bailed-out; specifically, the costs of insuring against default, plus credit rating. The breakdown by country was:

a.   US $15-70bn, 15bp lower interest rate costs

b.   Japan $25-110bn 25-60bps

c.   UK $20-110bn 20-60bps

d.   Eurozone $90-300bn 60-90bps

The NY FED estimated that each bond sale for the largest US banks was $60-80m cheaper over smaller ones.

6.   QE lowers the external value of the currency - boosting exports. This is not an explicit policy but has supporting benefits, closing output gaps, increasing inflation and employment. However, Brazil was most vexed about US QE, claiming that the world was in a midst of a currency war. Moreover, it caused major difficulties with the management of the Hong Kong dollar in April 2018. Since Dec 2004 it has operated a currency board, with a peg to the US$ at HK$7.80±5.

7.   An increase in money supply should raise price expectations and encourage consumption today rather than tomorrow. QE affects financial asset prices quickly, but goods and services are sluggish. Janet Yellen doubted whether a policy based purely on shifting expectations could ever work. Long-run inflation expectations become anchored at a particular level only after the actual rate has

been stable at a level beforehand. Sadly, as with the MTFS, another expectations dependent theory, expectations rise only if consumers believe in the model.

Alan Blinder and Mark Zandi for the US Centre on Budget and Policy Priorities find that without the fiscal stimulus, QE and the financial policies that resulted in a quickly recapitalised banking system:

- the US economy would have shrunk by 1000bps greater than the 4% recession in the US;
- twice as many people would have lost their jobs, and the unemployment rate would have been 600bps higher than the 10%;
- the federal budget deficit could have reached $2.8tn (20% of GDP);
- the recovery would have been slower, too. By 2011, the policies ensured that output was 1600bps higher than the crisis trend.

The BoE estimated that without QE GDP would be 8% lower and unemployment would have peaked 4% higher (12%). Cumulatively, over 2008-2012, incomes were 20% higher worth £23,000 to each household.

One might argue that the QE orthodoxy misses the main point. Japan lost two decades to stagnant growth and the BoJ is still seeking to buy up bonds.

- Greenspan, the former FED chair, suggested a Minsky thesis that a prolonged period of stability is a necessary and sufficient condition for an asset price bubble. Agents become used to a low risk environment, encouraging more reckless behaviour. QE weakens normal market disciplines.
- QE socialises the higher risk non-sovereign bonds, which may push up borrowing costs to other (European) nations.
- Banks lost interest in customer savings.
- Low interest rates, rather than an ageing population, precipitated a pensions' crisis.
- The preservation of *zombie companies* locks resources in to slow growing companies, slowing productivity growth. In the UK, R3 reported the number of zombies (which are not paying the principal on their loans) had fallen from 160,000 in November 2012 to 102,000 in August 2013. Begbies Traynor, using a broader definition, put the number at 432,000. These figures emerged as RBS was criticised for forcing viable companies into receivership. The BoE found that the largest 5 banks were offering forbearance on: 14% of loans to SMEs; 5 to 8% of secured household loans; 28% of leveraged loans; and 35% of commercial property loans. However, not all members of each group take out a loan: the 14% of SME zombie loans apply to only 6% of SMEs.
- Between 2007 and 2015, public investment in the Eurozone fell by around €20bn when €3tn of sovereign debt was issued. In the Eurozone plus the US, total non-finance sector debt increased from 225% of GDP to 250% but with tepid growth in output or wages.

The International Monetary Fund's Fiscal Monitor shows that the advanced countries' gross general government debt rose from 92% of GDP in 2009 to 106% in 2015. With the notable exception of Germany, all the big economies saw significant increases in government debt. Those most committed to austerity were among the least successful in preventing debt from rising, despite tightening budgetary policy. This was most notably true of the UK. Between 2009 and 2015, its gross general government debt rose at nearly double the rate of the Eurozone and much faster than the US or Japan. This affects credit ratings. All the ratings agencies downgraded UK government debt in July 2016 following the Brexit vote, including S&P which was the last of the AAA ratings for the UK. In 2015, Finland dropped out of the list of those with all three agencies assessing sovereign debt at AAA. In theory, this would put up government borrowing costs but as the central bank is the major purchaser and the interest rate is very low, this is not an issue. In 2016H1, Fitch (14), S&P (16) and Moody's (24) downgraded sovereigns at the highest rate since 2011. Fitch pointed to lower commodity prices affecting Middle East and Africa. Moody's was fined €1.2m by the European Securities and Markets Authority in June 2017 over a lack of transparency over their rating methods.

After a decade of QE, Swiss, Swedish, UK, central banks the FED, BoJ and the ECB held $15tn in debt, of which $9tn is sovereign debt. ECB $4.9tn, BoJ $4.53tn, and FED $4.47tn. Of the total sovereign debt of $46tn, these 6 hold 20% of it. In 2008, there was $25tn. This exposes central banks to interest rate rises. 40% of developed nations' sovereign debt is to be refinanced by 2021. In June 2018, the concern was both the FED and the ECB unwinding their balance sheets causing a liquidity crisis. The Treasury needs to sell $2.34tn in bonds by 2020, sucking $1tn out of the system.

Beyond refinancing, Portugal (€7.2bn), Ireland (€15bn) and Italy (€150bn) have a high exposure to Euribor, floating interest rates. There is €150tn worth of debt tied to this floating interest rate. A variant on Libor, it is to be replaced by 2020.

MONETARY POLICY 2019

Monetary policy has been marked by a shift away from central bank independence. This threatens a cornerstone of anti-inflationary policy. It could be viewed that there is no inflationary threat. Moreover, the QE that followed the 2008 crisis has favoured an asset-rich elite. House prices since 2010 have increase in real terms by 20% in the US while wages grew by 6% and the stock market has doubled. Wealth inequalities are widening. In June 2019, the FED held a conference on Monetary Policy targeting. Aiming for 2% inflation since 2012, with some flexibility over unemployment, its forward guidance was unhelpful indicating increases in 2018 and then cuts in 2019. Like Japan inflation is generally below target. Like Japan, there is an issue over whether it can deliver. Alternatives may assuage critics. Price-level targeting, entails picking a future price level to target. The BoE picked a rate of unemployment in 2013, which it met too early and abandoned it as an indicator for tightening the policy. Average inflation targeting entails aiming for inflation to average {2%} over a given period, allowing inflation to run above target during periods of strong economic growth to offset times when prices are weak. Targeting of nominal gross domestic

*product, [NGDP] combines both growth and inflation. A target of 4% could equal 0%
real growth and 4% inflation –2% above the current target.*

India

In January, the Indian Parliamentary Committee on Finance requested RBI to ease its
rules on capital requirements for banks so that they can increase lending. In December,
former governor Urjit Patel resigned over pressure over the same issue. The RBI was
preoccupied with a liquidity scare arising from a series of debt defaults by
Infrastructure Leasing & Financial Services (IL&FS) that sparked redemption pressure
at other shadow banking companies. Indian banks needed nearly $65bn in new bank
capital by March to meet regulatory requirements.

In February, the RBI reduced the repo rate by 0.25% to 6.25%, first reduction since
August 2017. The reverse repo rate has also decreased to 6.00% from 6.25% and the
Marginal Standing Facility Rate (MSF) and the Bank Rate has decreased by 25bp to
6.50%.The MPC lowered the repo rate again by 50bps to 5.75% across April and June.

Chinese Monetary Policy

As the trade war began hotting-up the PBoC decreased the RRR in April 2018 by 1%
from 17% for large and 15% for smaller banks. In July, a further 0.5% cut would boost
the money stock by $77bn+$31bn. Later that month China announced a fiscal stimulus
package of infrastructure projects and tax cuts for corporates, including $953m for
R&D. In October, the cuts were again 1%, injecting a net 750bn yuan ($109.2 billion)
in cash into the banking system = 1.2tn yuan minus 450bn maturing medium-term
lending facility (MLF) loans. In June 0.5tn yuan minus 463bn maturing debt pumped
more liquidity in to the market. This followed the failure of Inner Mongolia-based
Baoshang Bank on May 24th. In January, RRR was reduced by a full percentage point,
taking the ratio down to 16%. In May, there were staged cuts in RRR from 10-11.5%
for some small and medium-sized banks.

UK

The BoE raised the repo rate from 0.5% to 0.75%, the highest level since March 2009
and the second increase in a decade.

Japanese Monetary Policy

The PM of Japan, Abe, has claimed there are three arrows aimed at economic policy:
fiscal, monetary and industrial reform. His monetary policy has entailed the following:
1. Inflation targeting. In February 2012, the target was 1%, which was *raised* in
   January 2013 to 2%. There cannot be many economies raising their inflation
   target.
2. Asset purchase programme. In July 2016, BoJ doubled its annual purchase of
   exchange traded funds to ¥6tn. In September, the BoJ announced that it would
   continue buying bonds at ¥80tn/ year. Dubbed yield curve control (YCC), it is a
   new kind of monetary easing as it set a cap on 10-year bond yields at zero and

vowed to overshoot its 2% inflation target on purpose. In effect, this is unlimited money printing.

3. In January 2016, Japan adopted a Negative Interest Rate Policy of a –0.1% deposit rate. This, in part, was an exchange rate policy also.
4. In April 2018, it removed any time frame around the 2% target, having shifted it 6 times.
5. In July 2018 it allowed bond yields to move more flexibly around its target. It slowed its bond buying to less than half the amount it loosely pledges to buy each year, as its dominance in the market allows it to cap yields with fewer purchases.

After more than five years of QQE the BoJ, in August signalled the 2% target for inflation was not achievable. At the beginning of July the BoJ found from its tankan survey consumer prices expectations to be 1.1%/yr over the next 5 years. The BoJ cut their projection for core consumer price growth the fiscal year 18/19 from 1.3% projected in April 2018 to 1%. The following year, core inflation was 0.3% below the expected 1.8% despite unlimited money supply increases. An index of residents' livelihoods measuring households' confidence in current economic conditions improved from -12.4 in March, to -9.9 in July, but remained in negative territory. With 1.63 vacancies for each applicant, Japan is at over full employment – perhaps a 1% inflation target is more sensible.

US

Having appointed Jay Powell, a businessman to be FED chair in late 2018, Donald Trump demanded the FED stop raising interest rates. The FED raised the repo rate by ¼% to 2.5%, fourth increase in 2018. It also stated it would continue to reduce its balance sheet by $50bn/month, prompting Trump to nominate former campaign aide and conservative commentator Stephen Moore for a seat on the FED board. That threatens to inject politics into the heart of the central bank.

European Monetary Initiatives

The ECB began buying government bonds in March 2015, initially at a rate of €60bn/month. A year later this was raised to €80bn. By September 2016, the ECB had purchased €1tn in bonds. The signal in 2017 was to taper to €60bn until Dec 2017. In December, it announced further tapering to €30bn. In June 2018 it announced that it would not buy bonds from December. Price expectations stood at 1.2414%, a record low. In March, targeted longer-term refinancing operations (TLTRO-III) was announced. Starting in September 2019 and ending in March 2021, the aim is to preserve favourable bank lending conditions for small and medium-sized banks

South Africa

The SARB has used an inflation-targeting framework since 2000, with a range of 4.5%±1.5%. In June 2017 the Reserve Bank took legal action against a change of its mandate from protecting value of the Rand to 'meaningful socio-economic transformation.' In June 2019, SA Communist Party claimed that be expanded to explicitly include job creation, forcing the Reserve Bank governor to reiterate that price stability is the goal.

Others

Due to unexpectedly low inflation Egypt's central bank cut key interest rates in mid-February. This shift was in line with other developing economies. The Georgian, Paraguayan, Jamaican, Kyrgyzstani and Indian regulators lowered key interest rates by 25bps on March 13, 22, 19 February 26, April 4 respectively. The Nigerian the central bank cut its benchmark interest rate by 0.5% on March 26. By contrast, the Pakistani central bank raised its rate to 10.75% on March 29, citing continuing inflationary pressures and a high fiscal and current account deficit. Policymakers in Tunisia raised the key interest rate by 1% to combat high inflation.

NEGATIVE INTEREST RATES

There have been over 700 reductions of interest rates since the Lehman's collapse around the world but this has not secured a recovery. The BoE's Andrew Haldane suggests that these are the lowest real interest rates for 5,000 years.

Negative interest rates on deposits in the bank are a charge on saving. Negative interest rates are a concern on a number of levels. In a sense, negative interest rates have been with us for years. Real rates have been negative without causing unusual outcomes. The financial markets were imperfect and there were heavy regulations over retail borrowing. What is new is that following the Swiss, Swedish, Danish and ECB policy changes, nominal rates of interest rates from January 2016 for debt became negative. Issues:-

❑ In [old] theory, there is a lower bound with a liquidity trap to nominal rates so that a bond purchaser, at that bound, would only make a loss so monetary policy becomes impotent. If buyers believe that interest rates *can* go lower, then they might buy what appears to be an over-priced bond. So is there a liquidity trap any more? Perhaps yes. It was suggested that the Swiss lower bound could close to − 0.75%, but this is not clear.

❑ An interest rate regulates the time-preference of consumption. A positive rate encourages a consumer to forgo current consumption for greater future consumption. Investment is, in effect, future consumption – so saving is converted to investment today for consumption tomorrow. A negative interest signals that today's consumption is too little and this needs to be rebalanced.

❑ Using DCF/NPV criteria, low interest rates should foster longer term projects. From a MEI perspective, the economy should benefit from more investment. An excess of investment in production could be deflationary, driving up output and prices down.

❑ A negative interest rate can imply that the borrower is paid for borrowing. Nationalbanken in Denmark reduced its deposit rate, so did Danske Bank. Lending to Eva Christiansen at –0.0172, the borrower would *receive* interest per month of 7DKr. Sadly, there will be arrangement fees that will off-set this income stream but still, Eva is the first to receive a reward like this for borrowing. Anyway, Swiss domestic lending rates went up, not down.

- ❑ With deflation, the real value of loans increases over time.
- ❑ Before 2008, many current bank accounts entailed charges for their use. Negative rates act as a charge for using the bank to store your money. In effect, it is a *Gesell tax*; a tax on sight deposits. As deposits present an opportunity cost, this puts interest rates into the same category as inflation, so there should be a shift in portfolio structures:-
  - o As with inflation, consumers will convert cash into goods. There should be an increase in the velocity of money, V ($MV = PT$).
  - o Consumers will prefer holding cash, so there will be an increase in cash holdings.
  - o Gavyn Davies argued that if central banks pushed the yields on bank deposits too far into the negative zone, the entire economy would become a cash-based system.
  - o Businesses prefer holding assets that hedge against price rises.
  - o Smaller banks in Germany had imposed a Gesell tax. In Skatbank in 2014 and the co-op bank in Gmund am Tegernsss in September 2016 imposed a 0.4% tariff on large deposits. By August 2017, 20% of German companies had been threatened with this tax but only a tenth of those actually paid it.
- ❑ Large depositors, such as banks, may prefer paying a *Gesell tax* to other outcomes, particularly the non-repayment of loans. In 2014Q2, the US non-financial sector (corporates) held $2.58tn in cash and money market funds. This was up from $2.3tn in 2009. Fears that are most acute include:-
  - o The UK breaking up following an exit from Europe
  - o The Ukrainian crisis getting worse – Russian disruption of Brexit and Trump elections
  - o There is a financial crisis ahead in either housing or commercial property
- ❑ Negative rates may be deployed for differing reasons. A lack of lending presents a coordination problem. Some customers are likely to default on existing debt. Lower (negative) rates reduce that risk. To off-set deflation Sweden (repo rate) and the ECB (deposit rate) use negative rates. But… QE is causing Denmark and Switzerland exchange rate pressures. Negative interest rates discourage investors from buying the DKr and SFr.
- ❑ However… in a time of deflation the real value of money rises. As interest rates tend to shadow prices, falling prices can off-set negative interest rates.
- ❑ However… the combination of falling prices and rising exchange rates may mean that buying Swiss debt at negative nominal rates still generates a positive yield. A Polish 3 year bond, on offer in SFr @ –0.213%, would be attractive if the Swiss deposit rate was –0.75%.
- ❑ An interest rate is both a rationing and a signalling device. The criticism from Capitol Hill was that US forward guidance was unpredictable for financial markets. The demand was for [Taylor] rules-based monetary policy. A bill before the house could enforce this demand. Guidance has moved away from guidance to a pledge. Once the FED put interest rates up, what next? Under Greenspan and Yellen, ¼-point increases followed steadily. Powell is threatened by Trump.

❏ The setting of a low rate of interest should discourage savings. In theory, the fall in deposit rate should drive savers' and borrowers' rates in to negative territory. However, central banks will not want banks to pay people to borrow. This will be rather destablising for the banks. Indeed, the central banks were not making statements about passing these changes on to customers.

❏ Negative interest rates could also be seen as a punishment. The banks prospered whilst the rest suffered during the recession that they caused. Now negative interest rates are an ideal tool. Without negative savings rates, the banks must absorb the pain. The pain for a 0.25% reduction in repo rate is 2-3% of bank earnings. A Gesell tax of €7.5bn/yr.

❏ Lower bond yields reduce the tax payer's liabilities, shifting wealth from global investors to governments keen to reduce their debt ratios. Fitch estimated that in July 2016 across 34 countries with nearly $13.2tn [out of a total of $34tn] debt with a negative yield, annual interest on sovereign debt was reduced by $500bn/yr compared with 2011. So a 10-year bond in 2011 would yield 3.87% in 2011 and 1.17% in 2016 at the median. For Japan this amounts to $95bn/yr and Germany, the UK and the US combined $104bn.

But what if borrowing, not saving was the source of funds? Borrowing at low rates would lead to an over, not under investment. One such investment is in corporate debt. It has been reported that the biggest buyers of shares in the US market have been not real investors but companies buying-back their own shares with cheap, borrowed debt. McKinsey estimated that global corporate debt has more than doubled from 26% to 56% of GDP. One by-product of this is over-valued shares. Moreover, around ¼ of dollar denominated corporate bonds were issued by non-US firms. Emerging markets had issued around $4.5tn in dollar denominated debt: an increase of 100% in five years.

Lending institutions, such as those in the leasing sector, upon which Japan's SMEs rely on for liquidity, are squeezed. The Japan Lending Association provided funds equivalent to 7% of Japanese GDP in 2015. For the year to August 2016, volume was down 10.6%, an outcome of the negative interest rate policy but the opposite objective.

Pensions and Penalties
Some major institutions are obliged to buy government debt for reserve purposes, such as banks. But there is a key reason, these bonds are liquid and are preferable to holding cash in the vault or cash with the central bank – which earns a negative return.

McKinsey Global Institute considered the implications of low returns among lenders and borrowers. Net debtors, such as the State and non-financial corporations, have gained whereas net creditors, such as insurance companies, pension providers and households, lose. The Institute estimated that the UK government benefited by £120bn whereas UK households had lost £110bn. Due to low interest payments, profits of non-financial corporations have risen by 20%, *but then black holes in pensions schemes have emerged.* Why? Income in perpetuity – or until you die is related to interest rates. As rates fall, the capital sum that is required to meet the obligations rises, so more capital has to be put aside by the fund managers for this.

The BIS suggests that low long term interest rates may be a function of insurance companies covering their liabilities and the risk of falling yield in the future. They had to buy bonds, lowering yields. Yields have been too low for too long, crucifying pensions.

Final salary schemes are, therefore, a large problem. Blackrock, the fix interest rate bond trader, pointed out that negative interest rates affected savers, particularly those preparing for retirement. A typical 35 year old has to save over $3\times$ as much to have the same retirement income if rates are 2% compared with 5%. Hymans Roberts estimated that total pension deficits of UK companies over the past 15 years have risen from £250bn to about £900bn despite £500bn being injected in to them.

The collapse of Tata Steel shone a light on British Steel's £485m pension deficit. The fund, worth £15bn covers 130,000 members (85,000 retired + 45,000 to retire), would go with the sale of the steel interests. This was the key issue. The Pension Protection Fund, set up to support funds in this position would have its reserves wiped out. It was estimated that if loss of the pension fund was 5% that would amount to the loss £750m, double the previous loss the protection scheme has to deal with. BHS went down with a £591m pension black hole soon after. In June 2017, the Hoover pension scheme went into the Pension Protection Fund. Those under retirement age would receive an immediate 10% cut in their pension pot and those already retired, would receive less. The Hoover scheme has a deficit of about £250m with the scheme's liabilities around £500m (just below BHS's). Hoover Candy stopped producing washing machines in Merthyr Tydfil in 2009, but a head office and a distribution warehouse remained. Of the 7,800 members, 5,319 are pensioners and 2,184 who have deferred their pensions. Pensions' liabilities are now a severe impediment to corporate rescues.

The same lump sum problem applies to NHS medical negligence claims. They present a significant cost (£4.5bn over the past five years). But the lump sums that should provide set incomes for the lifetime of the patient-claimants must increase as the interest rate decreases.

EXCHANGE RATES

The implicit idea in textbooks is that most exchange rate dealings relate to economic fundamentals, but De Grauwe suggests that this is a misconception. According to BIS, in 2007, daily trades in FX were worth $3.2trn. This was up by 71% from 2004. International trade did not increase by 71% in 3 years. The breakdown of trades is as follows: spot (for immediate delivery) makes up ⅓; forwards 11% and the rest are swaps. In other words, FX trades are largely OTC (bilateral deals), not based on auction prices. By April 2016, turnover/day of foreign exchange was valued at $5.067tn, down from 2013. The US £ making up almost 44% of trades.

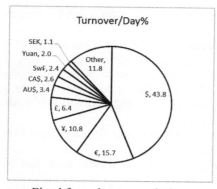

Turnover/Day%

SEK, 1.1
Yuan, 2.0
SwF, 2.4
CA$, 2.6
AU$, 3.4
£, 6.4
¥, 10.8
€, 15.7
Other, 11.8
$, 43.8

It is also normal for textbooks to talk about two [extreme] forms of exchange rate regime: fixed and floating. But, as the IMF observes, there are a variety of fixed forms:

- Float
- Intermediate – soft peg or managed float (Managed or dirty float – no predefined management rate; Crawling bands - predefined band movements; Crawling peg – predefined movement; Horizontal bands – predefined bands; Adjustable peg – predefined rate)
- Fixed for unknown period
- Hard Peg – currency unions, currency boards, dollarisation.

The distinction between 'pegged' and 'fixed' rates lies in the adjustment system. A fixed rate is one where intervention in the exchange market is allowed to affect the money supply. If a country runs a BoP surplus, the central bank has to intervene in the Foreign Exchange (ForEx) markets to prevent its currency from appreciating. In exchanging domestic for foreign currency, the increased supply of domestic coinage swells the reserves of the banking system and increases domestic expenditure. This leads to an increased demand for imports and, hence, correcting the surplus, automatically. Thus, a fixed exchange rate system is a monetary rule that contains a self-adjusting equilibrating mechanism of the BoP.

A pegged rate is an arrangement whereby the central bank intervenes in the exchange market to peg the exchange rate but still keeps an 'independent' monetary policy. If a country runs a BoP surplus, the central bank has to intervene in the ForEx as before. To neutralize the monetary effects of intervention, the central bank sells an equal quantity of domestic assets (say government bonds), cancelling the effects of the money supply. To maintain an independent monetary policy it may offset the monetary effects of intervention in the exchange market by sterilization operations.

Convertibility is a unilateral fix. The degree of convertibility is the ease with which a country's currency can be converted into gold or another currency. Non-convertibility implies a barrier to international trade. Government restrictions can often result in a currency with low convertibility. For example, a government with low reserves of hard foreign currency often restricts currency convertibility because the government would not be in a position to intervene in the foreign exchange market (i.e. revalue, devalue) to support their own currency if and when necessary.

Fischer (2001) suggested that, with open, small economies, an adjustable peg as an exchange rate regime choice is not sustainable. A shift to a harder peg is the trend. Prophetically, Fischer notes that, when borrowing in a foreign currency, lulled by a stable regime, investors reduce their perceptions of risk. When the crisis does come it is exceptionally damaging for the banking system. Poeck *et al.* (2007) divide currency crises into three groups:-

1. weak fundamentals based on excessive expansion of credit. Speculation of a devaluation follows a fall in interest rates and an outflow of reserves;
2. self-fulfilling expectations with multiple equilibria. Central banks fulfil the expectations of speculators and devalue, following a loss of confidence. There is no one equilibrium exchange rate. The current one is abandoned when the costs of maintaining it outweigh the costs of deserting it;
3. beyond weak fundamentals, a weak banking sector and poor financial regulation leading to moral hazard and over-indebtedness abroad.

Importantly, when internal objectives outweigh external the central bank has an incentive to devalue.

A currency board demonstrated a higher level of commitment to monetary rectitude than a pegged rate. The characteristics of a currency board are:

- A fixed exchange rate – tied to one other or to a basket;
- Monetary base can expand to no more than 100% of the foreign currency reserves;
- It precludes any lender-of-last-resort facility. The lack of a lender-of-last-resort facility makes the banking sector more vulnerable to a confidence crisis;
- Loss of monetary policy;
- Cannot use the exchange rate for BoP adjustment.

Estonia, Lithuania, Bosnia, and Bulgaria all established currency board-like systems from 1992 to 1997. QE, reducing the interest rate to zero and printing money, is not possible under a currency board regime. If hard-wired to a currency engaged in QE, the economy may suffer grievously. The central bank would have to absorb additional foreign currency, with potentially inflationary consequences. Alternatively, when bonded to an appreciating currency, the impact of higher interest rates etc. could lead to a recession and a potential speculative hot money outflow, which must be neutralised.

The characteristics of Dollarisation/ Currency Union are like those of a currency board, but by taking another country's currency, the domestic central bank cannot print money. Examples include Ecuador ($), Kosovo and Montenegro (€) (without permission). Scotland could be in this position.

Long Run Trade Deficit
At the end of 2016 the UK faced a 5.9% current account deficit, the greatest level since 1948. It is also experiencing a drop on external investments that it is paying to foreign investors in the country. The ONS explained that this is due to rates of return being better in the UK than elsewhere. The decline in FDI credits since 2011 has been entirely driven by a fall in the rate of return UK investors achieved on their overseas investments. In contrast, increases in FDI debits have been due to increased investment. This suggests that the current account deficit is increasing because the UK economy offers better rates of return than others. Thus, Carney argued that the UK was relying on the kindness of strangers (overseas investors). However, an alternative view

is that, much like Japan, the UK can dispose of foreign assets. Between 2012 and 2016 there was a net outflow of foreign investment of £82bn. However, UK investors divested £526bn in foreign assets. As UK investors hold overseas assets worth 420% of GDP the UK can continue on its current path.

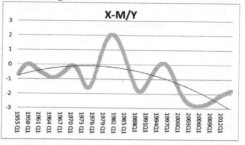

The diagram above shows the net exports divided by GDP filtered to remove the cyclical/erratic elements. The long run appears worrisome with a general decline from the 1980s despite the UK's holding of overseas assets. A widening external deficit also makes it harder to close the fiscal deficit, since the domestic private sector (households and/or companies) must run larger deficits to compensate.

Exchange Rate Diagrams
The free market forces of demand and supply determine floating Exchange Rates. Since one country's residents, say those of the US, demands the currency of another's on the foreign exchange market, say the UK's, it follows that demand for US$s implies supply of Sterling and supply of £s suggests a need for $s. Assuming costless trading, if the exchange rate is £1 = $2, then a TV in UK priced at £150 sells for $300 in the USA and a US fridge price $400 sells for £200 in UK.

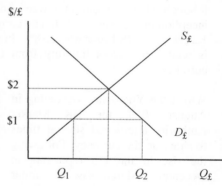

The diagram right reflects the workings of the foreign exchange market for Sterling (£) and US Dollars $. The supply curve slopes upwards as UK residents supply MORE £s to buy MORE US goods when they appear cheaper to them, i.e. when a £ buys more $s. The demand curve for Sterling slopes downwards as US residents will demand £s to buy more British goods when they appear cheaper to them, i.e. when a $ buys more £s. The equilibrium exchange rate occurs where the demand and supply for Sterling is equal, i.e. at $2/£. If the exchange rate was at $1/£, the *Balance of Payments* will be in surplus (excess demand for Sterling on the foreign exchange market of $Q_2 - Q_1$).

A rise in disposable income among UK residents will increase the demand for US exports, i.e. the supply curve for Sterling on the foreign exchange market shifts to the right (to $S_£^2$). The consequence for the exchange rate is a decrease from £1 = $2 to £1 = $1 in the diagram below.

The depreciation in the value of the £ makes imports relatively dearer and exports relatively cheaper. The UK TV sells for $150 in USA. The US fridge sells for £400 in UK. If the £ buys more foreign currency, the £ is said to have appreciated.

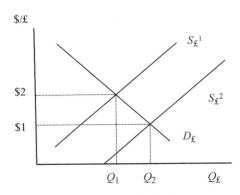

Fixed Exchange Rates
The rules of the Hong Kong currency board peg require the Hong Kong Monetary Authority to use its reserves to buy the currency once it hits the lower limit of the HK$7.75 to HK$7.85 band against the US dollar. In April 2018, it slumped as low as HK$7.85. Hong Kong is the world's least affordable housing market. House prices rose nearly 13% over the past year, and 146% over the past decade. About 90% of mortgages in Hong Kong are linked to Hibor, the local interbank rate.

HK shows the links between internal and external changes in the interest rate. Purchasing HK$ would remove some excess liquidity from the financial system (QE from China), lifting local short-term interest rates and making the currency more attractive to hold. Raising interest rates directly would hurt (slow) the property market. In the event, the HKMA raised its base rate by 0.25% to 2%. When this failed to work, it bought HK$51.33bn in the week from the 12th April, the first interception since its inception in December 1984. The currency climbed to 7.8498 and 3m Hibor stood at 1.21% when US Libor was 2.38%. In principle, one should track to other but the gap is related to excess liquidity from Chinese investments, putting pressure on the currency.

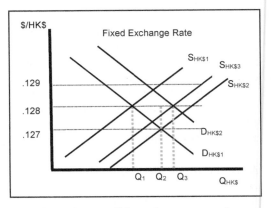

Whilst the Yuan was weakening in August 2018, the HK Market Authority intervened several times to shore up the currency. Following the rise in the US repo rate in December, March saw a similar defence, spending $2bn to maintain the rate.

In the diagram right is an analysis. Note that central rate (peg) of 7.8:$ is the same as one HK$ buying @ 0.128 US$. There is than an upper (.129) and lower (.127) rate. The rate slumped to .127, possibly on better rates of return in the US. To increase demand (demand curve right from $D_{HK\$1}$ to $D_{HK\$2}$) first interest rates were raised and then the authority bought currency. Note that because interest rates rose, the supply curve should shift left. Mortgage costs should diminish disposable income, reducing the demand for imports. Thus, if these policies moved the currency back to peg, equilibrium would be at Q3 where S_{HKS3} intersects with D_{HKS2}.

Venezuela
In January 2011, the Venezuelan Bolívar was devalued. Venezuela had three exchange rates.
1.   The DIPRO rate of the Bolívar was devalued from 2.15 to 2.6 to the Dollar. This rate was reserved for necessities like foods and medicines.
2.   The Oil rate was pegged at 4.3Bvrs:$ for non-essentials.
3.   The parallel or black market rate which was over 6Bvrs:$ but would be managed officially by the central bank.

In February 2013, the official fixed exchange rate of 4.3 bolívars to the $ was repegged to 6.3 bolívars. It still might be over-valued with an estimated 9 bolivars: $ as an 'equilibrium' exchange rate and 22.36 bolivars on the informal market. We can explore these numbers in the diagram, below. The diagram is constructed with the US$ not the bolívar as its base. Therefore, the initial position has it that the US is in surplus to Venezuela at 4 bolívars to the $ of $Q_1 - Q_2$. A devaluation of the bolívar amounts to a revaluation of the dollar to 6 bolívars to the $. This reduces the surplus to $Q_3 - Q_4$. Operating at equilibrium would require a higher revaluation of 9 bolívars to the $. With the exchange rate at 4 bolívars to the $ there would be excess demand. This could result in a black market in dollars. Under these circumstances, the rate of exchange could rise to 22 bolívars to the $.

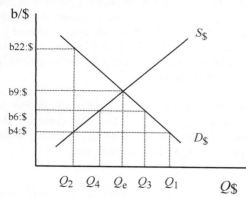

Capital controls could be an alternative, or used in combination. Assume that the target exchange rate is 4 bolívars to the $. To ensure there is no net outflow of funds, Venezuela should restrict the demand for Dollars to the supply. This entails only allowing Venezuelan to acquire Q_2 Dollars. In effect, this shifts the demand curve for Dollars to the left D_{S1} to D_{S2}. This results in balance of payments equilibrium, but the currency is not convertible.

The combination could result in the diagram left where the new exchange rate with currency restrictions addresses some of the problems, but a black market exchange rate persisted. On 18 February 2016, the bolívar was devalued from 6.3 Bvrs to 10 Bvrs. The inflation rate was 2,616% in 2017, over 2% a day. The consequences are evident in the exchange rate. In January 2018, the heavily subsidized DIPOR rate of 10Bvrs:$

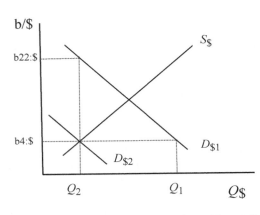

was scrapped and the central bank relaunched an exchange system known as DICOM, which most recently sold dollars at 3,345Bvs: $. The central bank said the first auction of the DICOM system yielded an exchange rate of 30,987.5Bvrs:€ (around 25,000Bvrs:$). The black market rate stood at 228,000Bvrs:$.

In June 2018, inflation was at 128.4% (annualised 46,305%). In July, the market rate of 119,900 Bvrs, was not close to the black market rate of 4mBvrs:$. At the end of July, the President, Nicolas Maduro announced plans to delete five zeros from the bolívar, two more than planned in March. Countries facing hyperinflation have done this in the past. On August 30th, 1924, Germany removed 12 zeros creating the new Reichsmark. On January 1st 2005, Turkish Lira lost six zeros. On February 2nd 2009, the Zimbabwean dollar was redenominated for the third time in three years equivalent to removing 25 zeros from the note.

The Venezuela problem continues. The inflation rate for 2018 was 130,060%. In January 2019 the annualised inflation rate was 2,688,670%. The new currency, the sovereign bolívar, introduced on August 20th 2018, stood at 637:$, in but by May, 5190. According to the UN of the 32m population, 3.3m emigrated after 2015.

Turkey
At the end of July 2018, Turkey's Central Bank raised its inflation expectations to 13.4% when that actual rate was 15.4% and the target rate = 5%. The GDP growth rate of 7.4% in 2017 though mitigated inflation. Concurrently, its foreign currency reserves raised concerns. These reserves are there to protect currency or the fulfil balance of payments imbalances. There are three measures that are used to assess threats in this regard.
1. Relate reserves against upcoming debt payments – can it meet its interest and debt payments. 100% is generally considered the minimum. Covering $200bn/yr Turkey was at 90% in January 2018; by June it was 74%.
2. The IMF has its Reserve Adequacy Measure (RAM) which tries to capture the total resources a country has available to meet asymmetric shocks. This covers gold and foreign currency reserves; Central Bank swap lines; Sovereign wealth fund ammunition; and access to IMF and other protective financing to calculate an overall ratio. Between 100% and 150% is the safe zone, again Turkey was at 75%
3. A third method it to measure the 'time' that would relate to coverage of the import costs. Three months' import cover is safe. At five months, again Turkey looked vulnerable.

Société Générale calculated corporate and sovereign debt repayments of nearly $3.8bn on foreign currency bonds were due in October. In January 2018 average weighed cost of fixed-rate bonds was 12.8%. By 2019Q1 it was 18.9%. Over the same period the average weighted maturity fell from 5 years to 2½.

In April, the FT estimated that the central bank was using unconventional tactics to bolster its reserves: swaps. Of the $26.9.1bn in net reserves the non-swaps were worth $16bn. Gross reserves stood at $75.57 when the expected external debt coming due over 12 months of $177bn. Both net and gross reserves are not sufficient to repel currency speculation.

It was suggested that the 40% fall in the exchange rate over 9 months was sufficient to resolve the 7% current account deficit. Also, the collapse adversely affects GDP reducing inflation. A drop in the Lira from 6 to 7 to the dollar would increase the debt repayments and put pressure on banks. Adding to pressures was the threat that a dispute over an American pastor detained in Turkey could see the US withdrawing Turkey's favourable access to the US under GSP. With some $1.66bn threatened, the Turkish Lira tumbled. (It was cancelled on May 17th). Then, on August 10th, Trump doubled the tariffs on steel (50%) and aluminium (20%), on national security grounds putting unprecedented economic pressure on a NATO ally and deepening turmoil in Turkish financial markets, where the Lira fell 18% at worst on the day. Turkey was the 6th largest steel exporter to the US. In retaliation five days later Turkey raised the tariffs on passenger cars to 120%; alcoholic drinks (140%) and on leaf tobacco (60%). Tariffs were also increased on goods including cosmetics, rice and coal. On September 13th the repo rate rose to 24%. As the traders were anticipating 22%, the currency rose 3.2%. Turkey banned the use of foreign currencies in the country's property market and on contracts for sales, rent and leasing must be made in Lira. In October, the Finance minister asked retailers to stick to price rise of 10% - a prices policy.

Corporate Support
For companies, the cost of servicing foreign debt had risen by a quarter in Lira terms over July and August. 85% of the $293bn in corporate foreign currency debt was held by 2,300 firms. Many of the 403 shopping malls, most of which sprang up this century, were funded by $15bn in foreign currency loans, so that the falling Lira would put up the costs of servicing the loans. In October, banks were asked to give a 10% discount on high interest rate loans.

In April, a support package worth about $4.9bn was offered to (f)ailing banks. In May, $4.9bn was offered to *inter alia* automotive and chemical sectors, which before they are able to export processed goods are largely dependent on imports of raw materials. In June, Twelve Turkish banks were offered $4.31bn (TL25bn) to lend to up to TL50m for 3 yrs @ CPI+4% and 4ys @ CPI+4.5%. Some 80% of the loans were backed by the government's Credit Guarantee Fund. Credit card repayments were also eased from 35% to 30% of the monthly bill.

Foreign Currency Savings

By March, TL1tn in residential bank deposits were held in foreign currencies – just under 50% of deposits – by May 55%. Currency theory might not work where domestic savings are held in a non-domestic currency. To avoid the devaluation of savings Argentines have historically saved in dollars. Turks are following suit. Exchange rate depreciation leads quickly to increases in inflation, portfolio dollarisation and higher interest rates. This means that a large depreciation quickly causes flight to dollar safety that often becomes permanent. To offset this May also saw the RRR for Forex deposits raised by 2%, imposing a Tobin tax of 0.1%, and a one-day settlement delay on Forex.

Argentina

In mid-June 2018 with the currency @ 28.45peso: $

- the central bank of Argentina began raising the RRR from 20% to 25% to reduce the money stock by up 100bnpeso (£2.7bn).
- The central bank also sold $175bn in an unusual auction of reserves.
- The government sold $4bn in bonds on the week before @ up to 32.92% in peso terms.
- The central bank lowered the cap on banks' foreign currency holdings from 10% to 5% of total assets.
- Asked for a $50bn IMF loan

On the 13th August in the wake of the Turkey's crisis it raised interest rates to 45% and sold $500m to support the peso. In the last week in August, it accelerated the disbursement of the $50bn IMF loan; auction off over $1bn in reserves to support the peso and raised interest rates to 60%. Having depleted its reserved by $13.5bn, it was left with $54.3bn at the start of September. One driver was the lack of confidence in the markets about Argentina's ability to finance its $24.9bn projected 2019 deficit. The primary fiscal deficit, projected at 2.6% of GDP for 2018, with a falling currency, increased the likelihood of default.

At the end of September, with the ForEx at 41p:$, the RRR was raised by 3% to 44%. To curb the expected 40% inflation and in an effort to restore market confidence in the country, it agreed to a bigger, faster IMF bailout than initially planned. It raised its 36-month financing package to $57.1bn, making about $50bn in credit available through 2019 - $19bn more than previously anticipated.

New Regime

From October 1st, as stipulated in the standby agreement with the IMF, the Central Bank adopted a rigid monetary rule that sets a 0% monthly growth for the monetary base. With a 'non-intervention' band, of 30% around the (non-pegged) exchange rate, whenever the market rate hits the ceiling, the bank has a modest stock of dollars available for sale. LELIQ seven-day interest rate became the policy rate. As a classic case of currency support, the central bank on 16th October issued $3.666bn worth of seven-day Leliq notes at an average interest rate of 72.198%. The peso rose by 2.19% to 36: $.

Price inflation in March was 54.7%. Central Bank set out the following policies:
- Seeking to reduce the monetary base by an additional 10%
- Extending its target for zero growth in the monetary base until December 2019
- Reducing its currency band from 2% to 1.75%/month
- Reducing the amount of dollars the central bank can buy if the peso falls below the currency band floor from $75m to $50m/day
- Expanding the limit Leliq banks can hold

At the end of the month the central bank offered Leliq notes @ 68.237% to boost demand for the currency again. President Mauricio Macri imposed a price fix on 60 essential' products for at least six months, and public service prices steady for the rest of the year. These include cooking oils, flour, yogurts, jams, biscuits and Yerba mate tea. There were also separate measures to help keep domestic meat prices low. However, the peso was hitting all-time lows of 43.97:$. In April, the Bank announced that the Leliq rate wound not drop below 62.5%.

India
The RBI sold nearly $19bn from the ForEx reserves between April and August 2018 to support the Rupee, draining roughly $1.4tn from banks, creating a cash crunch. In August, it raised its repo rate by 25bp to 6.5% the second increase in as many meetings. The CPI in June hit 5%, the 8th straight month it was over target rate of 4%. Moreover, oil hit $80/b in May and the monsoons were erratic. It also, in September, raised tariffs on 19 items to curb non-essential imports, reducing capital outflows. Unexpectedly at the October meeting RBI did not change the rate leading to the Rupee depreciating to a record low R74.23: $. Most commentators expected a rise of 50bps. Rather, it switched its ForEx intervention policy, increasing its participation in the derivatives market in relation to the spot market. In March and April, RBI for swaps of Rupees for $5bn injected close to 700bn Rupees into the banking system. In May, plans for swaps of 500bnRupees in OMO were not announced, but leaked.

The Capital Account
Although we pay great attention to goods and services, when discussing a balance of payments, in actual fact, for economies like ours, capital flows are far greater in value than their current account counterparts. Capital is captured by two accounts:
- Capital account: acquisition and disposal of fixed assets, e.g. land, remittances and EU transfers
- Financial account (which was the capital account until 1998): acquisition and disposal of other financial assets

In the diagram below there is a representation of how a common exchange rate affects the current and the capital accounts.

The balance of payments on the current account is in equilibrium at E_1, while the capital account is only in balance when the exchange rate is at E_3. With only one exchange rate for the economy, the price of the currency will gravitate to E_2. At this rate, the current account is in deficit $(q_2 - q_1) = q_3$ and the capital account is in surplus

$(q_5 - q_4) = q_3$. In 2015Q1, China ran a balance of payments deficit of $80bn whilst enjoying a surplus on the current account of $80bn. There was an exit of $179bn in capital.

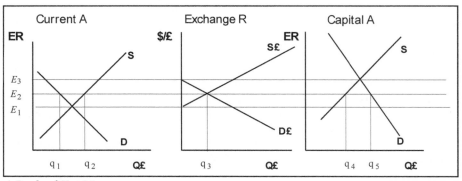

A Rush of Hot Money
If there is an increase in the demand for portfolio investments, (there is a rush of hot money into the economy) the demand curve in the capital account shifts to the right, in the diagram below. This drives the D£ schedule upwards. The result is a rise in the equilibrium exchange rate from E_2 to E_4. There will be a larger surplus on the capital and a greater deficit on the current account. This rush could be related to interest rate increases in the domestic market.

The Traditional Exchange Rate Models
The 'traditional', flow-oriented approach focuses on the current account and trade. The exchange rate affects, and is affected by, the relative competitiveness of the internationally traded goods and services. This can be seen in terms of the assets and liabilities denominated in foreign currency, or of the competitiveness of exports and imports. Even non-international traders would be affected, indirectly, through costs of materials purchased from importers. Export-oriented firms benefit from a fall, and importing ones from a rise, in the exchange rate.

The Portfolio Approach
The stock-oriented approach reflects the operations of the portfolio manager. The manager is concerned about returns and risk. Risk is reduced through diversification, within and across asset classes and within and across countries. The exchange rate is a mediator between domestic and international markets for bonds and stocks. Expectations of future incomes from these assets are affected by relative currency values. Following a fall in the share price, such that a company is undervalued, foreign investors will switch to domestic currency to purchase the under-priced shares, causing

an inflow of funds. Thus, there should be a negative relationship between stock prices and exchange rates.

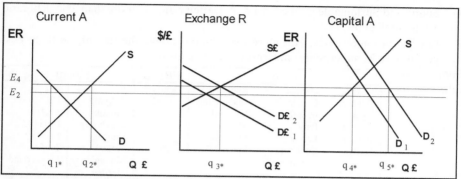

Large speculative flows follow, if not lead, exchange rate changes. A devaluation increases nominal GDP, pushing up the demand for money and interest rates, leading to an inflow of capital. Before a devaluation, speculation would precipitate large outflows. This encourages residents to move their (savings) capital abroad to retain some of its value. A devaluation pushes up the price of imports with a consequential rise in costs of some exports. There is a decline in real income. The costs of servicing debt denominated in other currencies to the Sovereign and others increases (such as a mortgage in Hungary in Swiss Francs). The value of that debt denominated in the local currency falls in foreign currency terms, lowering the value of investments of international portfolio investors. To invest further in assets denominated in the local currency, the portfolio investor will expect greater returns.

ERMII

With the creation of the single European currency, the Euro, there needed to be a successor to ERM to prepare new accession countries for entry to the single currency. The accession country should not disrupt economic stability within the single market. As such, a convergence criterion on exchange rate stability requires participation in ERMII.

Participation in ERMII is voluntary but all Member States of the European Union, except Denmark and the United Kingdom, are required to adopt the Euro. This would apply to a detached Scotland. Before it can qualify to adopt the euro, a country must participate in ERMII without severe tensions for at least two years. The exchange rate of a non-Euro area Member State is fixed against the Euro and is only allowed to fluctuate within set limits (±15%). In theory, interventions are coordinated by the ECB and the central bank of the non-euro area Member State. The non-Euro area Member States can opt for a narrower band. Denmark operates a band of ±2.25%.

Beyond the 2-year membership, convergence criteria are required to be met. They are:-

- Price stability: Not more than 150bps above the rate of the three best performing Member States as measured by the CPI;
- Sound and Sustainable public finances: Deficit ratio not more than 3%; debt ratio not more than 60%;
- Long-term interest rate: Not more than 200bps above the rate of the three best performing Member States in terms of price stability.

Some have fulfilled the

Euro			ERMII	Floating	
Austria	Germany	Malta	Denmark	*EU:*	*EU:*
Belgium	Greece	Netherlands	±2.25%.	Bulgaria	UK
Cyprus	Ireland	Portugal		Croatia	*EEA:*
Estonia	Italy	Slovakia		Czech Rep.	Iceland
Finland	Latvia	Slovenia		Hungary	Norway
France	Lithuania	Spain		Poland	*EFTA:*
	Luxembourg			Romania	Switzerland
				Sweden	

requirements recently. Divided by currency regime, the table above provides a guide to countries.

The Baltic States paid a particularly high price to join the Euro. Their convergence period coincided with the financial crisis. Maintaining currency stability with speculators expecting a devaluation proved costly. The countries engaged in an internal devaluation to maintain their currencies in very tight bands. In a sense, the Euro was political rather than an economic project. Given the turmoil in the Ukraine, with a significant number of Russian speakers, for the Baltic States joining the Euro was part of a political separation. April 2013 saw a call from all three States urging NATO to build a base in their region. These are the only three members of the former Soviet Union that have joined NATO.

A devaluation is losing its potency.
We teach that a devaluation can correct a balance of payments. Really, this concerns the current account. The requirement of the Marshall-Lerner condition relates to price elasticity of demand. As the exchange rate changes relative prices, goods should be price sensitive. The change in exports and imports should be positive. QE/QQE presents another set of results. British QE led to a 25% decline in Sterling's value but the current account failed to improve. Japan, the former great exporting powerhouse, seems to be facing the same problem. The World Bank, after reviewing 46 countries, concluded that a devaluation is only half as effective at boosting exports as it might have been 20 years ago. Why?

- For Japan, many of its great industrial companies are based overseas. The falling Yen helped Toyota's profits. Although 60% are built overseas, of the remaining 40% of vehicles built, over half are for export. For a depreciation of one Yen, operating profit would rise by 2%. Honda, which produces 80% of its vehicles overseas does not benefit as much. Sony, which produces ¾ overseas and pays its suppliers of its games and digital camera divisions in $, loses ¥3bn per depreciation of one Yen.

- Supply chains are global with parts made in units, so a devaluation leads to the cost of imports increasing as well as exports being boosted. Over a third of exported goods are assembled with components from other third party countries. An Apple phone, assembled by Foxconn, would see a rise in the costs of it components possibly off-setting the cost advantage a devaluation might offer Apple phones in the US. To address this, 'real value added' profit is the new focus. One can contrast China and Japan. Japan's supply chain is interwoven with China's. With their QQE a 17% depreciation over a year is associated with, in the quarter to June 2015, the largest drop in exports in five years. By contrast, as China moves up the value added chain, the import intensity of exports would decline.

- An alternative view is that, rather than boost output, prices are adjusted. Given the exclusivity of the product might be tarnished by greater volume, companies might prefer moving up-market. Phillippe Martin of Sciences Po finds that French multinationals prefer pocketing the profit rather than upping the volume. In a sense, a branded good should not be price sensitive. Non-price competition may be the basis of rivalry. By implication, the law of one price, which relies on homogeneity of product and zero transport costs, would not apply.

Purchasing Power Parity

In principle, an exchange rate should reflect the cost of the same product in both countries. A car in the US costing $15,000 should be priced at £10,000 in the UK if the exchange rate of $1.5: £ is an accurate measure of relative prices. Of course, if this is a car built in the US, there should be a difference related to transport costs. But this would be the only explanation of difference. In a transport cost free perfect model, arbitrage would drive the price for the same good to be identical – the law of one price – for all goods. So exchange rates should then reflect what a given sum of money (possibly gold) would purchase in either country. There are two versions of PPP, absolute and relative.

- ❑ Absolute PPP entails the above; the equalization of goods purchased with the same amount of funds;
- ❑ Relative PPP posits that *changes* in the exchange rate reflect *changes* in relative costs – inflation. A relatively high rate of inflation would lead to a corresponding depreciation of the exchange rate.

The assessment of this model has presented problems. The price indices would include prices of traded and non-traded goods, so not an accurate measure of changes in relative prices of traded goods. Relative Unit Labour Costs (RULC) would be an interesting alternative. This would give some idea of the wage cost per hour. Of course, not all workers are equally productive in that hour. Some workers are more productive and have access to superior capital. Also, climate may make certain activities difficult. Pricing goods in hours of labour to produce them would be a further alternative.

CHANGING VEHICLES

In 2004, it was argued that the difficulties of replicating human perception, such as executing a turn against oncoming traffic, involves so many factors that it was hard to imagine discovering the set of rules that can replicate a driver's behaviour. By 2010, Google announced that it had modified several Toyota Priuses to be fully autonomous. In 2013, the phrase 'self-driving car' was nowhere to be found in documents published by the US Dept. of Transportation. Today the FT is full of this phrase. The business model is also changing Electric cars built by other producers may turn car manufacture into a low-margin business. Competitive advantage may come through suppliers and new foci. After a century of stability there are great global trends in the car industry: *electrification; autonomous driving; and car sharing and renting.*

Gapper in the FT in December 2016 was asking why own a self-driving car at all. If a car does the driving (so Top Gear is irrelevant) and is available when you want it, why own? An Uber taxi costs $250/mile to hire. Ford estimate that driverless taxis will cost $1/mile. Without the thrill of driving ownership is likely to decline. A city dweller may only use their car for 3% of the time but the financing and depreciation continue inexorably. Rented vehicles can be on the road for a higher proportion of time. The role of marques is likely to change also. Why care about the car you rent?

Sharing
Car builders are looking to renting – taxi or minibus services are the future. Ford estimate that each of minibus vehicle will displace 25 cars in China and 11 in the US. In May 2017, Ford, looking at a new business model, advocating taking cars off the road, emphasised moving away from car owners and switching to sharing. Ford purchased Chariot for £50m in 2016. It then announced a minibus shuttle service across London in 2017 and 2018 it announced Argo will be a robo-taxi firm operating at scale by 2021, transporting goods and people. Maven has been launched by GM, which has purchased a taxi-booking firm (Lyft) for $500m.

Daimler owns taxi apps MyTaxi and Hailo. With other facilities and in alliance with Bosch it aimed to focus on shared fleet. Rather than taxis, BMW focused on owners renting out their own BMW vehicles. These strategies merged with the creation of a joint venture covering 5 major areas (sharing, on-demand mobility, parking services, electronic charging, on-demand ordering and payment component of the business). They recognise the threat that car sharing is to them. The merger combined Car2go (D) and DriveNow and ReachNow (BMW).

McKinsey estimates that car sharing could be worth $30bn by 2030. Saudi Aramco, the largest oil producer is not worried about electric cars, but car sharing and renting. It affects ownership and the number of vehicles on the road. Riyadh Sovereign Wealth fund has a 5% stake in Uber. Uber sold its South East Asia ride-share and food delivery businesses to Grab, which is South East Asia's most popular ride-sharing firm with millions of users across eight countries, including Singapore, Malaysia, Indonesia and Vietnam. Uber took a 27.5% stake in Grab. In June 2018, Toyota invested $1bn in Grab to offer financing, insurance and maintenance services to drivers based on data collected through recorder devices already installed in some Grab vehicles. More interestingly, the data could also help Toyota develop its own next-generation mobility services, including a self-driving electric vehicle aimed at companies for use in tasks such as ride hailing, package delivery and mobile shops. Softbank bought into this project in October.

In a different dimension to delivery, Amazon with Volvo and GM in 37 cities in the US in 2018 rolled out an app that allows delivery of goods to motor vehicles. Uber and Volvo have a $300m joint venture to develop driverless vehicles. Uber ordered 24,000 Volvo SUV driverless taxis to be delivered between 2019 and 2021.

Uber spent $100m on Jump Bikes – electronic scooters. These could disrupt the self-driving taxis/ bus model. Ford was joining the race by purchasing Spin. But this market shows how hype outpaces reality. Bird worth $2bn but only 2 years old and Lime already aiming for this renting market. Tier (Germany) raised €25m in two weeks in November to enter the market. Over slightly longer periods others achieved similar placings: Yellow (Brazil) raised $63m; Grin (Mexico) $45m. With low barriers to entry, profit could be short lived.

Electrification
International Energy Agency estimate that in 2017 there were 2m electric cars on the road. This would rise to 50m by 2025 and 300m by 2040 – around 20% of cars vehicles. This would curtail oil demand by just 2%.

Not all car companies are going the same way. Volvo, in July, pledged to end the production of combustion engines by 2019 and Daimler is building a platform for the EQ by 2022 for electric vehicles only. BMW are developing powertrains that can insert hybrid, combustion, and electric engines.

Batteries are a problem. They limit the distance one can travel; they are expensive; and must be replaced. Progress at making batteries more powerful occurred at a rate of 15%/yr for a decade and has reduced the cost to $150-250/kwh. Lithium battery components are dependent on China. In anode, cathode, electrolyte solution and separator supply China has increased its market share to 50-77% by around 10 percentage points between 2014 and 2016. Goldman Sachs forecasts that China will increase its market share of world electric car production from 45% in 2016 to 60% in 2030. China intends on making rare earths the equivalent of oil to the Arabs. In March 2018, it signed an agreement with Glencore to supply 50,000 tonnes of Cobalt over 3 years. This represents half the world's output in 2017. It appears that they could control the raw material and be strong in its use. South Crofty was the last of hundreds of Cornish tin mines to close in 1998. The price of tin continued to fall to a low of $3,730.80/tonne in February 2002. Things have changed. In two years to 2018, price

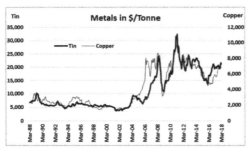

has risen 25% to $21,000. Tin can be used in electric batteries. Also, such mines contain deposits of lithium. Mining is expanding in developed countries. For example, lithium at the Zinnwald project in Southern Saxony, and Kaustinen, in Finland. A nickel mine in Sotkamo, Finland and in Serbia jadarite (boron and lithium). In Cornwall there is investment in copper and tin mines and tin, tungsten and copper near Plymouth. South Crofty will reopen in 2019.

Autonomous Driving
There are different levels of autonomy.
0.   No automation – human does the driving
1.   Car able to take limited control of the steering or speed e.g. cruise control
2.   Car able to take control of the steering and speed but the driver must monitor the road at all times
3.   Driver can take their eyes of the road but must be able to retake control if needed
4.   The car is de facto the driver but for poor conditions e.g. snow or country roads the driver must be able to retake control
5.   The car drives itself

Cars without pedals and steering wheels will be on the road. California approved new rules that allow for level 5 vehicles in April 2018. This will encourage car manufacturers to relocate to where the beasts of Silicon Valley are already ensconced. The Dept. of Motor Vehicles wants an enforcement interaction plan. What responsibilities will the companies have if the car is involved in an accident should be outlined.

Many cars already have level 1 autonomy. Mercedes and Tesla have level 2 capability in some vehicles. Audi unveiled an A8 in July 2017 with level 3 capability. It will operate at low speeds (<60kph) and only if the car can sense white lines and guardrails. The system must judge when the human should revanche control, which is an area of weakness. How to achieve this and will the human be alert enough to deal with what is a non-standard situation in 10 seconds are at issue. It may be better to skip level 3 and move to 5. Daimler is aiming for level 5 vehicles, whereas BMW is designing vehicle with wheels and pedals with level 3-4 capability.

In July, Baidu announced that it would be mass producing a self-drive bus. Without a driver's seat, steering wheel or pedals it has level-4 autonomy. It runs on electric power and can travel up to 100km after a two-hour charge, at up to 70km/h. Softbank is to buy 10 of these Apolongs buses for 'demonstration tests' within Japan by early 2019.

The First Fatality
In March 2018, the first fatality blamed on autonomous cars occurred in Arizona when a 49-year-old woman was hit by a car and killed as she crossed a street. A human monitor was behind the wheel. It turned out he was pratting with his phone. In the near-term, buses have a greater chance of public acceptance than self-drive cars. Car and truck manufacturers seemed to have backed away from level 5 autonomy. Cars need 3-dimensional maps that are continuously updated and accurate to a centimetre. GPS is not precise enough for self-driving cars so for car systems data must be shared among the vehicle eco system. Those on the road provide updates for others. The amount of information collected by a car by its Light Detecting and Ranging (LIDAR) sensors in a day is over a terabyte. This cannot be sent through the internet efficiently. As yet there is no agreement among map companies on standards and data sharing, so this information is proprietorial.

The maps are needed to reduce the amount of work that the autonomous software has to do to recognise the world around it. As with animals and movement, the software could focus on differences between known and perceived. So that the stored 'memory' could tell the car what should be there, which the car measures against the perceived, including the ephemeral pedestrians and cyclists. This though is predicated on recognition. Snowflakes can confuse scanners and snow banks and drifts can alter the appearance of objects. What software do you write for skidding or spinning? So winter in much of the rich world is a challenge.

MARKET FAILURE-EXTERNALITIES

Markets allocate resources efficiently when the benefit from the marginal activity = its extra cost i.e. MB = MC. However, this presumes that there are no spillovers that affect third parties; clear property rights; perfect competition; and people are the best judges of their own well-being.

Externalities – Short Run
Social costs and benefits emerge from the exchange process. An externality occurs when a cost or benefit from an activity or transaction impacts on parties not involved in that activity or transaction. The market mechanism may have produced at the most efficient point of production so that private MB = MC but do social MB = MC? In other words, do these externalities leads to a market failure – the over or under production/consumption of the good in question?

To begin a discussion of a perfectly competitive world with externalities there will be some definitions:

MNPB: Marginal Net Private Benefits = P – MC or (MR – MC) = Mπ (marginal profit)
MEC: Marginal External Cost, the damage from producing an extra q units of output.

MEC + MC = MSC

MSC: Extra cost to the firm plus extra cost to society as a result of producing the extra unit of output.

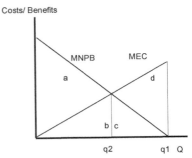
Costs/ Benefits

In the diagram right, profit maximisation occurs when MPNB = 0 at q1. (Assuming no fixed cost) Profits will then be areas a + b + c. However, as there are external costs, b + c + d, q1 cannot produce a social maximum, only a private maximum. The net social benefit (NSB) at q1 is a − d. The NSB is maximised at q2 where MNPB = MEC. Here, NSB = a + b − b = a. The removal of c & d are said to be a Pareto improvement.

How is q2 achieved by society? A standard 'Pigouvian' response to this market failure is to impose a penalty, a tax on the polluter. Demand for the good is the same as the benefit to society i.e. the MSB. Not only will this raise revenue, but also reduce the output and so pollution to a less undesirable level.

Setting standards and imposing penalties

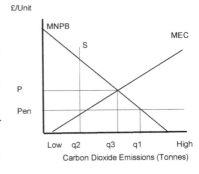
£/Unit

The problems of setting standards and imposing penalties are illustrated right with carbon emissions.

- Penalty: Assume the penalty for polluting is set at Pen. This is a lump sum tax on whatever is produced. The firm has the incentive to produce up to q1 tonnes of carbon as beyond that the penalty is greater than the net private benefits from greater output.
- Standards: Assume the polluter is allowed to emit q2 tonnes of carbon (Standard = S). This is sub-optimal.
- Obviously, if Pen = P, or S = q3, the Pigouvian optimal is achievable. With an administered rather than auction (market) prices, one wonders how the socially efficient output is achieved.

Carbon Trading

Carbon trading is a market solution to the above problem of achieving q3. Carbon trading entails a regulatory authority issuing (selling) rights to pollute the environment. Not only would this facilitate the drifting of rights to where they offer the highest NSB, but also this could encourage the installation of pollution control (abatement) equipment, such as by removing pollutants using scrubbers. In practice, firms do not buy all the credits they need. A company may receive credits under, say, the European Trading System for most, but not all, of its emissions. To deal with the shortfall, it could reduce its emissions by producing less, install abatement equipment, or buy more emissions permits. These can come from other firms within the scheme or from elsewhere.

In the diagram right, the Marginal Abatement Cost (MAC) is the extra cost of cleaning up the process when producing the extra unit of emission, or the cost of avoiding producing an extra unit of emission.

The MAC can be seen as the demand curve for carbon emission permits. If the price of permits = 0, the firm will pollute up to the level of q1. It is assumed that government supplies S permits and no one reneges on their responsibilities. The demand for permits, at that level, will result in a carbon permit price = P1 and the firm will pollute up to the level of q2. To achieve the socially acceptable level of pollution q* permits need to be sold, resulting in P* price per permit.

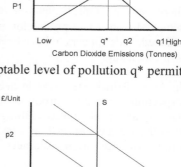

In the diagram right, there is an increase in demand for some product that entails a great deal of carbon emitting. The demand curve for permits shifts to the right from MAC1 to MAC2. The price, not the quantity of emissions, rises: there are no more emissions. Thus, the carbon permit supply determines the level of pollution.

Externality with Variable Technology

A different picture can be examined if, over a long run, improved technologies can be adopted. Like the LRAC curve and moving away from the restriction of the fixed factor, the firms can choose from a menu of technologies. Each offers a cost of producing the good and the amount of CO_2 emitted. In the diagram below, MSB curve reflects the benefits to society of reducing CO_2 emissions. When emissions are high the benefits to society of reducing them are considerable. But when they are low, the benefits are only slight. MSB curve slopes downwards. The MSC curve represents the cost of cleaning up the air/ reducing the pollutants/ shifting to more expensive but less polluting processes. As the move towards greener processes is subject to DMR, the costs of reducing air pollution further increases.

The optimal level of pollution is q1 tonnes of CO_2, where the MSB of lower emissions level equals the MSC of achieving it. If the current position is q2 tonnes of CO_2, it is socially efficient (globally) to reduce carbon emissions. One way this can be achieved is for a group, a country, or group of countries to bribe another to reduce their emissions. The area 'a' can be used to bribe others to reduce their emissions.

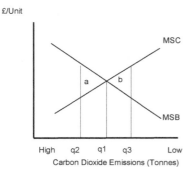

£/Unit

MSC

a   b

MSB

High   q2   q1   q3   Low

Carbon Dioxide Emissions (Tonnes)

Theoretically, this is a good solution and exists with the UN carbon off-set system. However, a Chatham House report pointed out that this carbon off-set that pours money into the developing world might make a bad situation worse if the third world country is badly run (corrupt).

By contrast, if the climatologists got it wrong and we set a level of CO_2 emissions at q3, the excess social cost for this would be area 'b.' If there was an improvement in technology and CO_2 emissions could be reduced/removed from some production processes, the efficient level of pollution would be reduced. This appears to have been the US position under President Bush; technology will find away.

In April, British Steel was in need of £100m bailout over a Brexit problem. It was expecting some free carbon credits but because of the suspension of this from 1st January and a bet on prices falling, it required permits by 30th April it could not afford. It collapsed anyway in May due to uncertainty over the Brexit process, a slump in orders from European customers, a weaker pound, and the steel tariffs.

The Efficient Level of Recycling

The marginal private cost of disposing of rubbish is, to most householders, negligible. However, the social costs, the costs of disposal storage burying or incineration will be higher. Where the marginal private costs (MPC) of rubbish disposal are lower than the marginal social cost (MSC) the market level or recycling will be at a socially inefficient level. This is analysed right. Where the marginal cost of recycling (MPCr) crosses MPC we find the market percentage level of recycling = q1% so the percentage of rubbish buried is 100–q1. More should be recycled. The socially efficient percentage level of recycling will emerge at q2%, when the full cost of disposal is imposed on the householder. This implies a tax on

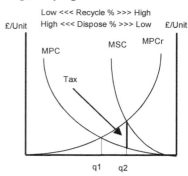

Low <<< Recycle % >>> High
£/Unit   High <<< Dispose % >>> Low   £/Unit

MPC   MSC   MPCr

Tax

q1   q2

burying rubbish, as indicated. However, as the marginal cost is virtually zero, a flat tax is not efficient. A solution to this is for the government to impose a tax on the refuse collector, the local authority, who then has an incentive to monitor rubbish and recycling.

Around 45% of plastic production is for packaging and a further 7% for electronics. By 2015, of the 8.5bn tonnes of plastic produced globally throughout time 6.3bn had gone to landfill and only 9% had been recycled. In October, the Chancellor Philip Hammond vowed to impose a tax on all plastics that does not include 30% recycled material. The electronics use though is likely to grow.

THE DEATH OF DIESEL – ANOTHER FINE

The cost of diesel is set to rise (see elasticity and shipping), but the falling demand for diesel cars means that this is already a headache for car manufacturers. They fell foul of a nitrogen oxide emission requirement. But diesel is less of a carbon emitter than petrol. So, as diesel is phased out, the 2021 requirement of 95g/km of CO_2 looms large. The fine of €95/g×no. of cars could impose a cost of €30bn, so by promoting pretol, EU manufacturers are going the wrong way. You might expect that with modern materials that the car was getting lighter. In 2018, the average car weighted 1,392kgs, 122kg heavier than 20 years previously. This is, in part, a wealth thing. A sports utility vehicle is relatively more popular. A Range Rover weighs 2,300kg. Smaller cars such as the Golf (1,335kg) are heavier than they could be because of the safety features that we expect. Also, we want more 'performance' – which means a heavier engine. In 2017 CO_2 g/km were on average 118.5g and in 2018 121g. UBS expects car company earnings for 2021 to be €7.4bn (14%) lower because of the cost of meeting the carbon target. Peugeot is most exposed (25% lower) with VW (13%) Renault (10%) Daimler (9%) and BMW (7%) being better off. Electric cars also have a weight problem – the battery. A Tesla X has one weighing 2,300kg – the same weight as a Range Rover. The performance of an electric car falls by a fifth if 300kg is added to a 950kg car. The cost of installing a small car with battery and electric motor is €2500-4000, so small cheap cars will be squeezed out.

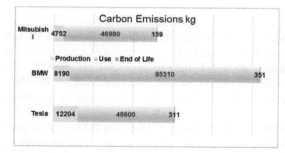

Electric Dreams
According to Trancik Lab at MIT, the Tesla Model SP100D, a battery-electric vehicle, emits 48,600kg of CO_2 over its 270,000km road life. This is around half of the BMW 750i xDrive and broadly similar to the Mitsubishi Mirage, both of which have internal combustion engines. However, when higher production emissions are taken into account the Tesla emits 226g/km but the petrol engine Mirage is notably less at 192. The concern is that larger electric vehicles are not that green. Rare earths are dirty and carbon-heavy in their production. Indeed, by 2030 the Mirage could be banned in Europe whilst the Tesla won't be. For the electric car it is the battery that causes green concerns. A top of the range vehicle will need 60kg of lithium and 10kg of cobalt. Moreover, the full life cycle assessment should take into account the generation of electricity itself. It

could be coal or wind powered. An e-Golf is estimated to produce 9,700kg of carbon over its lifetime: when powered by renewable sources, there could be a 61% reduction over the standard Golf. If powered by EU electricity, it is only a 26% reduction.

In May a merger of Fiat-Chrysler and Renault was announced. Worth $35bn the merger was driven by the costs of far-reaching technological and regulatory changes. The combine company would have the capacity to produce 8.7m vehicles/yr. F-C in Europe was operating at below 50% capacity. Economies of scale could be based on building similar models on a common vehicle architecture so that various vehicle sizes could be constructed on the same assembly line. For example, Renault's next electric car platform being launched at its Douai site in France. Renault and Nissan have jointly invested more than $5bn in electric cars whilst F-C has little in the way of components or intellectual property. Renault could use F-C's body-on-frame platforms, which underpin the automaker's big pickups and SUVs in North America. This combined with common purchasing of parts could save €5bn/yr. This was scuppered in June by a 'France first' French government.

With echoes of the 1990s there could be a flurry of mergers that follow this. F-C were approached by Peugeot in 2019. The latter may look to Jaguar Land Rover shifting some Vauxhall brands to Europe and consolidate in the UK. Emissions demands are a key driver.

In July 2016, MAN, Scania Daimler, DAF, Iveco and Volvo/Renault were found guilty of colluding on prices and passing on the costs of emissions-reducing technology. In September, the EU launched a formal investigation into collusion in delaying the development of clean emissions technology. The plaintiffs were BMW, Daimler and VW.

Shipping Problems
One large container ship emits more sulphur dioxide than 50m diesel cars. Although things have been slow, from March 2020 the International Maritime Organisation has prohibited 94,000 ships from burning untreated high sulphur fuel oil (HSFO). The regulation came in on 1st January 2019 but will take effect 22 months later. In effect, the threshold of sulphur emissions drops from 3.5% a 0.5%. This leaves three options available to shippers:
1. Abatement - Install scrubbers (exhaust gas cleaner systems that extract the sulphur as the HSFO is burned). Scrubbers take 6-9 months to install. From an industry supply perspective, the best possible outcome is around 1200 are installed before the 2020 deadline (out of the +60,000 needed).
2. Switch to liquid natural gas (LNG) propulsion systems. Given the capital expenditure requirement and uncertainty around enforcement of the regulation, plus volatility in the LNG markets over the next two years and availability at ports, this is unlikely.

3. Switch fuel intake to low sulphur fuel oil (which is equivalent to distillate). This is the most likely outcome.

The base global demand for distillate (diesel, kerosene, heavy and light gas oil) is around 30m b/day. The bunker (ship engine) fuel market accounts for around 5.5m b/d, with 70% (4mb/day) accounted for by around 70,000 ferries, cruise/container ships, dry bulk transport and oil tankers. These ships consume over 50% of the total global fuel oil demand.

Fuel oil is obtained during petroleum distillation, and has traditionally been the bottom of the barrel, high sulphur by-product formed along with gasoline and distillate by refiners. Given crude availability is skewed to light crude, refiners' supply of distillate is inelastic; they are already operating near maximum utilisation rates. It is estimated that refiners will see an additional 2.5mb/d demand for low sulphur/middle distillate demand from shippers in 2020. This will provoke a large change in price. Moreover, there will be a surplus of high sulphur fuel oil.

Impact[9]

Relative prices are as follows: With Brent crude at $77.29, Rotterdam 3.5% HSFO oil price was $67.18 and more expensive LSFO $69.25/b. By December 2021, Brent is estimated to fall to $65.88, with the 3.5% $15.95 below crude and $14.55 below 1% LSFO. Higher fuel costs will greatly affect total shipping costs, altering incentives. Fuel costs make up approximately 70-80% of total transport costs so as shippers moderate their speed to economise on fuel, perishable goods (like agricultural produce) cannot be transported so far and manufacturers may alter production facilities as geographical proximity becomes more important. In May 2019, a speed limit was proposed. Taking 24 days to cross the pacific rather than 20 increases the number of cargo ships needed by 20%.

Before, these oil derivatives were complements in supply; now they are substitutes. Middle distillate demand covers diesel and jet fuel. As such, other forms of transportation will see an increase in costs. According to the IATA, in 2018 the global airline industry's net profit was $32bn. The fuel bill was around $180bn accounting for around 23.5% of operating expenses at $73/b Brent. A notable increase in this could push some to the wall. Industries dependent on airlines, such as tourism will also be adversely affected, particularly as this tends to be price sensitive (high price elasticity). The Select Committee on Climate Change reported in May that Britain could exceed its CO_2 aviation target for 2028-32 by 20%. A Pigovian passenger tax of £26/seat would hurt the shorter intra-UK/European routes. However, the fuel rise might make that unnecessary.

---

[9] FT 15 4 19 Cleaner shipping will push up the cost of flying and driving, by Dizard

Diesel cars are being squeezed out of the market already, so automobile manufacturers may actually see a bump in demand for electric cars. In February, the EU agreed to CO_2 emissions from new trucks and buses by 30% by a 2030. Rail transportation is not so easy. Rail transported 16.95bn tonne-km of freight in 2017/18 equating to 10% of freight surface transport. But then, as with cars, there is a commitment for diesel trains to be phased out in the UK.

With a rise in demand for LSFO and a corresponding drop for HSFO will impact on other markets. Again substitutes in supply, the power generation market will benefit, and coal lose. As HSFO contains around 50% more energy per unit than coal, it will be switched to be a fuel for power generation, competing with coal in emerging markets (HSFO emits less CO_2 than coal). Schroders estimate that HSFO prices would need to decline to around $100/tonne to be competitive with coal fired power stations with coal @ $50/t coal. This requires a significant fall from a spot of $400/t.

Coase's Theorem
Coase proposed that an externality could be internalised if the person that caused the externality incorporated it into their personal costs and benefits. Through trade, a social optimum can emerge. Two teenagers in a room can illustrate Coase's trading approach. One wants to watch to the television and the other wants to study for a test. A solution is for the candidate to persuade the viewer to turn the television off. Another solution is for the viewer to persuade the candidate to go elsewhere or study later. One must relent otherwise both lose.

Property Rights
The tragedy of the commons emerges from lack of ownership; as no one owns the common land, there is a tendency to overgraze it. Without some rationing of the use of the land today, the land will be barren tomorrow. It makes sense for an authority to allocate grazing rights. If a sheep farmer wished to graze more sheep, they would have to pay others to use their portion of the land. They would only do this if the benefit of grazing more sheep was greater or equal to the cost.

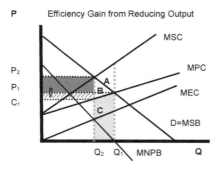

In the diagram left, where MPB=(MSB)=MPC the level of output is Q_1. However, as there are negative externalities produced this is an inefficient level of output for society. The socially efficient level of output is Q_2 where MSB=MSC. The reduction in consumption reduces wellbeing (total benefit) by areas B+C. However, there is a reduction in private production costs of area C and a reduction in social costs of area A+B. If the fall in costs outweighs the fall in benefits, this produces a favourable outcome. Fall in costs = A+B+C. Fall in benefits = B+C. Therefore, the fall in output to Q_2 leads to a net increase in well-being by area A. This is a Pigouvian outcome.

Coasian Solution
If there are two parties, Coase argues that an internalisation of the problem can lead to an improved outcome. Assume a polluting steel mill adversely affects the well-being of a neighbouring fishery. The steelwork will operate at Q_1 until it is in its interests not to. Also, the fishery will bribe the steelwork not to produce as long as the damage done to the fishery is greater than the bribe.

Together: so long as the bribe is greater than the lost benefit of not producing steel there exists the opportunity of a bargain.

The loss to the steelwork from reduced output is areas B+C. The reduction in costs is area C. The benefit to the fishery from less pollution is areas A+B. Thus, as A+B is greater than B+C–C there is scope to bribe and be better off (A).

Assigning property rights to the steel mill and, hence, the option to pollute the fishery's waters, the fishery has to bargain with the steel mill not to pollute. It is in the steel mills interest to produce Q_1 output. However, if bribed, the steel mill would produce less. As long as the amount the fishery is willing to bribe the mill (MEC = MSC – MPC) is greater than the benefit to the steel mill of producing steel (P – MPC) then bargaining will exist. The optimum level will occur at Q_2 when the bribe = P_2–C_1.

Assigning property rights to the fishery, the steel mill has to bargain with the fishery to pollute its waters. Now the payment has to be no greater than the damage. There is scope to increase output up to the point where the benefit to the steel mill of producing steel (P – MPC) is equal to the damage done to the fishery (MEC = MSC – MPC) so the bribe is paid.

In either case the output is the same. The difference is the bribe paid by different parties. As area A+B (the external cost of excess production) is greater than B the benefit from excess production there is an improvement in well-being of area A.

Pigou taxes and subsidies should be used to address an externality. Coase stated that it was not clear that taxing the perpetrator of the negative externality would produce the optimum outcome. Typically an externality entails costs jointly produced by the actions of both parties. There would be no pollution without the steel mill but there would be no problem without the fishery. It appears to be logical to remove the polluter. Pigou's approach creates a fixed price for pollution and a variable quantity. Reducing or, at the extreme, removing the source of the problem may not be the solution. The do nothing solution puts the burden on the fishery, but the tax solution puts the burden on the polluter. A better way could be for both parties to bear some of the adjustment costs.

We do not know the best (most efficient) way of addressing the externality the least worst solution is to get the parties to negotiate. The Pigouvian tax is a special case where the best case is where the polluter pays only.

MARKET FAILURE-DEMERIT GOODS

Demerit activities are those that are over consumed by consumers. Whatever gambling responsibly is is a moot point. In April, Fixed Odds Betting Terminals stakes dropped from £100 to £2. It was scheduled to come in in October 2019 by the government, but under pressure from parliament including Sports minister Tracey Crouch resigning in protest, the date was brought forward. Fixed-odds betting terminals generated £1.8bn in revenue a year for the betting industry and taxes of £400m for the government.

Price Minimum
In December 2017, the UK Supreme Court accepted the Scottish Government's right to impose a minimum of 50p a unit on alcoholic beverages. The court accepted that there would be market would be subject to distortions but the policy was a proportionate means of achieving a legitimate aim. The 2016 UK guidelines recommend no more than 14 alcoholic units a week (six pints of beer or seven glasses of wine). A Cambridge University study in the Lancet of 600,000 drinkers estimated that having 5-10; 10-15; and over 18 drinks/wk shortens life expectancy by 6 months; between 1 & 2 years; and 4-5yrs respectively. Also, every 12.5 units above the guidelines increases the probability of: a stroke by 14%; fatal hypertensive disease by 24%; heart failure by 9%; and a fatal aortic aneurysm by 15%.

The industry, obviously keen to argue for free trade, suggested that this contravened EU Law and would have no effect on drinking problems. It would affect ordinary drinkers, not the alcoholics. Given that cider can cost as little as 18p/unit this strikes one as misleading. Anyway, the ONS found that 80% of rich (those earning >£40,000) workers had had alcohol the week before whereas

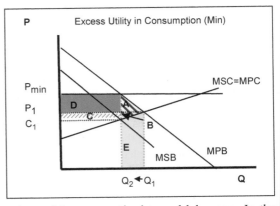

the proportion was only 50% among lorry drivers receptionists and labourers. In the diagram right, a price minimum P_{min} could force consumption down from Q_1 to Q_2 but, the welfare outcomes are different to a tax. Consumer surplus would fall by triangle A + box D. Producer surplus would fall by triangle B + box C. There would also be a decline in expenditure, which is the same as the reduction in costs (area E). From the producer's perspective, this is at the expense of output and jobs. Areas A+B+E are lost, but the supermarket gains areas C+D in higher profit. Thus, if $[Q_2 \times P_{min}] > [P_1 \times Q_1]$, the supermarket is better off.

A Sweetened Pill Swallowed Partly
As part of a healthy balanced diet, NHS recommend an adult's *reference intakes* (RIs) for a day are: Energy: 8,400 kJ/2,000kcal; total fat: 70g; saturates: 20g; carbohydrate: 260g; total sugars: 90g; protein: 50g; and salt: 6g. The Behavioural Insight Team found that people under-report their calorie intake by up to 50% affecting policy initiatives. One benefit of poorer health is that people do not live as long. The PwC estimate that the shortfall in Defined Benefits pension schemes, valued at £530bn, could be £310bn smaller. For example, a previous estimate of a 40 year old living to 90 is revised downwards to living to 84.

In April 2016, Mars took the unusual step of advising to its customers that some of its products should only be consumed *weekly*, not *everyday*. As part of its ambition to create and promote healthier food choices, it wanted to reduce the consumption of high salt, sugar or fat content produce such as Dolmio's carbonara, lasagne sauces, pesto, and macaroni oven kits, and Uncle Ben's oriental sauces.

The fizzy drinks industry is illustrative of an amoral approach to marketing. The sugar tax announced in the April 2016 budget prompted the Soft Drinks Association to describe it as 'the misguided campaign on sugar.' This would include Coco-Cola, Britvic and Suntory. Secretly, they have been taking steps. 50% of the sugar intake of the average US citizen comes from fizzy, energy and sports drinks, plus tea.

Depending on how much extra sugar has been added, bottled drinks had 18p or 24p/ltr tax added in April 2018. When George Osborne announced the sugar tax in 2016 the expected revenue was about £500m/yr. By November 2017, the anticipated figure had dropped to £275m/yr. Again, firms responded with reduced sugar recipe. Irn Bru stopped making the original full-sugar version. AG Barr, the brand owner, expected 99% of its drinks range, including other brands, to be below the threshold by the time it came into force. Suntory had reduced the sugar content of Ribena and Lucozade by 50%. Britvic, owners of Robinson's, J2O and Fruit Shoot, has pursued this policy since 2013. By November, the tax raised £153.8m imposed 7 month previously.

Mexico has high rates of obesity and sugar consumption. Over 70% of the population is overweight with more than 70% of the added sugar in the diet derived from sugar-sweetened drinks. A sugar tax was introduced in 2014. The University of North Carolina and the Mexican Instituto Nacional de Salud Pública (National Institute of Public Health) found that a 1 peso (4p)tax / ltr of sugary drink, led to a decline in consumption by 18.8ml/person in 2014 and 29.3ml in 2015. Purchases of other untaxed drinks went up on average by 2% over the two years. Euromonitor reported that a 33¢/ltr tax introduced in Berkeley, California reduced sweetened beverage consumption by 21% and increased water consumption by 63%. In comparison, other cities in the US reported a 4% increase in SSB consumption, and only 19% increase in water consumption in that time. That said, the Mexico tax raised £880m/yr; the French, £263m, Belgian £87m; and the Finish £79m. Since the beginning of 2018 when Norway's tax on sweets and sugary drinks rose dramatically, Norwegians make a day trip to Sweden to get their sugar fix. All sweetened drinks are now taxed at about 43p/litre. Also, all sweets and chocolate, chewing gum and sweet biscuits are now taxed at £3.34/kg.

Below is a social welfare diagram. The marginal social cost (MSC) of manufacturing sugary drinks is the same as the marginal private costs (MPC) (we'll ignore the cost of bottle disposal, say – but see plastics and coffee). However, the costs to the individual (and to society) from drinking are not fully borne by the consumer. Additional costs, such as time off work, poorer well-being, and time in hospital receiving treatment for diabetes are borne by both the individual (and society). There are, thus, two elements that are blended together: the over consumption by individuals; and the impact on society's medical and other services that over indulgence brings.

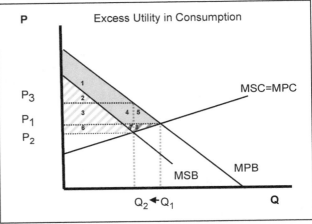

As a point of exploration, the following entails considering the marginal social benefits merely as the socially defined appropriate level of sugary drink consumption, not that defined by individuals. Thus, the over consumption can be viewed as excess utility.

Individuals consume the drinks up to point Q_1 where the cost of the drink (P_1) provides that level of marginal utility. A lower level of consumption is socially desirable (Q_2). This is where the extra cost of producing a unit of sugary drink reflects the full net benefit to the consumers, including the demerit of weight, a shorter life etc..

Welfare can be judged from the excess consumer and producer surplus. Assuming no negative externality in production, total revenue is $Q_1 \times P_1$ and consumer surplus comprises areas 1+2+3+4+5. However, if the level of consumption was more socially acceptable, there would be a lower price and quantity. Then, total revenue would be $Q_2 \times P_2$ and consumer surplus would be areas 2+3+6, a clearly smaller total area and, hence, fewer resources allocated to drink's production. The well-being accounting is not straight-forward. Society must benefit from the correction in the assessment of utility. As the triangles do not overlap perfectly, we end up with the measure of the excess as 1+4+5–6. However, producer surplus falls because of the reduced consumption by 6+7+8. Thus, as measured by individuals, there is a net fall in well-being of 1+4+5+7+8.

A Tax in a Coffee Cup

Because of their plastic lining, some 2.5bn coffee cups are thrown away annually in the UK, almost none of which are recycled. Consistent with a Pigouvian solution the Environmental Audit Committee (EAC) had proposed a charge of 25p for disposable coffee cups. Starbucks started charging 5p for disposable coffee cups in 35 London stores as part of a trial in January 2018. Waitrose, over several months from April 2018 year stopped using (52m/yr) disposable coffee cups. The government was hoping for a more Coasian solution. If they found some way of reducing cup use coffee vendors could sell more coffee. A solution is for the consumer to bear some of the recycling cost – reuse old cups. Pret a Manger (50p) Costa Coffee (50p) and Starbucks (25p) were already there, offering discounts for using reusable cups. An independent coffee chain Boston Tea Party (BTP) found that only 5% of customers took up 25p discount for its reusable cup scheme. It stopped supplying disposable cups and saw sales drop by £250,000 over 10 months to April.

In effect, the coffee vendor and consumer share the benefits of reducing the tax burden. The vendor sells fewer cups per litre of coffee sold and the consumer consumes more coffee per £1 spent on coffee. The outcome is that more coffee is sold than Q_2. In the diagram right for

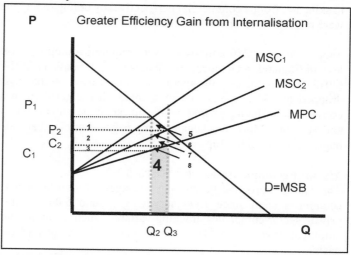

the sake of ease assume that the cost of coffee cups is zero. As before there is still the cost of disposal inherent in MSC_1 but now, assume that that cost can be halved as everyone reuses a cup once. So that the new MSC curve is MSC_2. The Pigouvian tax is P_1-C_1. By reusing, more coffee is consumed than before $Q_3 > Q_2$. There is a rise in costs of = 4+7+8. Rise in benefits = 4+5+6+7+8. Therefore, the higher Coasian output to leads to a net increase of 5+6+7+8. The new price is P_2. Lower than the Pigouvian tax price. However, recycling costs remain. The Coasian tax is P_2-C_2. This raises revenue of areas 2+5+6+7. So with the greater coffee consumption, society is better off by 5+8.

Externalities and Public Opinion

If David Attenborough says there is a problem; there is a problem. BBC documentary Blue Planet II raised consumer understanding of the issue, with 10.3m viewers. Following this, new targets hit the headlines. KPMG banned plastic cups. Using 3m/yr that cost £60,000 it is providing reusable water bottles. Diageo announced in that it would phase out the use of plastic straws and stirrers from all its offices, events, promotions, advertising and marketing globally – and is advocating the same for its partners and customers. Iceland found when it surveyed 5,000 people 80% were in favour of the retailer getting rid of plastic. It went with public opinion with its own brand products. Pizza Express, Morrisons, Waitrose, and McDonalds followed suit in June 2018.

Unilever's 'Sustainable Living' brands accounted for 60% of the company's growth in 2016, and they grew more than 50% faster than the rest of the business. Bulldog Skincare for Men has developed sugarcane packaging as a replacement for plastic. Not only does this get rid of the issue of plastic waste, but sugarcane saves carbon dioxide, rather than releasing it into the atmosphere. Bulldog's marketing research suggests that in skincare, from a commercial perspective, by opting to buy their products consumers were rewarding companies that take a positive stand.

Shops with over 250 employees were required to impose a plastic bag charge of 5p levy in England in October 2015 Wales (2011), Scotland (2014) and Northern Ireland (2013). Before the levy the average consumer used 140 bags/yr (7.64bn in 2014). This dropped to 25. The outcome of a small charge resulted in a notable reduction in consumption. Having phased out the 5p carrier bags in the past year in England, Wales and Scotland, Morrisons began selling paper shopping bags also side plastic reusable bags – both types for 20p.

Markit Economic Research 17/08/2015

The Markit Eurozone Purchasing Managers' Index has been compiled by Markit's economics team since 1998 surveying around 5,000 manufacturing and services private sector companies, tracking variables such as output, new orders, stock levels, employment and prices. The index can be used to estimate GDP change on a quarterly basis

GDP (quarterly %Δ) $= -5.93 + 0.118$ PMI
(adjusted $R^2 = 0.725$)

A PMI would be interpreted as below
$-0.266 = -5.93 + 0.118 \times 48$. In other words, a

PMI	GDPΔ%	PMI	GDPΔ%
40	-1.2	52	0.2
42	-1.0	54	0.5
44	-0.7	56	0.7
46	-0.5	58	0.9
48	-0.3	60	1.2
50	0.0		

drop of around 0.3% on a quarterly basis or 1.2% on an annual basis. A PMI of 50.0 is indicative of GDP being unchanged on the previous quarter.

Reserve Bank of India estimated the following:
http://www.rbi.org.in/scripts/AnnualReportPublications.aspx?Id=896

The Export Demand Function for India: Some Inferences on the Impact of the Global Recession on India Box II.32
An estimate of India's exports for the period 1980-81 to 2007-08 reveals a long run elasticity of demand for India's exports with respect to world GDP. RBI uses the following abbreviations:
X = Quantity index of India's exports, YW = World GDP at constant prices in US$ terms, RXP = ratio of India's export price (unit value index of India's exports deflated by the Rupee-US$ nominal exchange rate) to world export price (unit value index of world exports in US$ terms). ln = natural log.

The dependent variable is quantity (of exports), which is a function of income, and relative price. As RBI used natural logarithms, the expression can directly assess elasticities. The expression is

$$ln\,X = -56.96 + 3.73\,ln\,YW - 1.94\,ln\,RXP + 0.81\,AR(1)$$
$$(-7.72)\quad (8.43)\qquad (-1.78)\qquad\quad (7.28)$$
$$R^2 = 0.99\quad DW = 1.65\qquad SEE = 0.07$$

Interpretation:- High R^2 indicates a robust model, but the DW is low (need dof and a critical value to judge). The t-ratios are in brackets. We have not got a critical value, but let us use the notional one of 2. This suggests that exports are influenced by income but not prices. The income elasticity of 3.73 would indicate that it exports luxury goods. The −1.9 suggests India exports price sensitive goods (*but* −1.78 suggests that value is not significantly different from zero).